John M. Lawrie.

D1348864

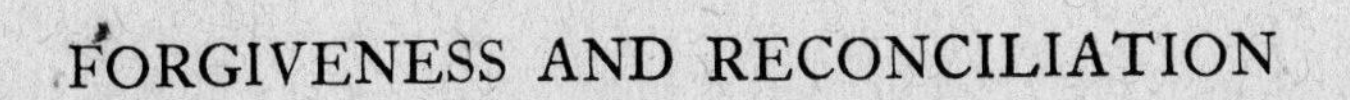

FORGIVENESS AND RECONCILIATION

OTHER BOOKS BY
DR. VINCENT TAYLOR

THE FORMATION OF THE GOSPEL TRADITION. 7s. 6d.

JESUS AND HIS SACRIFICE: A STUDY OF THE PASSION-SAYINGS IN THE GOSPELS. 10s. 6d.

Macmillan and Co.

THE HISTORICAL EVIDENCE FOR THE VIRGIN BIRTH. 12s. 6d.

BEHIND THE THIRD GOSPEL: A STUDY OF THE PROTO-LUKE HYPOTHESIS. 16s.

Oxford University Press

THE FIRST DRAFT OF ST. LUKE'S GOSPEL. 1s.

Society for Promoting Christian Knowledge

THE GOSPELS: A SHORT INTRODUCTION. 3s. 6d.

THE ATONEMENT IN NEW TESTAMENT TEACHING. 8s. 6d.

THE DOCTRINE OF THE HOLY SPIRIT (in collaboration with H. WATKIN-JONES, H. ROBERTS, and N. H. SNAITH). 3s. 6d.

The Epworth Press

FORGIVENESS AND RECONCILIATION

A STUDY IN NEW TESTAMENT THEOLOGY

BY

VINCENT TAYLOR

PH.D., D.D. (LOND.), HON. D.D. (LEEDS)

PRINCIPAL AND FERENS PROFESSOR OF NEW TESTAMENT LANGUAGE AND LITERATURE AT WESLEY COLLEGE, HEADINGLEY, LEEDS

MACMILLAN AND CO., LIMITED

ST. MARTIN'S STREET, LONDON

1941

COPYRIGHT

PRINTED IN GREAT BRITAIN

PREFACE

In the present work I have carried a stage further the investigation begun in *Jesus and His Sacrifice* and continued in *The Atonement in New Testament Teaching*. In the former of these books I treated the Passion-sayings in the Gospels against the background of Old Testament thought; in the latter I examined the testimony of the Primitive Church and the special teaching of St. Paul, the writer of the Epistle to the Hebrews, and St. John, with reference to the work of Christ; and in each of these volumes I ventured to put forward a constructive statement of the doctrine of the Atonement which would account for the evidence under discussion. In the course of these investigations, now extending over seven years, the conviction deepened in my mind that there was yet another, and equally important, approach to the doctrine which must be made if the subject was to receive adequate attention. Was it possible that a clearer light might be thrown upon the Atonement by a careful investigation of New Testament teaching concerning forgiveness and reconciliation; and how far would the results, provisionally reached, be supported by this inquiry? I was well aware that in modern theology it is usual to identify forgiveness and reconciliation, and to regard justification simply as a Pauline version of forgiveness; and I suspected that the acceptance of this threefold identification not only obscures the teaching of the New Testament, but also creates formidable difficulties in apprehending the doctrine of the Atonement. It seemed necessary, therefore, to ask: What does the New Testament teach regarding forgiveness, justification, and reconciliation; and how are these experiences related to the death of Christ? The same question presented itself also in the case of the ideas of fellowship with God and of sanctification, inasmuch as, demonstrably, New Testament teaching upon each of these themes is far too full to be included under the idea of reconciliation.

Chapter I is assigned to the study of the idea of forgiveness, as it appears, first, in the Acts and Epistles, and then in the sayings and parables of Jesus; and the conclusion reached is that forgiveness is primarily, if not exclusively, presented as the remission of sins. It is not suggested that we ought to abandon that richer conception of forgiveness as restoration to fellowship with God, to which, under the influence of other aspects of New Testament teaching, Christian thinking has been led. None the less, it is of decisive importance for theology that we should be in no doubt as to what actually is the teaching of the New Testament.

In Chapter II the Pauline doctrine of justification is investigated. I must confess to have undertaken this study in the first place from a sense of duty, in a series of lectures given to my students on the Epistle to the Romans; but I must also state that by degrees the sense of obligation was enlarged by a quickened interest which ultimately became a feeling of fascination. Our apprehension of the greatness of St. Paul's thought on this subject is made difficult by our almost incurable habit of speaking of 'justification', whereas St. Paul uses the noun rarely, and prefers to speak of 'being justified' and of God's gracious activity in 'justifying' men. In itself, the phrase 'justification by faith' does not give us an adequate characterization of the doctrine, since it is meant to distinguish the idea from 'justification by works'. The faith in question is not simply faith in God, in a broad and general sense, but faith resting in, and dependent upon, God's redemptive activity in Christ; and it is of immense importance to ask how this faith can be related to righteousness. So regarded, justification is not merely a Pauline equivalent for forgiveness; it is a distinctive moment in the story of God's dealing with the soul of man. The special interest for our inquiry is the connexion in which justification stands to the work of Christ.

Chapters III, IV, and V treat, respectively, the ideas of reconciliation, fellowship, and sanctification. In considering reconciliation it is obviously necessary to examine all that the New Testament teaches about peace with God, freedom, and sonship, as well as the Pauline treatment of reconciliation. The teaching concerning fellowship also cannot be excluded, although here the subject-matter is so full, including as it does the ideas of fellowship with Christ, living and dying with Him, abiding and being in Him, and seeing and knowing God, that separate treatment is necessary. Sanctification also must be discussed, since, while it cannot be included under reconciliation, it cannot possibly be excluded from a discussion of the nature of fellowship with God.

The final chapter, Chapter VI, represents an attempt to consider the relation of the Christian experience as a whole, as well as in its several aspects, to the doctrine of the Atonement. It is here maintained that the doctrine which meets the deepest needs of man is one which interprets the redemptive work of God in Christ as the supreme revelation of divine love, as an objective revelation in history, and as a Godward and representative ministry in which men participate by faith, worship, and service.

It may be that, in their anxiety to reach constructive results, some readers will find these discussions tedious and will be inclined to question their value. Can we possibly distinguish in our experience, it may be asked, between forgiveness, justification, and reconciliation? How can we have a sense of the remission of sins which stops short of fellowship with God; and can we know justification at all apart from its results in forgiveness and reconciliation? The answer to these questions is that, undoubtedly, forgiveness, justification, and reconciliation form an indissoluble unity; but that it by no means follows that we can afford to neglect to ascertain the true character of justification. The temptation to think otherwise arises from the tendency to rest theology exclusively upon 'the Christian experience'; and, in consequence, to imagine that anything which cannot be consciously known and felt is of little theological importance. This obsession, which perhaps has only to be stated to be recognized as such, is very costly; it has led many of us to neglect justification, and, in turn, I believe, this neglect has compelled us, not without misgivings, to acquiesce in limited conceptions of the work of God in Christ. The fact that we are not conscious of justification is irrelevant, provided that we perceive that justification is the gracious act of God which makes reconciliation ethically possible. If we do not appreciate the necessity of this divine activity, our conception of reconciliation will be painfully inadequate; and we shall be unable to descry in the Atonement more than the revelation of divine love upon the stage of history. If, however, we see that, in His graciousness, God has given to us a standing-ground in relation to Himself which makes fellowship with Him an ethical and spiritual possibility, our understanding of reconciliation will be greatly enriched, and we shall welcome, in the work of Christ, a redemptive ministry which gives this standing to those who trust in Him. The development of this thought is doubtless a matter for theology, but we cannot usefully begin the task until we have inquired what St. Paul means by saying that we are 'justified by faith'.

It is with these preliminary inquiries that this book is concerned. Questions relating to the history of doctrine and to systematic theology are touched upon, but only incidentally; the investigation is not intended to be more than is described by the sub-title. New Testament theology is a legitimate sphere for a teacher of the New Testament; and, in his enthusiasm for source-criticism, form-criticism, grammar, and exegesis, he must never renounce it to the care of any one else. The need for this discipline to-day is as great as ever, and all the more so because we have now absorbed the results of literary and historical criticism. If theology is to regain the position it deserves, and if preaching is to be rescued from its decline, we must spare no pains to understand the teaching of the classical Christian writings.

Naturally, there are introductory questions which must be considered before the study of forgiveness and reconciliation can be profitably undertaken, including the doctrine of God, the nature of sin, and the right use of Scripture. These questions I have treated in outline in the Introduction.

I should like to explain that I have followed the example of the English edition of Huck's *Synopse* in using the symbol S to indicate Codex Sinaiticus, and in some cases, when referring to well-known commentaries, have simply added the page number after the writer's name.

In conclusion, I desire to express my deep gratitude to friends who have read the typescript and have given to me the benefit of their criticisms, and, in particular, to the Rev. Dr. H. Roberts, the Rev. S. G. Dimond, M.A., and my junior colleague, the Rev. C. D. Bacon, B.A., B.D., who has also been kind enough to prepare the Index of Proper Names. I am also deeply indebted to them, and to my wife, for help in the correcting of the proof sheets, and to four of my students, Messrs. W. Lillie, A. Tuley, R. P. Woods, and D. E. Wright for supplying me with a copy of a considerable portion of the typescript. I desire also to acknowledge my debt to the printers, the firm of Messrs. R. MacLehose & Co., for their great skill and constant courtesy, and to my publishers, Messrs. Macmillan & Co., for undertaking to publish such a work as this in the difficult conditions of the War. In sending forth this book, I do so with the prayer that it may be of some service to many within the Church of Christ who desire to understand their faith better, and to commend it more adequately to others.

VINCENT TAYLOR

College House,
Wesley College,
Headingley, Leeds.
May 26th, 1941.

CONTENTS

PAGE

PREFACE - - - - - - - - v

INTRODUCTION - - - - - - - - xv

I. FORGIVENESS

INTRODUCTION - - - - - - - - 1

(*a*) FORGIVENESS IN THE ACTS AND THE EPISTLES - - 2

(*b*) FORGIVENESS IN THE SAYINGS OF JESUS - - - 10

(*c*) FORGIVENESS IN THE PARABLES - - - - 18

(*d*) FORGIVENESS IN THE OLD TESTAMENT AND IN LATER JUDAISM - - - - - - - 23

(*e*) THE PLACE OF FORGIVENESS IN MODERN THEOLOGY 27

II. JUSTIFICATION

INTRODUCTION - - - - - - - - 34

(*a*) THE MEANING OF THE VERB 'TO JUSTIFY' (*δικαιόω*) - 36

(*b*) THE USE OF *δικαιόω* IN THE NEW TESTAMENT, APART FROM THE PAULINE EPISTLES - - - 40

(*c*) ST. PAUL'S USE OF *δικαιόω* - - - - - 41

(*d*) ST. PAUL'S USE OF *δίκαιος*, *δικαίωμα*, *δικαίωσις*, AND *δικαιοσύνη* - - - - - - - 48

(*e*) ST. PAUL'S TEACHING CONCERNING IMPUTATION - 52

(*f*) JUSTIFICATION BY FAITH - - - - - 56

(*g*) JUSTIFYING FAITH AND RIGHTEOUSNESS - - - 65

(*h*) THE PLACE OF JUSTIFICATION IN MODERN THEOLOGY 72

III. RECONCILIATION

PAGE

Introduction - - - - - - - - 83

(a) The Pauline Doctrine of Reconciliation - - 84

(b) Reconciliation and Peace with God - - - 100

(c) Reconciliation and Freedom - - - - 108

(d) Reconciliation and Sonship - - - - 110

(e) Reconciliation and Fellowship with God - - 117

(f) Reconciliation and Sanctification - - - 117

(g) The Place of Reconciliation in Modern Theology 118

IV. FELLOWSHIP

Introduction - - - - - - - - 130

(a) Fellowship or κοινωνία - - - - - 131

(b) The Pauline Phrase 'In Christ' - - - 135

(c) The Pauline Idea of Dying, Rising, and Living with Christ - - - - - - - - 139

(d) Johannine Teaching about 'Abiding' and 'Being in Christ' - - - - - - - - 143

(e) New Testament Teaching on Seeing and Knowing God - - - - - - - - 146

(f) Fellowship in the Christian Community - - 151

(g) The Origins of New Testament Teaching concerning Fellowship with God - - - 156

(h) The Place of the Idea of Fellowship in Modern Theology - - - - - - - - 166

V. SANCTIFICATION

PAGE

Introduction - - - - - - - 172

(*a*) Sanctification and the Ethical Life - - 173

(*b*) Sanctification and Life in the Spirit - - 180

(*c*) Sanctification and the Christian Ideal - - 185

(*d*) Sanctification and Sinless Perfection - - 190

(*e*) Sanctification and the Vision of God - - 198

(*f*) Sanctification and Perfect Love - - - 203

(*g*) Sanctification and the Community - - - 215

(*h*) The Place of Sanctification in Modern Theology 220

VI. ATONEMENT

Introduction - - - - - - - 226

(*a*) The Doctrine of the Atonement - - - 226

(*b*) The Unity of the Christian Experience - - 232

(*c*) Forgiveness and the Atonement - - - 233

(*d*) Justification and the Atonement - - - 238

(*e*) Reconciliation and the Atonement - - - 247

(*f*) Fellowship with God and the Atonement - 254

(*g*) Sanctification and the Atonement - - - 260

(*h*) Forgiveness and Reconciliation as the Heart of the Gospel - - - - - - - 266

Index of New Testament References - - - 276

Index of Proper Names - - - - - - 286

INTRODUCTION

Forgiveness and Reconciliation can be justly said to be a comprehensive description of the Christian experience, provided regard is paid to all that these terms imply. In modern theology the two ideas are commonly held to be synonymous, and to describe man's restoration to fellowship with God. Forgiveness, however, has the advantage of suggesting also the thought of the remission of sins, which by general consent is essential to reconciliation. It also reminds us of justification, which, so far as it is considered at all, is widely, but not accurately, held to be a Pauline equivalent for forgiveness. Further, forgiveness and reconciliation raise the question of fellowship with God, and imply, at least, that perfect communion with God which is in mind when we think of sanctification. A study, therefore, of forgiveness and reconciliation inevitably means an investigation of the remission of sins, justification, reconciliation, fellowship with God, and sanctification. It is also essential, for reasons which will appear, to consider the relationships of each of these experiences to the Atonement, a doctrine with which they are vitally connected.

A wide field is obviously opened out by the inquiry which is proposed. Moreover, it is neither possible nor desirable to limit the theme to forgiveness and reconciliation with God, for all kinds of human relationships, personal, religious, social, and international are suggested by it. These topics will be constantly in mind, but they will not receive the same detailed attention as the question of reconciliation with God, partly because, in themselves, they are far-reaching enough to warrant independent study, but mainly because, in the writer's view, for purposes both of understanding and of practical treatment, they depend upon the primary question of forgiveness and reconciliation with God. This latter subject will be the one mainly in mind, and it will be treated on the basis of New Testament teaching, in the belief that in this, interpreted critically and historically, is given the best guidance for such an inquiry.

In the Introduction to his invaluable work, *A History of the Doctrine of the Work of Christ*, Principal R. S. Franks has drawn attention to the need for the study of particular doctrines from the point of view of the whole. As far as possible, that principle has been steadily kept in mind in the present investigation. There are, however, limits within which it can be observed. The study of forgiveness and reconciliation requires at least three preliminary inquiries before it can be profitably undertaken. First, it is necessary, and indeed indispensable, to consider the doctrine of God, for again and again this doctrine has profoundly affected all that has been taught concerning forgiveness and reconciliation. Secondly, the doctrine of Sin is also deeply influential in its bearing upon this theme. If sin is lightly esteemed, a shallow treatment of forgiveness and reconciliation is inevitable; if it is associated with total depravity, everything will be made to depend on the will and power of God; if neither of these positions is taken, problems of the greatest complexity must arise, as we try to relate the sovereign grace of God to human freedom and responsibility. In all these cases the inquiry is decisively affected. Thirdly, the use of Scripture, to which reference has been made, needs to be explained and vindicated. It is necessary to indicate what degree of authority is assigned to the various New Testament writ-

strangely good and evil are mingled in the human heart. In lives apparently abandoned to evil there are unexpected manifestations of divine grace, gleams of sacrifice and desires after good which prove that man is not bereft of the ministries of the Spirit. Moreover, in the heart of most men there is a mingling of motives, self-regarding interests being crossed with altruistic purposes, with the result that deeds of heroism or quieter acts of service appear side by side with works of the flesh and sins of the spirit. The division of men into sheep and goats is picturesque and popular, but it does not correspond with facts. In thinking of sin, it is easy to forget these things, since our attention is concentrated upon sin in itself, its nature and character. But besides evil there is a prevenient grace ever at work in the heart of man. Long ago, in a well-known passage, the Puritan divine John Howe compared man to a ruined palace, in which lie neglected fragments of a noble pillar and scattered pieces of curious imagery, which, he declares, by its desolation and faded glory show too plainly that 'the Great Inhabitant is gone'.[1] The description is eloquent and impressive, but in the mercy of God it is not true. When the palace is in ruins, the Great Inhabitant does not go. He lingers by the broken pillar, and sometimes when least expected He speaks in the silent galleries.

The divided character of man's heart must be recognized frankly and unreservedly, and judgment left to a holy and a loving God; but this recognition does not preclude the analysis of sin or invalidate the view that it is egoistic and destructive of fellowship with God and men. Such an estimate of sin is the presumption of the good news of Christianity. The apostles of a genial humanism are the false friends of humanity, in that they minimize the

[1] *The Living Temple*, Part II, iv. 9.

facts of sin which are the cause of frustrated lives and a disordered world. The true friends of man are those who, while rejecting the doctrine of total depravity, see with clear eyes the sin in individuals and communities which is the cause of all our woe. Such, at least, is the second doctrinal principle which underlies this investigation.

Lastly, consideration must be given to the question of the use of Scripture. What is the value of a study of New Testament theology?

For the modern student of the Gospels and Epistles it is not possible to hold a doctrine of verbal inspiration and infallibility. The New Testament writings have decisively shaped the life of the Church, but no less certainly has the Church influenced the formation, canon, and text of the New Testament, and, in some respects, of the revelation contained therein. We owe these books to the Church, in the sense that they were written to satisfy its religious needs, and to the Spirit, in that thereby the needs were met. For the most part the influence of the Christian Church has proved to be the elucidation of the Gospel, and nowhere so much as in the Gospel of St. John; but to some degree also the tradition has suffered corruption, notably in the narrative tradition of St. Matthew, the accounts of nature-miracles, and details in the Resurrection-stories; and, in this work, full recognition is made of this human element. None the less, and along with many other New Testament students, the writer is conscious of a growing appreciation of the authority of these books. As one of the main sources of Christian doctrine, the inspiration of devotion, and the treasure-house of worship, the New Testament has an authority comparable with that of the Christian Church and the Christian experience. Indeed, it is upon these three closely united foundation stones that the authority of Christianity depends. The justification for this claim is far more than tradition and impressionism. In the first place, the New Testament enshrines the revelation made by the Spirit to the greatest personalities of the Church; for so, at least, must we esteem St. Paul, St. John, and the writer of the Epistle to the Hebrews, not to speak of the other writers. Infallibility, and verbal inspiration are vain dreams, but the belief that the New Testament writers were Spirit-inspired men is well founded. It is supported by the marked contrast between these writings and those of the second and third centuries A.D. The former are creative and original; the latter derivative. This view explains also the spiritual depth and religious insight of these writings, and the controlling influence they have exercised upon doctrine, devotion, and worship. Especially notable is the unity of their teaching. What is wanting in St. Paul is supplied by St. John or the writer of the Epistle to the Hebrews, and these, in turn, depend upon the tradition of the primitive communities. Moreover, the teaching can give the Christian of to-day a satisfying grasp of the Christian Message, capable of being translated into the thought of our time. Finally, it is highly significant that almost every great revival in the life of the Church has followed a close study of the New Testament. So it was at the Reformation, that decisive movement in the sixteenth century; so it was also in the Evangelical movement in the eighteenth century; and if the Tractarian movement of the nineteenth century is an exception, the same influence is illustrated in its later history, in the exegetical work of the late Bishop Gore. To this effect exerted upon religious movements we must add the stimulating influence of the Gospels and Epistles upon the minds and beliefs of countless individual Christians throughout the ages, the feebleness which overtakes faith when its Biblical roots are cut, the signs of renewed life which appear when its witness is accepted, always provided it is received with intelligence and in close association with the life of the Christian Society. One of the greatest needs of the Church to-day is first the study, and then the findings, of New Testament theology; for when this discipline is accepted, a new grasp of the Gospel is gained, a truer piety is engendered, and a fresh enthusiasm for missionary and social enterprise is born.

On these three convictions, in relation to God, to sin, and the New Testament, the investigation which follows is based.

I

FORGIVENESS

The question: What is forgiveness? is less easy to answer than one might suppose, especially if we desire to relate our answer to the teaching of the New Testament. In modern theology the distinction between forgiveness and reconciliation is far from clear, and many would affirm that there is no difference at all. Evidence for this statement can easily be found in current definitions of forgiveness. W. H. Moberly interprets it as 'the full restoration of delicate personal relations between friends or between parent and child'.[1] W. Temple explains that forgiveness does not consist of remission of penalty; 'to forgive is to restore to the old relationship.'[2] R. S. Franks defines it as 'a restoration of the sinner to communion with God; it is the breaking down of the barriers between them'.[3] R. N. Flew maintains that 'God's forgiveness is never a mere passing of the word, a dumb turning of the back, a formal cancelling of a debt. It implies *a personal relationship, violated and now restored*'.[4] 'Forgiveness', he writes, 'means the reception of the sinner into a personal relationship with God: and means, too, that this relationship is richer than it was before the relationship had been broken'.[5] E. B. Redlich, the most recent writer to treat the subject, states the idea

[1] *Foundations* (1914), 293.
[2] *Christus Veritas* (1925), 257.
[3] *The Atonement* (1934), 156.
[4] *The Forgiveness of Sins* (Manuals of Fellowship), 5.
[5] *The Idea of Perfection in Christian Theology* (1934), 23.

succinctly when he says: 'Forgiveness is full restoration to fellowship'.[1]

It may well be that the opinion that forgiveness is reconciliation, or restoration to fellowship, has fully established itself; and it is not the purpose of this investigation to dispute its truth. It is, however, of the utmost importance that we should see if this identification is supported by New Testament usage, or whether in Scripture forgiveness has a well-defined meaning which gives it a content of its own. Only by means of a patient inquiry directed to this end can we protect ourselves from the danger of confusion in Christian theology. In the present chapter, therefore, we shall examine the New Testament conception of forgiveness, first, as we find it in the Acts and the Epistles, and, secondly, as it appears in the sayings of Jesus. The special problems which arise must then be considered, in order that we may see the bearings of the inquiry upon the larger theological issues.

(*a*) *Forgiveness in the Acts and in the Epistles*

According to the New Testament the Apostolic preaching included a message of forgiveness. In Acts ii. 38 men are exhorted to repent and be baptized unto the remission of sins. Christ is proclaimed as a Prince and a Saviour 'for to give repentance to Israel, and remission of sins' (Acts v. 31; cf. xiii. 38). Those who believe on Him are promised this gift 'through his name' (Acts x. 43); and to open men's eyes that they may receive it, is part of an apostle's commission (Acts xxvi. 18). In all these cases the phrase used is *ἄφεσις ἁμαρτιῶν*. In the Epistles the only other examples of the use of the noun are Eph. i. 7: 'in whom we have our redemption through his blood, the forgiveness of our trespasses', Col. i. 14:

[1] *The Forgiveness of Sins* (1937), 104.

'in whom we have our redemption, the forgiveness of our sins', Heb. ix. 22: 'And apart from shedding of blood there is no remission', and Heb. x. 18: 'Now where remission of these is, there is no more offering for sin'.

The material for consideration is not greatly extended if we include *ἀφίημι* and *χαρίζομαι*. The former is used in Acts viii. 22 with reference to Simon: 'Repent . . . and pray . . . if haply the thought of thy heart shall be forgiven', in Rom. iv. 7 in an Old Testament quotation: 'Blessed are they whose iniquities are forgiven', in James v. 15: 'And if he have committed sins, it shall be forgiven him', and in 1 John i. 9: 'If we confess our sins, he is faithful and righteous to forgive us our sins', and ii. 12: 'I write unto you, my little children, because your sins are forgiven you for his name's sake'.

If we add the passages in the Gospels apart from sayings of Jesus, we have the available material in full. *Ἄφεσις ἁμαρτιῶν* is used by St. Mark in describing John's baptism: 'the baptism of repentance unto remission of sins' (i. 4; cf. Lk. iii. 3), and in the L tradition, in the Song of Zacharias in Lk. i. 77: 'To give knowledge of salvation unto his people in the remission of their sins', and Lk. xxiv. 47: 'And that repentance and remission of sins should be preached in his name unto all the nations'. The verb is also used in the scribes' question: 'Who can forgive sins but one, even God?' (Mk. ii. 7; cf. Lk. v. 21), and in the quotation of Isa. vi. 10 in Mk. iv. 12: 'And it should be forgiven them'.[1]

The material is much less in extent than is commonly supposed, especially if we leave aside the general references in Mk. i. 4, iv. 12, Lk. i. 77, Acts viii. 22, Rom. iv. 7, and Heb. ix. 22, x. 18. The important passages are Lk. xxiv. 47, Acts ii. 38, v. 31, x. 43,

[1] Isa. vi. 10 reads: 'and be healed'; LXX: 'and I shall heal them'.

xiii. 38, xxvi. 18, Eph. i. 7, Col. i. 14, Jas. v. 15, 1 John i. 9, ii. 12.

It is noteworthy that in none of these passages is forgiveness represented as the remission of penalties; what is remitted is sin. It is also significant that forgiveness is not presented as the equivalent of reconciliation, or as the restoration of fellowship between persons. At the most it can only be described as action directed to the removal or annulment of some obstacle or barrier to reconciliation. This obstacle, or to speak more precisely, the object of the forgiveness, is variously described as 'sins', 'trespasses', and 'the thought' of 'the heart' (Acts viii. 22). Everywhere it is implied that, if this object is removed, covered, or in some way adequately dealt with, the forgiveness is accomplished. Forgiveness, therefore, in these passages cannot be identified with reconciliation; it is a stage antecedent to reconciliation; it is that which makes reconciliation possible. Another marked feature is that forgiveness is not directly connected with the death of Christ; it is nowhere said that He died that men might be forgiven. The association is indirect. Instead of being connected immediately with the death, it is associated rather with Christ Himself as the Risen Lord and Saviour of men. Baptism is offered 'in the name of Jesus Christ' unto remission of sins (Acts ii. 38). Christ bestows this gift (Acts v. 31, 1 Jn. i. 9). It is 'through his name' (Acts x. 43; cf. Acts xiii. 38, Lk. xxiv. 47), and 'for his name's sake' (1 Jn. ii. 12), that it is imparted: 'in him' that it is received (Eph. i. 7, Col. i. 14). In most of these cases the thought of Christ as the Risen Lord and the conqueror of death is the undertone of the proclamation, especially in Acts v. 31 where He is spoken of as 'a Prince and a Saviour'. In Eph. i. 7 and Col. i. 14 we must be careful not to read too much into the word 'forgiveness' because of its close association with the term 'redemption' (ἀπο-λύτρωσις).[1] It is not sound exegesis to explain it as meaning full restoration to fellowship, and then to read 'redemption' in this sense. Rather must we take 'redemption' as indicative of the meaning to be assigned to 'forgiveness'. If we do this, the passage falls into line with those already considered. Originally an eschatological term[2] (cf. Eph. i. 14, iv. 30, Rom. viii. 23), ἀπολύτρωσις is used in Eph. i. 7 and Col. i. 14 of a present spiritual possession, which consists in 'deliverance' or 'freedom', as also in 1 Cor. i. 30 and Rom. iii. 24. 'We *have*', says St. Paul, 'our redemption'. We need not wait for it until the End-time: here and now we have it in Christ! The thought is clearly that of deliverance from the guilt of trespasses and sins. This is the ἀπολύτρωσις, and the Apostle is simply interpreting the expression when he adds: 'the forgiveness of our sins'. Thus the meaning is that conveyed elsewhere by ἄφεσις ἁμαρτιῶν. Forgiveness is only indirectly associated with the death of Christ in so far as deliverance or freedom is one of its blessings. It is clear from the evidence as a whole that, while the Apostolic preaching did associate the message of forgiveness with the Crucified and Ascended Lord, it did not expressly teach that Christ 'died that we might be forgiven'.

The conclusions already reached are of such interest and importance that it is desirable to see if they are supported by an examination of the passages where χαρίζομαι appears.

In classical Greek χαρίζομαι is commonly used with the meanings 'to show favour', 'to gratify', 'to give freely'. Liddell and Scott give no examples of the verb with the

[1]See later, p. 45.

[2]Cf. F. Büchsel, *Theologisches Wörterbuch*, iv. 355.

meaning 'to forgive' (Lat. *condonare*) except those usually cited in the New Testament,[1] and none is instanced by Moulton and Milligan[2] from the Papyri. In view of the richer content of χάρις in the New Testament it is reasonable to expect that χαρίζομαι also will express deeper and more intimate relationships, but whether it has the meaning 'to forgive' is a matter for inquiry. The verb is used twenty-three times in the New Testament, of which sixteen are found in the Pauline Epistles and seven in Luke–Acts. Eleven of these are used in the usual classical sense, and for our present purpose may be disregarded. Of the remaining twelve, translated in the Revised Version by some part of the verb 'to forgive', two are in Lk. (vii. 42, 43) and ten in the Pauline Epistles (2 Cor. ii. 7, 10 (*ter*), xii. 13, Eph. iv. 32 (*bis*), and Col. ii. 13, iii. 13 (*bis*)).

Although the Lukan instances appear in a parable of Jesus they may be treated here, especially as it is possible, and even probable, that they represent the Evangelist's vocabulary. It is, on the whole, doubtful if we ought to render the verbs in Lk. vii. 42, 43 by 'forgive'. The classical meaning 'to deal graciously with' is entirely adequate, and both A. Plummer and H. K. Luce adopt this meaning.[3] The same appears to be true of 2 Cor. ii. 7: 'so that you should rather deal graciously with him and comfort him'. 2 Cor. ii. 10 is also patient of the same interpretation: 'But to whom you show any graciousness, I do also; for what graciousness I have already shown, if I have shown any, for your sakes have I shown it in the

[1]Those given are 2 Cor. xii. 13, Col. ii. 13, and absol. 2 Cor. ii. 7, etc.

[2]*The Vocabulary of the Greek Testament*, 684.

[3]Plummer suggests: '"he made them a present" of what they owed', for Lk. vii. 42, *St. Luke*, 212; Luce: 'he made them a free gift of what they owed', *St. Luke*, 162.

presence of Christ'. Moffatt translates 2 Cor. xii. 13: 'Pray pardon me this terrible wrong'! The sting of the words in this sarcastic passage would be quite well expressed by the rendering: 'Deal graciously with me in respect of this wrong'! If, however, we prefer 'forgive' or 'pardon', the verb means little more than would be conveyed by ἀφίημι, with the added ironical suggestion that a little indulgence might be necessary. Eph. iv. 32 and Col. iii. 13 may be taken together. Moffatt renders the former: 'Be generous to each other', and the same meaning suits both passages. Eph. iv. 32 might, then, be translated: 'Be ye kind one to another, tender-hearted, dealing generously with each other, even as God also in Christ dealt generously with you'. It is in harmony with this claim that nowhere else does St. Paul summarize the blessings which Christ confers upon men under the idea of forgiveness. Undoubtedly, the generous dealing in question has to do with sins, trespasses, and offences, and this fact is the justification for the rendering: 'forgiving each other, even as God also in Christ forgave you'; but it is significant that, instead of ἀφίημι, St. Paul uses a new verb in this connexion. This preference indicates his recognition of the limitations of the current idea of forgiveness, and at the same time marks the beginnings of a richer development. He is evidently thinking of much more than forgiveness as he understands the term. Col. ii. 13 is the only passage where the proposal to translate the verb by 'forgive' is impressive in view of the accusative πάντα τὰ παραπτώματα. Even here the translation: 'having dealt graciously with us in respect of all our trespasses', is possible, but if we prefer: 'having forgiven us all our trespasses', we must recognize that the use of χαρίζομαι suggests only a more gracious expression of the idea which otherwise would have been indicated by ἀφίημι.

The thought is that of the setting aside through love of barriers in the way of fellowship. What is suggested by χαρίζομαι in the passages under consideration is the forgiving spirit which is ready to remove obstacles. To the meaning conveyed by ἀφίημι there is added the suggestion that, in setting aside wrongs, χάρις or 'grace' must be in the mind and heart of those who are wronged. There is no case in which χαρίζομαι is used to suggest the full restoration of broken relationships; action leading to this end, and necessary to it, is the meaning implied.[1]

In the passages which have been under review the condition of forgiveness is *repentance*, by which is to be understood not only a change of mind, but a turning of mind and heart to God, or to those who are wronged, and a desire for amendment.[2] In several of these passages μετανοέω or μετάνοια is used in close connexion with the reference to forgiveness. John's baptism is one of 'repentance unto remission of sins' (Mk. i. 4; cf. Lk. iii. 3, Mt. iii. 2). On the day of Pentecost Peter bids his hearers repent and be baptized unto remission of sins (Acts ii. 38; cf. viii. 22), and Christ is declared to have been exalted to give the dual gift of 'repentance to Israel, and remission of sins' (Acts v. 31; cf. Lk. xxiv. 47). The same idea is expressed by ἐπιστρέφω in Acts xxvi. 18 (cf. Mk. iv. 12), and by ὁμολογέω with reference to confessing sins in 1 Jn. i. 9. Along with these passages must be considered about thirty more where repentance is mentioned alone with the idea of forgiveness lying in the back-

[1]It is a matter for regret that it is not yet possible to check the above by the treatment of the verb in Kittel's *Theologisches Wörterbuch*.

[2]Cf. R. N. Flew: 'I accept the argument of J. Kosnetter, *Die Taufe Jesu* (Vienna, 1936), that though the word "metanoein" is usually a translation in the LXX of "nicham" the sense of "shub" better suits the N.T. passages', *Jesus and His Church*, 50 f.

ground.[1] In all these cases it is a question of repentance towards God and throughout it is implied that He is ready to forgive whenever men turn from sin to Him.

One important feature remains to be noticed. In all the passages which have been considered there is no case, apart from those in which χαρίζομαι is held to be used in the sense of 'forgive',[2] in which the forgiveness mentioned is forgiveness between man and man. This strange feature is partly explained by the fact that in the Apostolic preaching divine forgiveness is naturally prominent; but this is not a complete explanation if we have regard to the strong ethical interests of primitive Christianity. How is it, one asks, that the first Christians are so rarely exhorted to forgive one another? This question becomes even more pressing when we observe that there are no references at all to forgiveness or to repentance in Galatians, 1 Corinthians, 1 and 2 Thessalonians, Philippians, Philemon, 1 Timothy, Titus, 1 Peter, 2 and 3 John, and that in the Fourth Gospel there is a single reference to forgiveness in xx. 23 and none to repentance. These interesting facts support the contention that in the New Testament forgiveness is an ethical activity of limited content if we compare it with the richer developments of subsequent Christian thought. It is not spoken of more frequently because it is not yet what subsequently it came to be.

Thus far we have not taken into account the sayings of Jesus, and the question becomes urgent whether, in His teaching, the meaning of forgiveness is deepened and enlarged. This point will be considered in the next sections.

[1]Cf. Mt. iii. 11, xi. 20, Mk. vi. 12; Acts iii. 19, xi. 18, xiii. 24, xvii. 30, xix. 4, xx. 21, xxvi. 20; Rom. ii. 4; 2 Cor. vii. 9 f., xii. 21; 2 Tim. ii. 25; Heb. vi. 1, 6; 2 Pet. iii. 9; and Apoc. ii. 5 (*bis*), 16, 21 (*bis*), 22, iii. 3, 19, ix. 20 f., xvi. 9, 11. Ten sayings of Jesus, containing references to repentance, will be considered later. See p. 16.

[2]Cf. 2 Cor. ii. 7, 10, xii. 13, Eph. iv. 32, Col. ii. 13, iii. 13.

In view of its importance it will be useful to summarize the results gained from the Acts, the Epistles, and the Apocalypse.

In these writings (1) Forgiveness is the removal or annulment of the obstacles in the way of reconciliation; (2) It is not represented as the main purpose of the death of Christ, but is included among its results, probably as one of the signs of the expected Messianic salvation; (3) Its condition is repentance; (4) It is thought of almost exclusively as the divine forgiveness; (5) As regards relationships between man and man, the few examples are expressed by χαρίζομαι, used in the special sense of generous dealing in respect of the barriers to a renewal of fellowship.

(*b*) *Forgiveness in the Sayings of Jesus*

The meaning of forgiveness in the teaching of Jesus must now be considered.

Obviously, the sayings in which it is expressly mentioned must be examined first. The Parables require separate treatment, especially those which are widely believed to illustrate forgiveness and yet do not actually use the word. In reading these parables it is fatally easy to find our own ideas in the teaching of Jesus; and just for this reason attention ought to be concentrated first upon the sayings in which references to forgiveness are definitely made. These sayings are determinative without necessarily being exhaustive in their significance.

We shall examine the sayings in which ἄφεσις and ἀφίημι are used in the four sources, Mark, Q, M, and L.[1]

[1]These are the sources used by the writers of Mt., Mk., and Lk. according to the Four Document Hypothesis: Q = the sayings-source used by Matthew and Luke in common; M = the similar sayings-source used by Matthew only; and L = the collection of sayings and narratives used by Luke only. Both Matthew and Luke used Mk. as a source. Cf. B. H. Streeter, *The Four Gospels: A Study of Origins* (1924), 223-70.

We shall also consider the teaching of Jesus regarding the conditions of forgiveness and the place which He gives to it in human relationships.

Ἄφεσις is found once[1] only, with the meaning 'forgiveness', in the sayings, in Mk. iii. 29: 'Whosoever shall blaspheme against the Holy Spirit hath never forgiveness'. Elsewhere in the Gospels the verbal form is used, and it appears in all the four principal sources.

In Mark there are three examples, apart from the references to forgiveness in the story of the Paralytic (Mk. ii. 1-12). There is the declaration that all sins and blasphemies shall be forgiven to the sons of men (Mk. iii. 28), which immediately precedes the saying regarding blasphemy against the Holy Spirit mentioned above (Mk. iii. 29), and the command: 'And whensoever ye stand praying, forgive, if ye have ought against any one; that your Father also which is in heaven may forgive you your trespasses' (Mk. xi. 25). In the story of the Paralytic, Jesus says to the man: 'Son, thy sins are forgiven' (Mk. ii. 5; cf. ii. 9), and as a proof of the power of the Son of Man on earth to forgive sins, He bids him take up his bed and go to his house (Mk. ii. 10 f.).

To all these passages there are parallels in Mt. and Lk., but these need not be considered here. Mt. xxvi. 28, however, must be mentioned, because in this passage 'Matthew' adds to the Markan saying: 'This is my blood of the covenant, which is shed for many' (Mk. xiv. 24), the interpretative words: 'unto remission of sins'.

In Q there are three sayings relating to forgiveness. First, there is the well-known passage in the Lord's Prayer: 'And forgive us our sins (Mt., "debts"); for we ourselves also forgive every one that is indebted to us (Mt., "as we

[1]It is used twice in the sense of 'release' in the quotation from Isa. lxvi. 1f. in Lk. iv. 18.

also have forgiven our debtors")' (Lk. xi. 4 = Mt. vi. 12).[1] Further, there is a parallel to the Markan saying on blasphemy against the Holy Spirit (Lk. xii. 10 = Mt. xii. 32). Finally, there is the saying about repeated forgiveness: 'Take heed to yourselves: if thy brother sin, rebuke him; and if he repent, forgive him. And if he sin against thee seven times in the day, and seven times turn again to thee, saying I repent; thou shalt forgive him (Mt., "until seventy times seven")' (Lk. xvii. 3 f. = Mt. xviii. 15, 21 f.).[2]

In M, besides a parallel to Mk. xi. 25 in Mt. vi. 14 f.,[3] are found the references to forgiveness in the Parable of the Unforgiving Servant (Mt. xviii. 23-35). Of this man Jesus says that his lord 'being moved with compassion, released him, and forgave him the debt (τὸ δάνειον)' (Mt. xviii. 27). The lord himself says: 'I forgave thee all that debt (ὀφειλήν), because thou besoughtest me' (Mt. xviii. 32); and Jesus applies the teaching of the parable in the words: 'So shall also my heavenly Father do unto you, if ye forgive not every one his brother from your hearts' (Mt. xviii. 35).

From the L Source comes the Prayer from the Cross: 'Father, forgive them; for they know not what they do' (Lk. xxiii. 34).[4] There are also four references to forgiveness in the story of the Woman in the City who was a Sinner: 'Her sins, which are many, are forgiven' (47); 'To whom little is forgiven, the same loveth little' (47);

[1]These sayings may, however, be from L and M respectively. Cf. Streeter, *The Four Gospels*, 239, 281 f.

[2]Mt. xviii. 15-22 may be from M. Cf. T. W. Manson, *The Mission and Message of Jesus*, 501-4.

[3]Mt. vi. 15 appears in some MSS. in Mk. xi. 26, but is omitted by S B W sy[s] sa bo.

[4]For the textual problem connected with these words see Streeter, *The Four Gospels*, 138.

'Thy sins are forgiven' (48); 'Who is this that even forgiveth sins?' (49). The last, of course, is the comment of the guests.

Such, then, are the references to forgiveness in the Synoptic Gospels. In the Fourth Gospel there is only a single reference in the words: 'Whose soever sins ye forgive, they are forgiven unto them; whose soever sins ye retain, they are retained' (Jn. xx. 23). This passage is probably a secondary version of the saying on binding and loosing in Mt. xvi. 19, xviii. 18.

If we omit parallels in the various Gospels and in the different sources, we are left with five sayings: those on blasphemy, on forgiving others, and on repeated forgiveness, that in the Lord's Prayer, and the words from the Cross; and in addition the references to forgiveness in the Lukan story of the Woman in the City and in the Matthaean Parable of the Unforgiving Servant. The extent of the material is less, I think, than might have been expected.

As in the passages previously examined the forgiveness is usually related to an object, variously described as 'sins' (ἁμαρτίαι, ἁμαρτήματα), 'trespasses' (παραπτώματα), 'blasphemies' (βλασφημίαι), 'debts' (ὀφειλήματα, cf. δάνειον, ὀφειλή). Only in the sayings in Lk. xvii. 3 f., xxiii. 34, Mt. xviii. 35 is the verb used absolutely, and in these cases definite actions are implied. The idea, therefore, of forgiveness is the same, the cancelling of obstacles to reconciliation. The forgiveness in question is usually that exercised between man and man, but in Mk. iii. 28, Lk. xi. 4, xxiii. 34 and Mt. xviii. 35 God's forgiveness is thought of, and in Mk. ii. 10 (cf. Lk. vii. 48) Jesus speaks of a forgiveness which He, as the Son of Man, exercises Himself.

In no recorded saying does Jesus connect forgiveness

with His death, for, as we have seen, the phrase: 'unto remission of sins', in Mt. xxvi. 28, is the addition of the Evangelist. This fact, however, may easily be misconstrued and misinterpreted. In point of fact there is no saying of Jesus in which He defines the meaning of His death, after the manner of a theologian, in relation to the blessings which it confers upon man. This fact does not mean that His death had no manward significance for Him, but rather that the meaning which He found in it can only be divined by a close study of His teaching and His actions as a whole. We cannot therefore assume that He saw no connexion between it and the forgiveness of sins. Moreover, while the phrase, 'unto remission of sins', is the Evangelist's addition in Mt. xxvi. 28, it is a correct interpretation of at least a part of what is involved in the words: 'This is my blood of the covenant, which is shed for many' (Mk. xiv. 24). Both the idea of a covenant and that of the shedding of sacrificial blood are inseparably connected with the thought of the forgiveness of sins (cf. Jer. xxxi. 34, Heb. ix. 22). The true conclusion to be drawn is that the absence of a saying of Jesus directly associating His death with forgiveness is so far a confirmation of the results gained from our study of the Apostolic preaching, that the forgiveness of sins is not the primary object of His suffering and death. This result of our investigation is easily understood if forgiveness, as Jesus understood it, and as the Apostles preached it, is not identical with reconciliation, but is a stage introductory to it, the removal of the barriers to fellowship between God and man.

This claim is so challenging to accepted views that we are not likely to accept its truth unless, in addition to linguistic considerations, it is confirmed by a sound exegesis of the sayings. This test, however, is conclusive. Naturally, there are cases where the reference is so general that various interpretations are possible; but the most distinctive sayings have only one meaning.

When Jesus declares that sins and blasphemies against the sons of men shall be forgiven, while those against the Holy Spirit shall not (Mk. iii. 28; cf. Lk. xii. 10 = Mt. xii. 32), He means that in the one case a barrier is surmountable and that in the other case it is not. When men standing at prayer are bidden to forgive if they 'have aught against any one' (Mk. xi. 25), they are commanded to remove definite obstacles to true fellowship. When, in the Lord's Prayer, we are invited to say: 'Forgive us our sins, for we ourselves forgive every one that is indebted to us' (Lk. xi. 4 = Mt. vi. 12), the meaning is: 'Let not our sins stand in the way, for in like manner we ourselves remit the debts of others'. When it is said that the wrong-doer must be forgiven 'until seventy times seven' (Mt. xviii. 22, cf. Lk. xvii. 3 f.), the injunction is that, because of his repentance, grounds of offence are repeatedly to be set aside; they are not to count against him. When the lord of the unmerciful servant is represented as saying: 'I forgave thee all that debt' (Mt. xviii. 32), the suggestion is that the debt was cancelled. When Jesus prays: 'Father, forgive them; for they know not what they do' (Lk. xxiii. 34), the meaning is that which is expressed in the prayer of Stephen: 'Lord, lay not this sin to their charge' (Acts vii. 60). When the paralytic (Mk. ii. 5) and the woman in the city (Lk. vii. 47 f.) are forgiven, they receive the word of absolution which makes reconciliation possible. It goes without saying that in all these cases wider horizons of peace and fellowship with God and man are opened, but it is not of these that the sayings speak; they are directed rather to the pre-conditions of reconciliation, to obstacles, barriers, stumbling-blocks which need to be annulled and taken away.

In its fundamental aspects, therefore, the teaching of Jesus in relation to forgiveness is like that found in the rest of the New Testament passages. It is positive, not negative, but it is concerned with the things which stand in the way of fellowship rather than with fellowship itself. Similar also is the emphasis laid on the necessity of repentance. In Lk. xvii. 3 f. forgiveness and repentance are mentioned together in the two sayings, but in eight other sayings repentance alone is named with the implication that where it is present offences and sins will be forgiven. Thus, at the outset of His public ministry Jesus bids men repent and believe in the good news (Mk. i. 15 = Mt. iv. 17). He declares that if Tyre and Sidon had seen the mighty works done in Chorazin and Bethsaida 'they would have repented long ago, sitting in sackcloth and ashes' (Lk. x. 13 = Mt. xi. 21). He commends the Ninevites because they repented at the preaching of Jonah (Lk. xi. 32 = Mt. xii. 41). He warns those who told Him of the slaughtered Galilaeans that, except they repented, they would in like manner perish (Lk. xiii. 3) and repeats the warning in the light of the eighteen on whom the tower in Siloam fell (Lk. xiii. 5). In the Lukan parable of the Lost Sheep He speaks of joy in heaven over one sinner that repenteth (Lk. xv. 7)[1] and uses the same words in the parable of the Lost Coin (Lk. xv. 10). Finally, in the parable of the Rich Man and Lazarus, He implicitly denies that men will of necessity repent because one should rise from the dead (Lk. xvi. 31). In all these sayings the kind of forgiveness in mind is the cancelling or passing by

[1]Note also the words: 'more than over ninety and nine righteous persons, which need no repentance'. This is the only instance of the noun in the sayings, since the addition in Lk. v. 32 is probably editorial.

of offences and sins from which men turn away in their penitence towards God.

While, however, the sayings agree in substance with those in the Acts and the Epistles, there are two important distinctive features in the former. The sayings give greater prominence to forgiveness as it affects human relationships, to forgiveness, that is to say, between man and man. Further, the condition of forgiveness is not only repentance, but also the presence of the forgiving spirit in relation to the offences of others.[1] The following sayings illustrate these two points:

Mk. xi. 25: 'And whensoever ye stand praying, forgive, if ye have aught against any one; that your Father also which is in heaven may forgive you your trespasses.'

Lk. xi. 4: 'And forgive us our sins; for we ourselves also forgive every one that is indebted to us' (cf. Mt. vi. 12: 'And forgive us our debts, as we also have forgiven our debtors').[2]

Lk. xvii. 3 f.: 'If thy brother sin, rebuke him; and if he repent, forgive him. And if he sin against thee seven times in the day, and seven times turn again to thee, saying, I repent; thou shalt forgive him.'

Mt. vi. 14 f.: 'For if ye forgive men their trespasses, your heavenly Father will also forgive you. But if ye forgive not men their trespasses, neither will your Father forgive your trespasses.'

Mt. xviii. 35: 'So shall also my heavenly Father do unto you, if ye forgive not every one his brother from your hearts.'

In the rest of the New Testament there are no passages of this kind; the presence of the forgiving spirit as a condi-

[1]E. B. Redlich has strongly emphasized this point in his recent book, *The Forgiveness of Sins* (1937), 139 ff.

[2]T. W. Manson thinks that the Matthaean form is to be preferred. Cf. *The Mission and Message of Jesus*, 558. 'There are also Rabbinical parallels (Billerbeck, i. 424 ff.). But generally the Jewish insistence is on the duty of the offender to seek forgiveness of the injured party; that of Jesus on the duty of the injured party to offer forgiveness', *op. cit.*, 462.

tion of the divine forgiveness is a note distinctive of the teaching of Jesus.[1]

Comparing our present results with those previously gained, we conclude: (1) In the sayings, as in the Acts and the Epistles, forgiveness is the covering or removal of the barriers to reconciliation; (2) It is not set forth as the purpose of Christ's death; (3) The conditions are repentance and the presence of the forgiving spirit; (4) While, as in the rest of the New Testament, much is said of the divine forgiveness, greater emphasis is laid on the duty of forgiving others.

(*c*) *Forgiveness in the Parables*

In considering the conclusions stated at the end of the previous section, and especially the first, it is natural to ask whether the investigation has not been carried out on too narrow a basis. Do we not gain a richer and a truer conception of forgiveness from such parables as the Unmerciful Servant, the Rich Man and Lazarus, the Pharisee and the Publican, and, above all, the Prodigal Son?

The sayings in the first two of these parables have already been examined, and it has been seen that they actually form part of the evidence for the view that, in the teaching of Jesus, forgiveness is the removal of the barriers which stand in the way of fellowship.

A fuller study of the parable of the Unmerciful Servant (Mt. xviii. 23-35) only serves to confirm this conclusion. The forgiveness of the king is the remission of the debt of ten thousand talents (xviii. 24), and it is to this action that

[1]Canon Redlich instances Eph. iv. 32 and Col. iii. 13. See *The Forgiveness of Sins*, 140. But in these passages the point of view is different. The divine forgiveness is not conditioned by the presence of the forgiving spirit; the spirit of forgiveness is invoked on the ground of the divine forgiveness already received. The common element is the emphasis on the duty of forgiveness in relation to others.

he refers when he says: 'Thou wicked servant, I forgave thee all that debt, because thou besoughtest me: shouldest not thou also have had mercy on thy fellow-servant, even as I had mercy on thee?' (xviii. 32 f.). Forgiveness, as here described, is the bestowal of mercy and the cancellation of indebtedness. Doubtless, when it is exercised, normal relations are restored, but it is not of this consummation that the terms used speak; the peculiar nature of the action described is that it makes the restoration possible. When the lord of the unmerciful servant asks: 'Shouldest not thou also have had mercy on thy fellow-servant?', he does not mean: 'Ought you not also to have restored him to fellowship?', but: 'Ought you not to have remitted his debt of one hundred pence?'. True fellowship, indeed, with the merciful lord is actually lacking. So little is it present that the servant can take his comrade by the throat and cry, for the sake of a paltry sum: 'Pay what thou owest' (xviii. 28). And yet, he has been forgiven! The conclusion is inescapable that Jesus is speaking of a stage antecedent to reconciliation when He applies the teaching of the parable in the sombre words: 'So shall also my heavenly Father do unto you, if ye forgive not every one his brother from your hearts' (xviii. 35).

The parable of the Rich Man and Lazarus (Lk. xvi. 19-31) does not supply much material for discussion since it is not intended to illustrate forgiveness. Indeed, as we have seen, it is only by implication that the idea of forgiveness arises in the words: 'And he said, Nay, father Abraham: but if one go to them from the dead, they will repent (xvi. 30). The suggestion is that the five brothers are in need of forgiveness. In the absence of any indications to the contrary we are entitled to infer that here forgiveness is conceived as elsewhere in the sayings of Jesus.

The parable of the Pharisee and the Publican (Lk. xviii. 10-4) is of interest in our discussion because of the statement: 'I say unto you, This man went down to his house justified rather than the other' (xviii. 14). 'Justified' here means 'declared in the right'. Strictly speaking, this description extends the idea of forgiveness, since not only are the publican's offences covered, but also a judgment is expressed concerning the man himself. We are appreciably nearer the Pauline conception of justification. The act of forgiveness has already been completed. It is because he is forgiven that the man goes down to his house 'justified'; and it is because he is both forgiven and 'justified' that he is restored to fellowship with God.

So far nothing has been observed which compels us to modify the conclusions previously reached. Is this also the case if we consider the parable of the Prodigal Son (Lk. xv. 11-32)? Is not this parable the classical example of forgiveness, and is not the forgiveness described full restoration to fellowship?

In view of the trend of our inquiries until this point this question needs to be considered with some care, and all the more because the words 'forgive' and 'forgiveness' are nowhere used in the parable. Unlike the parable of the Unmerciful Servant, this parable is not intended primarily as an illustration of forgiveness; what it describes is a lost son and the grace of a loving father. In such a story it is inevitable that both forgiveness and reconciliation should be represented, but it is important to determine at what points they appear and whether they are identified. Especially should we be on our guard against the danger of first identifying the two in our own minds, under the influence of modern teaching, and then of discovering signs of an identification which in reality may not be intended.

The restoration of the lost son to the joy of fellowship is described in the words:

> 'But the father said to his servants, Bring forth quickly the best robe, and put it on him; and put a ring on his hand, and shoes on his feet: and bring the fatted calf, and kill it, and let us eat, and make merry: for this my son was dead, and is alive again; he was lost, and is found. And they began to be merry' (xv. 22-4).

Here is a picture of reconciliation. The son is restored to the fellowship of the home; the broken relationship is re-established. It may even be that here is a representation which includes the heart of the Pauline idea of justification, since the father accepts the son as righteous: 'This my son was dead, and is alive again; he was lost, and is found'.

But have we here an example of forgiveness?

Undoubtedly, forgiveness is depicted in the above passage in the sense in which we understand the term to-day, as it is described, for example, in the quotations given at the beginning of the present chapter. If 'to forgive is to restore the old relationship', if forgiveness is 'the full restoration of delicate personal relations between friends or between parent and child', Lk. xv. 22-4 describes forgiveness. But does the passage describe forgiveness in the New Testament sense of the term? Would it have been recognized as such by the New Testament writers? Would St. Paul have so described it? Would Jesus?

It is difficult to answer these questions in the affirmative. It is a sound exegetical canon that material, where the presence of an idea is suspected but is not directly expressed, must be appraised in the light of passages where the actual terms are used and the meaning is explicit. If we apply this principle, we are at a loss to explain why the richer meaning found in xv. 22-4 is not found also in the sayings, to account for the fact that in every New Testament passage where forgiveness is actually mentioned it appears to denote the removal of the barriers to fellowship rather than reconciliation itself. Why should this passage, where the term is not used, stand alone? The presumption surely is that from the standpoint of New Testament usage it is not an example of forgiveness; it describes reconciliation, and in the New Testament the two are not the same thing.

Forgiveness is described in the parable at an earlier point, in the words of xv. 20:

> 'But while he was yet afar off, his father saw him, and was moved with compassion, and ran, and fell on his neck, and kissed him.'

Even here we have a warmer conception of forgiveness than anywhere else in the New Testament, and one which merges into a picture of reconciliation, but the essential characteristics of forgiveness are here plainly present. The wrong done by the son is cancelled by the father; it no longer stands between them; the son is forgiven. Moved with compassion at the evident sign of repentance, the father runs to meet his son, and in the kiss of love the wrong-doing of the past is covered.

The distinction we have traced would be fine and even trivial if our object were simply an exegetical treatment of the parable, because it concerns matters which have little interest or meaning for modern ways of thinking. To say that forgiveness is described in verse 20, but reconciliation in verses 22-4, sounds like hair-splitting if our object is the appreciation of the beauty and suggestiveness of the parable. If, however, as in our investigation, the purpose is to discover the precise sense in which the New Testament uses the term forgiveness, in view of its supreme importance for the study of theology, the value of the distinction cannot be exaggerated; it permits us to say that New Testament usage is consistent throughout. Nothing in this parable, nor indeed in any parable, can shake the conclusion that in the New Testament forgiveness is the cancelling or removal of barriers to reconciliation.

The study of this parable, however, adds a point of much importance for the story of the development of the idea of forgiveness. The parable of the Prodigal Son has contributed more than all other factors to the extension and enrichment of the content of forgiveness, so that in modern thought it is a synonym for reconciliation, and to such a degree that it requires an effort of mind to believe that it ever meant anything less. And the parable is a parable of Jesus! Jesus, therefore, who used the word forgiveness in a sense so different from our own, is directly responsible for the enlargement of the idea. It is significant, however, that He gives the impulse to this development in a parable in which He uses neither the noun nor the verb. Must we not say that He employs neither, tacitly or deliberately, just because their meaning was inadequate to such a story as the one He wished to tell? His silence is in line with the later practice of St. Paul, who deserts ἀφίημι for χαρίζομαι when he desires to speak of richer and more humane relationships. We shall see later that it is in harmony with St. Paul's preference for justification as a term of richer content than forgiveness as he understood the word.

(*d*) *Forgiveness in the Old Testament and in later Judaism*

We may now reasonably claim that the narrower content of forgiveness in the New Testament, as compared with modern usage, has been established. The question therefore arises: How is this limitation of reference to be explained? Why is it so consistent, and why is it overcome only with obvious difficulty?

The answer, or at least part of the answer, is that the limitation arises from the Old Testament antecedents of the idea and especially from the associations of the cultus. This fact is clearly seen from the use of ἀφίημι in the Septuagint, where it is used to render *nasa'* ('to take away') in Gen. iv. 13, Ex. xxxii. 32, Psa. xxiv. 18, xxxi. 5; *ṣalaḥ* ('to forgive') in Lev. iv. 20, v. 10, 13, Numb. xiv. 19, xv. 25 f., Isa. lv. 7; and *kipper* ('to cover, make atonement for') in Isa. xxii. 14. In these passages the objects of forgiveness are: ἁμαρτία(ι), ἀνομία, ἀσέβεια and αἰτία (Gen. iv. 13). The act of forgiveness is the covering or removal of these evils. Parallel with this usage is the use of ἐξαλείφω to render *maḥah* ('to wipe, blot out') in Psa. li. 3, 11, Isa. xliii. 25, xliv. 22.[1]

It is obviously not possible in the course of the present discussion to examine the Old Testament conception of forgiveness in detail, and the following list of passages is offered only as a selection illustrative of its main features.

'Forgive, I pray thee now, the transgression of thy brethren, and their sin, for that they did unto thee evil' (Gen. l. 17).

'The Lord, the Lord, a God full of compassion and gracious, slow to anger, and plenteous in mercy and truth; keeping mercy for thousands, forgiving iniquity and transgression and sin . . . ' (Ex. xxxiv. 6 f.).

'I said, I will confess my transgressions unto the Lord;
And thou forgavest the iniquity of my sin' (Psa. xxxii. 5).

'Have mercy upon me, O God, according to thy lovingkindness:
According to the multitude of thy tender mercies blot out my transgressions' (Psa. li. 1).

'Iniquities prevail against me:
As for our transgressions thou shalt purge them away' (Psa. lxv. 3).

[1] Cf. the use of ἐξαλείφω in Acts iii. 19 and Col. ii. 14.

'But he, being full of compassion, forgave their iniquity, and destroyed them not:
Yea, many a time turned he his anger away' (Psa. lxxviii. 38).

'Thou hast forgiven the iniquity of thy people,
Thou hast covered all their sin' (Psa. lxxxv. 2).

'Bless the Lord, O my soul,
And forget not all his benefits:
Who forgiveth all thine iniquities;
Who healeth all thy diseases' (Psa. ciii. 2 f.).

'If thou, Lord, shouldest mark iniquities,
O Lord, who shall stand?
But there is forgiveness with thee,
That thou mayest be feared' (Psa. cxxx. 3 f.).

'I, even I, am he that blotteth out thy transgressions for mine own sake; and I will not remember thy sins' (Isa. xliii. 25).

'Let the wicked forsake his way, and the unrighteous man his thoughts: and let him return unto the Lord, and he will have mercy upon him; and to our God, for he will abundantly pardon' (Isa. lv. 7).

'For they shall all know me, from the least of them unto the greatest of them, said the Lord: for I will forgive their iniquity, and their sin will I remember no more' (Jer. xxxi. 34).

'Who is a God like unto thee, that pardoneth iniquity, and passeth by the transgression of the remnant of his heritage? he retaineth not his anger for ever, because he delighteth in mercy' (Mic. vii. 18).

Such a list as this shows clearly where the debt of the New Testament writers lies. It reveals also the reason for their preoccupation with the idea of forgiveness as the cancelling of sins, transgressions, and iniquities. The Old Testament references to 'blotting out', 'purging away', 'covering', and 'remembering no more' determined this element in their thinking.[1] They were also deeply

[1] 'When a Hebrew thanked God for forgiving all his sin, he was giving thanks for the fact that no cloud obscured the brightness of his life', R. H. Kennett, *The Church of Israel*, 167.

influenced by the thought of the readiness to forgive of a God who 'delighteth in mercy'.

The influence of the cultus, however, in deepening the sense of sin, and in establishing the idea that forgiveness is the cancelling or covering of transgressions, must not be underestimated. '*All* sacrifices', write Oesterley and Robinson, 'whether bloodless or bloody, effect reconciliation (cp. Ezek. xlv. 15, 17); i.e. they are means of obtaining divine forgiveness'.[1] G. F. Moore says that the primitive expiations and purifications are perpetuated in the Mosaic laws, 'but they no longer possess in themselves a mysterious, or if we choose, a magical, efficacy; they are rites which God has appointed for men to seek pardon through, and are thus conditions of forgiveness'.[2] Repentance, however, came increasingly to be emphasized in association with the rites. Moore points out that Judaism 'made repentance the condition *sine qua non* of them all, and eventually the substitute for them all'.[3] Reparation was also held to be necessary and the performance of good works, especially charity.[4] The finest statement of the duty of the injured party to forgive the wrong-doer is the passage cited by T. W. Manson[5] from the *Testaments*

[1] *Hebrew Religion, Its Origin and Development*, 298. [2] *Judaism*, i, 117.

[3] *Op. cit., ibid.* Cf. Leo Baeck, *The Essence of Judaism*, 171. Moore says that, with the omission of the words 'in Christ', the definition of repentance in the Westminster Shorter Catechism 'completely embodies the rabbinical teaching', *op. cit.*, i, 515. This definition is as follows: 'Repentance unto life is a saving grace, whereby a sinner, out of a true sense of his sin, and apprehension of the mercy of God in Christ, doth, with grief and hatred of his sin, turn from it unto God, with full purpose of, and endeavour after, new obedience.'

[4] Cf. Moore, *op. cit.*, i, 514. In *M. Yoma*, 8, 9 it is said: 'Sins that are between a man and God the Day of Atonement expiates; sins that are between a man and his fellow the Day of Atonement does not expiate until he has conciliated his fellow.'

[5] *The Mission and Message of Jesus*, 504.

of the Twelve Patriarchs: 'Love ye one another from the heart; and if a man sin against thee, speak peaceably to him, and in thy soul hold not guile; and if he repent and confess, forgive him. . . . But if he be shameless and persisteth in his wrong-doing, even so forgive him from the heart, and leave to God the avenging'.[1]

If, however, the Old Testament and the best elements in Jewish teaching explain the character of the New Testament doctrine of forgiveness, there is another factor, closely connected with the former, which must be considered. This is the seriousness with which sin, transgression, and iniquity, as barriers to the enjoyment of fellowship, were regarded. It is not a limited or grudging conception of forgiveness which gives first importance to the removal of these barriers if true fellowship is to be attained. On the contrary, it is a conception wide and deep enough to take full account of the actual facts of life and experience. This is a consideration deserving of the most earnest attention by a generation such as our own which, until recently at least, has been inclined to esteem the problems of reconciliation too lightly. Grateful as we must be for the enrichment of the idea of forgiveness under the influence of the spirit and teaching of Jesus, we owe an immeasurable debt to the peculiar emphasis made in the Old and New Testament writings.

(*e*) *The Place of Forgiveness in Modern Theology*

The preceding discussion has revealed a wide difference between the meaning of forgiveness in the New Testament and its significance in modern theology. Whereas in the former it denotes the removal of the

[1]Gad vi. 3-7. This passage is of the greatest importance if Moore is right in dating the Hebrew original of the *Testaments* in the latter half of the second century B.C. *Op. cit.*, ii, 155.

barriers to reconciliation, in the latter it signifies full restoration to fellowship. We forgive the wrong-doer when by the action of love we repair the broken fellowship and re-establish it upon strong and enduring foundations.

Examples of modern usage have already been given, but it may not be without profit to recall a classical presentation of this view in R. C. Moberly's *Atonement and Personality*.[1] Moberly rightly insists that 'the simple idea of not punishing is too negative and external to touch the real core of the matter' (p. 51). Forgiveness 'is an attitude of a person to a person. It can only be understood in terms of personality' (p. 54). It 'is strictly and absolutely correlative to what may be called the "forgiveableness" of the person forgiven' (p. 56). Moberly even speaks of forgiveness as a process, at first inchoate and provisional, which requires to be consummated, and may be forfeited and reversed. 'Earthly forgiveness—real in the present, but real as inchoate and provisional—only reaches its final and perfect consummation then, when the forgiven penitent—largely through the softening and enabling grace of progressively realized forgiveness—has become at last personally and completely righteous. It is not consummated perfectly till the culprit *is* righteous . . .' (p. 61). Our forgiveness is found in our clear view and unswerving aim, of thought and heart, towards the end. 'And the end is the effectual realization at last of such absolute antithesis between the sinner and his sin, as only is perfectly realized when he, the real he, is no longer a sinner but righteous' (p. 70). It will be observed that, in this account of the matter, the term forgiveness covers, not only justification in the Pauline sense, but sanctification as well. It embraces the entire process of Christian

[1]In the chapter on 'Forgiveness', pp. 48-73.

growth and development, and is at once a possession and a hope, an earnest and a fulfilment.[1]

This account of forgiveness probably extends the content of the idea farther than is common in modern theology, but it serves to illustrate the enrichment that is possible, and it raises in an acute form the problem of the difference between ancient and modern conceptions. The question inevitably arises: Can the modern conception be justified, or ought we to return to New Testament teaching concerning forgiveness?

It serves no useful purpose to slur over the difference between the two views and to treat it as negligible. It is perfectly true that the idea of cancelling offences can only be a first stage in the process of reconciliation, and that, in consequence, the extension of the meaning of forgiveness was a perfectly natural and inevitable development. All the more remarkable becomes the failure of the New Testament to illustrate this advance within the terminology of forgiveness; its evident preoccupation with the act of the cancelling of sins and offences. There are, as we have seen, good reasons for this restriction—the influence of the Old Testament and of the cultus in particular, and the seriousness with which the fact of sin was regarded. The question, therefore, is important, whether theology is wise in using the term forgiveness in the wider sense. Is not the New Testament usage to be preferred?

Strong arguments can be put forward in favour of a return to New Testament usage. (1) We retain the marked emphasis upon the necessity, as a first step to reconciliation, of cancelling sins and offences. (2) We pre-

[1]One is reminded of the observation of Ritschl that the identity of the forgiveness of sins, justification, reconciliation, and admission to communion with God 'receives really classical expression in Calvin', despite the distinctions drawn elsewhere in his discussions. Cf. *Justification and Reconciliation* (Eng. Tr.), 73.

serve a useful terminology which distinguishes successive stages, discernible in thought if not always in experience, in what is certainly a complex and not a simple process, namely, forgiveness, justification, and reconciliation. (3) When we have worked out our modern conception of forgiveness in relation to the death of Christ, we are protected against the embarrassment of discovering that, so far as the term forgiveness is concerned, it entirely lacks foundation in the teaching of the New Testament. (4) We possess a complete answer to theologians who remind us that Jesus never taught that forgiveness was the purpose of His death, and that the sole conditions of forgiveness, on which He insisted, were repentance and amendment. In a word, the task of modern theology is relatively simplified and clarified. These are not small advantages and they ought not lightly to be surrendered.

On the other hand, there are compelling reasons why we should adopt the wider conception of forgiveness current in modern theology. (1) If we are alive to the facts of New Testament teaching, as revealed in the preceding discussion, we can avoid the entanglements described above. (2) The wider connotation of forgiveness has come to stay. It has definitely established itself, although not in the highly developed form favoured by Moberly; and it is dangerous, although not always avoidable,[1] to use a term in one sense in theology and in another sense in common usage. (3) The modern idea of forgiveness is closely related to our conceptions of personality as they have been developed by the study of philosophy and psychology. (4) While not directly taught in Scripture, this idea has been deeply influenced by the teaching of Jesus, in the parable of the Prodigal Son, His emphasis upon the Fatherhood of God, and the decisive place which He gives

[1]As, for example, the use of the term 'person' in Symbolic Theology.

to love as the supreme motive in all human relationships. It was under the influence of this teaching, and of the revelation made in Christ Himself, that Christian thought was able to revive the use of a dying terminology, hardly aware of the new life transfused into it, and to express by means of it the idea of restored fellowship with God. (5) As following upon the teaching of Jesus, the beginnings of this process of development are discernible in the New Testament, negatively in the virtual neglect of *ἄφεσις* and *ἀφίημι* in the Pauline and Johannine writings, and positively in St. Paul's preference for *χαρίζομαι* and, as we shall see later, for *δικαιόω*. (6) Religious terminology is by its nature organic, not static. It is the language of the Christian Society, the Church, nourished and sustained by the Christian Revelation and progressively guided by the Spirit of God. It is therefore to be expected, rather than otherwise, that a term like forgiveness will not remain at the level at which it appears in Scripture, but will be enriched in proportion as the work of God in Christ is increasingly apprehended.

These arguments, which rise above prudential considerations, are decisively in favour of the modern conception of forgiveness as full restoration to fellowship with God. In modern theology it is not possible to restrict its meaning to pardon or the remission of sins. Even in the New Testament the exultation with which it is proclaimed in the earliest preaching shows that it is associated with far more than a simple act of cancellation, although the positive blessings to which it leads are described by other terms. An extension, therefore, of the meaning of forgiveness was inevitable, and in modern usage it is fully established.

Just because of this extension of meaning, the earlier history of the idea of forgiveness is of the utmost importance, both as illustrating the development itself and because it helps to deliver us from serious mistakes in theology. It cannot be too clearly recognized that, if we use a term in one sense without perceiving that Scripture uses it in another sense, the consequences are bad exegesis, theological error, and religious confusion. These unhappy results, indeed, can actually be observed in the religious thought of to-day, and especially in connexion with the doctrine of the Atonement. Few things have contributed so much to the opinion that objective theories, which find a Godward aspect in the work of Christ, are obsolete and mistaken as the identification of the modern and the Biblical uses of the term forgiveness. Few tasks, therefore, can be so important as that of distinguishing these usages. To affirm that Christ died that we might be forgiven, is unscriptural, if we are thinking of the remission of sins; it is totally misleading, if by the forgiveness of sins we mean the restoration of sinners to the joy of fellowship with God. As thus used, forgiveness is synonymous with reconciliation; and the whole question is raised, how so great an end, involving as it does the remission of sins, the free grace of God in receiving sinners, entrance upon a life of fellowship with Himself, and progressive growth in perfect love, is brought to pass. This question is bound up in the closest possible manner with the doctrine of the Atonement. From first to last reconciliation is the work of God in Christ, and the same must be said of forgiveness if it is interpreted as restoration to fellowship with God. The relationship between reconciliation and the Atonement will be considered at a later stage, but before this inquiry can be usefully undertaken it is necessary to examine not only the idea of forgiveness, but also justification, reconciliation, fellowship with God, sanctification, and many subordinate subjects which are connected with these great themes.

In this inquiry one point will call for special attention. We have seen that the New Testament does not teach that Christ died in order that sins might be remitted, but that it does include forgiveness, in this sense, as one of the signs of the expected Messianic salvation. Here is a problem of the greatest importance which may easily be overlooked. It is clearly necessary to determine what is meant when it is said that Christ did not die in order that sins might be forgiven. For the moment we may content ourselves with the statement that the true meaning of the New Testament teaching is that the death of Christ was not necessary to enable God to remit sins. In view of the problems of repentance, it does not follow that there is no connexion between the Atonement and the remission of sins; and one of the questions for further discussion in Chapter VI will be the nature of this connexion.

II

JUSTIFICATION

Now that we have discussed the relation of forgiveness to reconciliation in Biblical and in modern usage, we must inquire what meaning can be given to justification. If forgiveness and reconciliation are synonymous, what room is there for this term; and, if they are distinguished, is justification more than pardon? This question inevitably leads to much more important considerations than those of terminology. It raises the issue whether justification is of more than historical interest. Is it an experience of vital moment in the story of God's dealings with the soul of man? Even the possibility that this may be true is sufficient to warrant a careful investigation of New Testament teaching in relation to this theme. It may well be that the blurring of the New Testament distinction between forgiveness and reconciliation, however much it may be defended, is in part responsible for our modern neglect of justification, to our great loss in Christian theology and experience.

As every one knows, justification is a characteristic Pauline idea. Whereas St. Paul uses ἀφίημι of forgiveness once only (Rom. iv. 7) and ἄφεσις but twice (Eph. i. 7, Col. i. 14), he uses δικαιόω twenty-five times, δίκαιος fourteen times, δικαίωσις twice, δικαίωμα five times, and δικαιοσύνη fifty-two times. As this enumeration shows, he is very sparing in his use of the noun 'justification'; he prefers to use the verbal and adjectival forms and is especially fond of the word 'righteousness'.

The abundant use of this terminology, instead of that

associated with forgiveness, is striking, especially as St. Paul knew his Old Testament so well and was familiar with rabbinic teaching. Why does he so markedly pass by many great Old Testament passages bearing upon this theme? Why does he speak of forgiveness actually less frequently than Jesus Himself? The explanation can only be that he did not think of forgiveness as full restoration to fellowship with God. Just because he was so familiar with Old Testament teaching, he perceived the limitations of a term which suggests little more than an opened door, blessed as this boon is when it is contrasted with the religious condition of men separated from fellowship with God by the barriers of unrepented sins. But if this is so, we must be bold enough to draw the conclusion that for St. Paul the idea of 'being justified' was a much richer conception than that of 'being forgiven', more adequate to express the ideas of God's gracious action in restoring sinners to Himself and of man's standing with God as a redeemed personality. This view is entirely contrary to that which is commonly held. In modern usage forgiveness is a rich ethical conception; justification is often contemptuously dismissed as a term of the law court, a forensic notion which belongs to a sub-Christian stage of religion. Few reversals of terminology are more surprising. To modern theological usage St. Paul is a stranger. If he could return to our world, he would feel like a visitor to a city of Babel smitten with the confusion of tongues. It is true, of course, that *δικαιόω* and its cognates are terms of legal content, although, even so, deepened and enriched by that more humane conception of righteousness which distinguishes the Hebrew idea from the Greek.[1] Terminology, however, must never hastily be assessed exclusively in the light of origins and

[1]Cf. C. H. Dodd, *The Bible and the Greeks*, 44.

associations. We have no more right to disparage δικαιόω because it comes to us from the law courts than we have occasion to apologize for ἀπολύτρωσις because it is used of the manumission of slaves, ἐλλογάω because it is associated with the counting-house, βεβαιόω because it is used by estate-agents, δόκιμος because it described tested metals, παρουσία because it connoted the visit of a potentate, and many other words with social or commercial associations. The origins of a word can never be ignored, but they are wrongly conceived if they are remembered with contempt, or if an aroma of disparagement is carried over to the religious ideas they are used to express. Derivation merely reveals the hole of the pit out of which they have been dug. We can learn more about their meaning by considering the use to which they have been put, since of words, as of men, it is true that 'rank is but the guinea's stamp'. In respect of δικαιόω and its cognates this principle is especially important, because repeated investigations have clearly shown that, while the terminology is legal, St. Paul's thought breaks through the forensic moulds into which it is poured in consequence of the Hebraic idea of righteousness which for him is determinative.

(*a*) *The Meaning of the Verb 'to justify'* (δικαιόω).

Among the more important studies of the meaning of δικαιόω and its cognates are those of Sanday and Headlam,[1] E. de Witt Burton,[2] C. H. Dodd,[3] and G. Schrenk.[4] These investigations are so thorough and comprehensive that it is not necessary to do more than to summarize the

[1] *I.C.C.*, *Romans*, 28-31.
[2] *I.C.C.*, *Galatians*, 460-74.
[3] *The Bible and the Greeks*, 42-59.
[4] Kittel's *Theologisches Wörterbuch*, ii. 176-229.

results which have been reached, as a basis for our study of St. Paul's teaching about justification.

Sanday and Headlam claim that the verb means properly 'to pronounce righteous', and that it cannot mean 'to make righteous'. 'There may be other influences', they say, 'which go to make a person righteous, but they are not contained, or even hinted at, in the word δικαιοῦν. That word means "to declare righteous", "to treat as righteous"; it may even mean "to prove righteous"; but whether the person so declared, treated as, or proved to be righteous, is really so, the word itself neither affirms nor denies.'[1] They speak of this as a 'rather sweeping proposition', but hold that it is made good by the nature of verbs in -όω, when derived from adjectives of *moral* meaning, by the regular use of the word in classical Greek, the Septuagint, the Pseudepigraphic Books, and by the 'no less predominant and unmistakable usage of the New Testament', and especially by Rom. iv. 5: 'But to him that worketh not, but believeth on him that justifieth the ungodly, his faith is reckoned for righteousness.' 'Here it is expressly stated that the person justified has nothing to show in the way of meritorious acts; his one asset (so to speak) is faith, and this faith is taken as an "equivalent for righteousness".'[2]

Burton also discusses classical usage, and that of the Hebrew Old Testament, the Septuagint, the Apocrypha, and the Pseudepigrapha. He maintains that 'in Hebrew usage and the Greek usage of Semitic writers the terms are prevailingly moral as well as forensic', and that in many passages in Isa. xl-lxvi and the Psalms righteousness is in content the equivalent of salvation.[3] In the New Testament the verb signifies: (1) 'to recognize or

[1] *Op. cit.*, 30. Cf. also F. A. Philippi, *Romans*, i. 80.
[2] *Op. cit.*, 31.
[3] *Op. cit.*, 466 f.

declare one to be (in the proper ethical sense) δίκαιος'; and (2), with a greater emphasis upon the forensic element, 'to recognize as acceptable (to God), to accept; in the passive, to be accepted (by God)'.[1] The close agreement with the results of Sanday and Headlam is manifest.

C. H. Dodd also carefully distinguishes between the usage of the Septuagint and that of classical Greek. Normally, δικαιόω means 'to deem' or 'pronounce right' with reference to an impersonal object, and 'to treat justly' or 'do justice to' in the case of a person; but in the Septuagint it is used in a favourable sense, with the meaning 'to redress' or 'vindicate' (cf. Psa. lxxxi. 3, 2 Ki. xv. 4), and again of putting a person in the right by declaring him righteous (cf. Ex. xxiii. 7, Isa. v. 23). 'This is a sense of δικαιοῦν strange to non-biblical Greek, in which δικαιοῦν τὸν ἄδικον would mean "to condemn or punish the unjust".'[2] The Septuagint, Dodd maintains, combines or confuses two different meanings of the causative verb. 'In the one, the quality τὸ δίκαιον belongs to the act or the agent, in the other, to the object of the action: in the one sense it means to do a person justice; in the other, to deem a course of action right or righteous.'[3] The Greek reader, he observes, would constantly find something a little strange in the use of the word, since its connexion with the narrower sense of 'justice' gives to the Greek-speaking world 'a thinner and poorer substitute for this characteristic Hebrew idea'.[4]

The discussion of Gottlob Schrenk not only treats the Greek terms, but also examines the New Testament passages in which they appear. With reference to the dis-

[1] *Op. cit.*, 473. [2] *The Bible and the Greeks*, 52. [3] *Op. cit.*, 53.

[4] *Ibid.* Earlier (p. 44) Dodd points out that the Hebrew idea of righteousness is 'more inward, more humane, and more inclusive' than the corresponding Greek conception.

tinctively Pauline usage, he stresses the forensic character of the thought. St. Paul does not think of the inflowing of ethical quality, of a *justum efficere* in the sense of the creation of correct conduct, but rather of declaring the justification of the godless man who believes, on the ground of the justifying action of God in the death and resurrection of Christ.[1] Justification is both an experience of the individual and a redemptive act of God, and the one cannot be understood apart from the other.[2] It is also closely associated with the Final Judgment, and is thus an eschatological idea as well as a soteriological concept.[3]

From the foregoing summary it appears that, on lexical grounds, the meaning of δικαιόω in the New Testament must be sought among such alternatives as 'to declare righteous', 'to treat as righteous', 'to vindicate'. It cannot mean 'to make righteous'.[4] This rendering, favoured by Roman Catholic scholars, is not adopted by Boylan in his recent valuable commentary on Romans, but it is implied where he speaks of justification as 'a sort of creative act on God's part',[5] or 'an actual qualitative condition',[6] or as 'inner sanctification'.[7] Such comments[8] have no support in the meaning of the Greek verb. If, however, we cannot accept the meaning 'to make righteous', it does not follow that the alternative renderings are free from difficulty. 'To declare righteous', 'to deem righteous', and even 'to treat as righteous', all tend to suggest the thought of an ethical fiction: someone who is

[1] *Theol. Wört.*, ii. 219. [2] *Op. cit.*, ii. 220.
[3] *Op. cit.*, ii. 221 f. [4] So Sanday and Headlam, 30, Dodd, 51.
[5] *Romans*, 80. [6] *Ibid.* [7] *Op. cit.*, 67.
[8] See also p. 57, where justification is described as 'a positive robe of glory', and p. 59, where Rom. iii. 26 is interpreted as meaning that God 'makes the believer just after the model of God'.

not righteous is said to be righteous. There is thus the suggestion of an innuendo in these renderings. This difficulty is real, but it is exegetical, not lexical; it can be met only by examining closely the relevant New Testament passages. The rendering 'to vindicate', although attractive, is not likely to prove helpful, since vindication implies that someone is under a cloud or has been misrepresented in some way or other. To 'vindicate' such a person is to bring his true character to light, and it is doubtful whether, even by the use of the word 'paradox', such a meaning can be extended to the Pauline, as distinct from the Synoptic, usage. It is clearly necessary, if further progress is to be made, to examine the New Testament passages in which the verb appears.

(*b*) *The Use of δικαιόω in the New Testament, apart from the Pauline Epistles*

The New Testament examples of the use of δικαιόω outside the Pauline Epistles raise few difficulties, and may be considered first.

The idea of acknowledging the righteousness of God is expressed in Lk. vii. 29: 'And all the people when they heard, and the publicans, justified God, being baptized with the baptism of John', and the thought of proving something or someone to be right lies behind Mt. xi. 19: 'And wisdom is justified by her works' (cf. Lk. vii. 35: 'of all her children') and I Tim. iii. 16: 'He who was . . . justified in the spirit.' To prove or claim oneself to be in the right is the meaning in Lk. x. 29: 'But he (the lawyer), desiring to justify himself', and in Lk. xvi. 15: 'Ye are they that justify yourselves in the sight of men'. In Lk. xviii. 14: 'This man went down to his house justified rather than the other', the suggestion is that of being acquitted, absolved, or pronounced legally right, and the same is true of Mt. xii. 37: 'For by thy words thou shalt be justified, and by thy words thou shalt be condemned.'

The remaining examples in Acts xiii. 39, Tit. iii. 7, and Jas. ii. 21, 24, 25, present parallels to the Pauline usage; but Apoc. xxii. 11: 'He that is righteous, let him do righteousness still' stands by itself with the meaning: 'to practise righteousness' as opposed to ἀδικεῖν 'to act unjustly'. Tit. iii. 7: 'being justified by his grace', is 'characteristically Pauline'.[1] In Acts xiii. 39: 'And by him every one that believeth is justified from all things, from which ye could not be justified by the law of Moses', it is not certain whether the idea is that of full acquittal or that of a deliverance which transcends the power of the Law. Lake[2] thinks that it is more natural to take the meaning to be 'forgiveness from everything—which the Law never offered', but others[3] accept the more limited interpretation, as indicating on the part of Luke an imperfect grasp of Paulinism, and this appears to be the truer interpretation. The passages in James all involve the idea of justification 'by works' (ἐξ ἔργων), and, in the opinion of Schrenk,[4] are not to be understood as a polemic against pseudo-Paulinism or as a misunderstanding of Paul, but as a parallel reaction to the tradition of the synagogue, emphasizing the active character of genuine faith.

(c) *St. Paul's Use of* δικαιόω

We turn now to the Pauline use of δικαιόω and its cognates. Its distinctiveness is due, not so much to St. Paul's characteristics as a writer, as to the fact that he is

[1] J. H. Bernard, *The Pastoral Epistles*, 179.

[2] *The Beginnings of Christianity*, Part I, Vol. IV, 157.

[3] Cf. A. C. McGiffert, *The Apostolic Age*, 186.

[4] *Theol. Wört.*, ii. 223. This view is hardly convincing. A pseudo-Paulinism appears to be in mind.

compelled to use an existing vocabulary for new purposes, in short, to describe a unique Christian experience based upon a redemptive work of Christ which has analogies but no true parallel. It is for this reason that lexical inquiries contribute so little to the determination of the Pauline conception; they serve to warn us away from profitless exegetical by-paths, but bring us to cross-roads where several ways diverge. Similarly, the study of the usages of the Septuagint, the Apocrypha, and the Pseudepigrapha merely provide a necessary preliminary discipline; while, outside the Pauline Epistles, we discover only parallels with earlier usage or echoes of St. Paul's thought. In the end we must go to the Apostle himself. St. Paul must be his own interpreter.

This account of the exegetical problem suggests the best, and indeed the only valid, method of approach. We must consider first passages where his thought is most clearly expressed, and, in the light of these, other statements where his expressions seem bare and even colourless.

The distinctive ideas in St. Paul's usage are as follows:

(1) *The activity is initiated by God; it is a manifestation of Divine Grace.* We are 'justified freely by his grace' (Rom. iii. 24). 'It is God', says the Apostle, 'that justifieth' (Rom. viii. 33), and of those who are called he says 'them he also justified' (Rom. viii. 30). In the prophecy that in Abraham all the nations would be blessed he sees a foreshadowing of the fact that 'God would justify the Gentiles by faith' (Gal. iii. 8). Although this truth is not often explicitly stated, it must be regarded as a dominating conception implicit in the barest statement regarding justification. In particular, it is implicit in all the negative passages in which it is denied that men are justified 'by works' (Rom. iii. 20, iv. 2, Gal. ii. 16 (*bis*)), or 'by

the law' (Gal. iii. 11), and in positive statements which associate the activity with faith and the work of Christ. From first to last justification is the act of God; men cannot secure or merit it (Rom. iv. 5). He, and He alone, brings it to pass.

(2) *The activity is a present experience, or, to speak more exactly, it is an eschatological act brought into the present, which has meaning for a man here and now.* The eschatological aspect of justification is present in the statement that it is 'the doers of a law' who 'shall be justified' (Rom. ii. 13), and perhaps also in St. Paul's admission that, though he knows nothing against himself, 'yet am I not hereby justified' (1 Cor. iv. 4).[1] So also the claim that 'it is God that justifieth' (Rom. viii. 33), and the assurance that, through the obedience of the one, 'shall the many be made righteous' (δίκαιοι κατασταθήσονται, Rom. v. 19), have an eschatological ring. But this hope, so characteristic of Jewish thought, without being obliterated, falls into the background in comparison with the confident affirmation that men are justified now. The tenses are frequently present. The immediate state of men who have sinned and fallen short of the glory of God is that of 'being justified freely by his grace through the redemption that is in Christ Jesus' (Rom. iii. 24). Christ Jesus is publicly set forth as 'a means of atonement' to show God's righteousness 'at this present season', 'that he might himself be just and the justifier of him that hath faith in Jesus' (Rom. iii. 25 f.).[2] The same Pauline emphasis on the present is evident in Rom. iii. 28, Gal. ii. 16,

[1]Robertson and Plummer (*I.C.C. I Corinthians*, 77) think, against Meyer, Beet, etc., that the verb is used in its general sense ('am I acquitted'), not its technical theological sense.

[2]I have discussed this passage in detail in an article in the *Expository Times*, l. 295-300.

iii. 8, 11, 24, and is reflected in Acts xiii. 39. While the solemn thought of the time when the Lord shall come, 'who will both bring to light the hidden things of darkness, and make manifest the counsels of the hearts' (1 Cor. iv. 5), deeply stirs St. Paul's mind, his distinctive conviction is that men can be justified by God here and now. Indeed, in his view, it is the fact of present justification which gives the assurance to men of final deliverance from the divine judgment. 'With all the more reason, therefore, shall we, now that we have been justified by His blood, be saved by Him from wrath' (Rom. v. 9, Boylan's translation).

(3) *As a divine activity justification is conditioned by faith on the part of men.* Faith is mentioned ten times in passages where the verb is used. A man is not justified by the works of the law, St. Paul says, 'but only through faith in Jesus Christ', and the purpose of believing on Christ Jesus is 'that we might be justified by faith in Christ, and not by the works of the law' (Gal. ii. 16; cf. iii. 8, 11, 24, Rom. iii. 28). God is the justifier of 'him that hath faith in Jesus' (Rom. iii. 26; cf. iii. 30). Faith, indeed, is 'reckoned for righteousness' 'to him that worketh not, but believeth on him that justifieth the ungodly' (Rom. iv. 5; cf. v. 1). The faith in question is not faith in general, for, although in six cases no object is mentioned (Rom. iii. 28, 30, v. 1; Gal. iii. 8, 11, 24), Gal. ii. 16 and Rom. iii. 26 clearly show that St. Paul is thinking of a personal faith-relationship with Christ, while Rom. iv. 5 speaks of a faith in God who justifies the ungodly. In the light of these passages we are warranted in thinking that in the other cases, where there is a bare reference to 'being justified by faith', a faith-relationship to Christ is implied. By this is to be understood more than an attitude, and more even than a relationship, of self-surrender and self-

committal to Him. St. Paul does not separate the Person and Work of Christ, and accordingly faith in Him must mean dependence upon Him both as Lord and as Redeemer. It is important to observe that faith is not described as the final cause, or ground, of justification. The phrase διὰ τὴν πίστιν is never used in this connexion by St. Paul;[1] it is 'by', 'from', or 'out of' (ἐκ) faith that men are justified by God (cf. Rom. iii. 26, 30, v. 1; Gal. ii. 16, iii. 8, 24). In Gal. ii. 16, διά *c. gen.* is used. Faith, therefore is at most a conditioning cause[2] of an activity which is grounded in God's grace, expressed and embodied in the life and death of Jesus Christ.

(4) *The ground of justification is the atoning work of Christ.* This thought is clearly expressed in Rom. iii. 24, 25 f., and v. 9 (cf. iv. 25, v. 16, 18)[3]. In iii. 24 St. Paul speaks of 'being justified freely' by the grace of God 'through the redemption (τῆς ἀπολυτρώσεως) that is in Christ'. In this passage, in view of the definite article and the words which immediately follow (iii. 25 f.), it is impossible to interpret ἀπολύτρωσις generally of spiritual deliverance gained in Christ. St. Paul is thinking of a particular deliverance accomplished by Christ by His death, in consequence of which God receives men as righteous. In iii. 25 he describes Christ as Him 'whom God openly

[1]Schrenk points out that the phrase δικαιοσύνη διὰ τὴν πίστιν is notably absent from the Pauline Epistles. Cf. *Theologisches Wörterbuch*, ii. 210.

[2]The same view must be taken of the phrase 'by works' (ἐξ ἔργων). It is a misrepresentation of the position which St. Paul assailed to suppose that 'works' were interpreted as the ground of justification. Here, too, the ground is the mind and will of God, and the error is in thinking that 'works' could be a conditioning cause of justification. In the case of ἐκ πίστεως the distinction pointed out above is more apparent because St. Paul so clearly relates justification to the redemptive work of Christ in Rom. iii. 24, 25 f., v. 9.

[3]The passages enclosed in brackets are examined in Section (*d*).

set forth as a means of atonement (ἱλαστήριον), through faith, by his blood', and he explains that the purpose in view was to show the righteousness of God, 'that he might himself be *just* and the *justifier* of him that hath faith in Jesus'. For our present argument it makes no difference whether ἱλαστήριον is rendered 'means of atonement', 'means of expiation', 'a propitiation', 'propitiatory', 'a propitiatory sacrifice', or 'a votive gift'. The point in any case is that the activity of God, 'the Justifier', rests upon the atoning ministry of Christ. Even if the improbable renderings, 'as one exercising reconciling power',[1] 'as one with power to reconcile',[2] or 'the Mercy Seat'[3] (*kapporeth*) are adopted, this claim still stands; but it is at its strongest if ἱλαστήριον and ἐν τῷ αὐτοῦ αἵματι point to a sacrificial meaning in the death of Christ. In favour of this interpretation is the statement in Rom. v. 9: 'being now justified by his blood'. Here the phrase, 'by his blood', cannot adequately be explained by the violent circumstances of Christ's death;[4] it bears a definitely sacrificial

[1]Cf. C. A. Anderson Scott, *Christianity according to St. Paul*, 72.

[2]Cf. C. A. Anderson Scott, *Foot-Notes to St. Paul*, 25.

[3]So Ritschl, *Die christliche Lehre von der Rechtfertigung und Versöhnung dargestellt*, ii. 171; Büchsel, *Theol. Wört.*, iii. 321f.; D. Smith, *The Atonement in the Light of History and the Modern Spirit*, 160-3. The objections to the rendering 'Mercy Seat' are as follows: (1) To translate ἱλαστήριον by 'mercy-seat', *Gnadenstuhl* (Luther), is misleading. τὸ ἱλαστήριον is 'the propitiatory' which covered the ark, the place where sacrificial blood was sprinkled. Cf. Deissmann, *Encycl. Biblica*, col. 3027-35. (2) As thus used the word invariably has the definite article, except in Ex. xxv. 16 (17) where the noun ἐπίθεμα is added. (3) Nothing in the context of Rom. iii. 25 suggests that St. Paul is thinking of 'the propitiatory' (contrast Heb. ix. 5). (4) It is not St. Paul's habit to allude to religious objects in the Levitical cultus, with the exception of the Temple itself (cf. 1 Cor. iii. 6, vi. 19). (5) The ideas of Rom. iii. 25 are unduly complicated if Christ is thought of both as an offering ('by his blood') and as Himself 'the propitiatory'.

[4]Cf. C. A. Anderson Scott, *Foot-Notes to St. Paul*, 25. See *The Expository Times*, l. 295-300.

meaning, and refers to the life of Christ freely offered for men upon the Cross.[1] In the light of the three passages in question the relation of justification in Pauline thought to the Cross is unmistakable. It is by reason of the atoning ministry of Christ that God justifies men. It would be absurd to object that in the majority of cases there is no reference to the Cross, for in many passages St. Paul's immediate interest is to rebut the suggestion that justification is 'by works'. We must read these passages in the light of those in which St. Paul expresses himself more fully. Moreover, Rom. iii. 24, 25 f., and v. 9 are not mere passing opinions, the isolated expressions of a mood; they are settled Pauline convictions. Accordingly, the barer passages must be read as charged with the same meaning. We must conclude that, whatever justification may mean, it is a divine activity grounded in the work of Christ and made possible on that account. There are, of course, Pauline passages in which δικαιόω is used in a general sense, without reference to justification. In Rom. iii. 4, for example, in the words, 'that thou mightest be justified in thy words', the meaning is 'proved to be right'; and the same usage is found in 1 Cor. iv. 4: 'For I know nothing against myself; yet am I not hereby justified'. Again, in Rom. vi. 7: 'for he that hath died is justified from sin', the verb is used in the sense of 'set free'.[2] Apart, however, from cases of this kind, our conclusion is that St. Paul uses δικαιόω to describe a present activity of God, conditioned by faith, which rests upon the atoning work of Christ.

[1]Cf. 1 Cor. x. 16, xi. 27, Eph. i. 7, ii. 13, Col. i. 20. The background of thought is the Old Testament principle that 'the blood is the life' (Gen. ix. 4, Lev. xvii. 10-2, Deut. xii. 23). Cf. *The Atonement in New Testament Teaching*, 92 f.

[2]Cf. Boylan, *Romans*, 100. See also Sanday and Headlam, *Romans*, 159: 'Sin loses its suit'.

(*d*) *St. Paul's Use of* δίκαιος, δικαίωμα, δικαίωσις, *and* δικαιοσύνη

Our next step must be to consider how far the results already reached are supported by St. Paul's use of the adjective δίκαιος and the three nouns δικαίωμα, δικαίωσις, and δικαιοσύνη.

(1) Of the cases where δίκαιος is used only four call for special notice. In Rom. i. 17 and Gal. iii. 11, by means of a somewhat violent use of the quotation: 'The just shall live by faith' (Hab. ii. 4), further illustrations are supplied of the connexion between justification and faith. Rom. iii. 26 explains the purpose of the sacrifice of Christ as that of showing that God Himself is δίκαιος as well as the justifier of him who believes in Jesus. Rom. v. 19: 'even so through the obedience of the one shall the many be constituted righteous (δίκαιοι κατασταθήσονται)', preserves the eschatological note in St. Paul's teaching about justification and grounds it in the work of Christ.

(2) Among the five cases in which δικαίωμα is used only two (Rom. v. 16 and 18) are of importance for our purpose, since in the remaining three instances the meaning of the word is 'ordinance' (Rom. i. 32, ii. 26, viii. 4). In Rom. v. 16 'the judgment' which came through Adam is contrasted with the 'free gift' which came through Christ; the former, it is said, was 'unto condemnation' (εἰς κατάκριμα), the latter 'unto justification' (εἰς δικαίωμα). The contrast shows that δικαίωμα is used in the sense of 'sentence of acquittal', or 'acquittal'; it is used not of the act of justifying, but objectively of its result.[1] It describes, that is to say, a state or standing into which men are brought by the obedience of Jesus Christ. In the second passage, Rom.

[1] Sanday and Headlam, 141; Schrenk, ii. 226 f.

v. 18, Sanday and Headlam[1] find the same meaning, again interpreting δικαίωμα as 'sentence of acquittal' or, as they paraphrase the passage, 'a single absolving act'. In the Revised Version, however, the translation is as follows: 'So then as through one trespass the judgment[2] came unto all men to condemnation; even so through one act of righteousness (δι' ἑνὸς δικαιώματος) the free gift came unto all men to justification of life'. As the examples cited by Schrenk[3] show, 'act of righteousness' is a meaning which the noun can well express, and the contrast with the word 'trespass' strongly supports this rendering. In any case, however the word is translated, the redemptive work of Christ is in St. Paul's mind, as also in v. 16. It is in virtue of Christ's death that men receive the justification which issues in life (εἰς δικαίωσιν ζωῆς).

(3) At the end of the passage we have been discussing the word δικαίωσις appears, and to this word we now turn. The free gift, says St. Paul, 'came unto all men *to justification of life*' (Rom. v. 18). As distinct from δικαίωμα, δικαίωσις describes the *act* of justifying. The word ζωῆς introduces a new idea, and raises the important question of the relation of justification to life. Most modern commentators accept the view of Winer,[4] that ζωῆς is a genitive of 'inner reference of a remoter kind'; it is a genitive, not of apposition,[5] but of effect or quality. Justification is not identified with life, but is described as an act which leads

[1] *Op. cit.*, 141 f.

[2] The two subjects, 'the judgment' and 'the free gift' are not expressed in the Greek, but are understood from the context (see verse 16).

[3] *Theol. Wört.*, ii. 224 f. See also Lightfoot, *Notes on the Epistles of St. Paul*, 292; Denney, *The Expositor's Greek Testament*, ii. 630; Philippi, *Romans*, i. 279.

[4] *Grammar of New Testament Greek*, 235.

[5] Cf. Lightfoot, *Notes on the Epistles of St. Paul*, 292.

to the enjoyment of life and has life for its goal.[1] The only other passage in which δικαίωσις appears is Rom. iv. 25: '(Jesus our Lord) who was delivered up for our trespasses, and was raised *for our justification* (διὰ τὴν δικαίωσιν ἡμῶν)'. The form of the sentence is probably affected by the fact that in the words, 'who was delivered up for our trespasses', there is an allusion to Isa. liii. 12 in the Septuagint version (διὰ τὰς ἀνομίας αὐτῶν παρεδόθη). This semi-quotation causes an apparent separation between the references to the death and to the resurrection, with the result that the latter seems to be specially related to justification. On this point the opinion of Johannes Weiss is very sound. 'The parallelism of members', he observes, 'according to which the death is connected with sin, the resurrection with justification, has no serious theological bearing—though much has been made of it in the past. It is merely the rhetorical expansion of a *single* thought: dead and risen (the two cannot be thought of in separation) on account of sins (or the forgiveness of sins) and of justification (these two also go together: forgiveness and justification)'.[2] If this view is accepted there is no reason to give to the preposition διά *c. acc.* the extremely rare prospective sense ('with a view to');[3] it is used in its ordinary causal meaning ('on account of'), and the thought is that, because of sin and of justification, Christ both died and rose again.

[1]Cf. Sanday and Headlam: ' "Life" is both the immediate and ultimate result of that state of things into which the Christian enters when he is declared "righteous" or receives his sentence of absolution,' *Romans*, 142; Denney: 'When God justifies the sinner, he enters into and inherits life,' *Romans*, ii. 630. Schrenk thinks that 'life' is described as the correlative of justification, as eschatological, but as beginning now, *Theol. Wört.*, ii. 228.

[2]*The History of Primitive Christianity*, 104.

[3]This is the commonly accepted view. Cf. Sanday and Headlam, 116; Denney, 622; Boylan, 73; Schrenk, *op. cit.*, ii. 228. For a further discussion see *The Expository Times*, l. 298, *The Atonement in New Testament Teaching*, 97. See also H. G. Meecham, *The Expository Times*, l. 564.

(4) It is not necessary to discuss all the passages in which δικαιοσύνη appears, since in many of them the meaning is quite general or is not specially related to justification. In other cases reference is made to 'the righteousness of God' (Rom. i. 17, iii. 5, 21, 22, x. 3 (*bis*), 2 Cor. v. 21; cf. Rom. iii. 25 f., 2 Cor. ix. 9). Phil. iii. 9 mentions a righteousness 'which is through faith in Christ, the righteousness which is of God by faith' (cf. i. 11). These passages illustrate the ethical and religious elements in St. Paul's thought; they describe both an attribute of the Being of God and a saving activity which it is His nature to exercise.

Turning to the passages more directly related to justification, we find some in which it is denied that righteousness is 'through' (Gal. ii. 21) or 'of the law' (Gal. iii. 21). In contrast with these passages are those in which faith is closely related to righteousness. The phrase 'the righteousness of faith' is used with reference to Abraham while he was still uncircumcised (Rom. iv. 13; cf. iv. 9, 11). In Rom. ix. 30 and x. 6 'the righteousness which is of faith' is mentioned, and in Rom. x. 4 it is said that 'Christ is the end of the law unto righteousness to every one that believeth'. In Phil. iii. 9 'the righteousness which is of God by faith' and which is 'through faith in Christ' is expressly distinguished from a righteousness which St. Paul describes as 'mine own, even that which is of the law'. In Gal. v. 5 the eschatological note appears in the words: 'We through the Spirit by faith wait for the hope of righteousness'.

In these controversial passages the importance of faith in relation to righteousness receives a decisive emphasis, and if less is said of the object of faith (cf. Phil. iii. 9), the reason is that the dominant intention is to reject the claims of a righteousness based on merit or the fulfilment of the demands of the law. The plea is 'Not works, but faith', and the nature of faith is left to be defined elsewhere as faith in God actively at work in the redemptive ministry of Christ.

Thus far, we have met with nothing but confirmation of the results already reached, and although much remains for discussion, no serious ethical difficulties have been encountered. It is safe to say that, if St. Paul had said no more about justification than is contained in all the passages we have examined in Sections (*c*) and (*d*), while many problems would have remained obscure, and therefore open to further inquiry, a theology concerned to preserve Christian values would find little difficulty in coming to terms with Pauline teaching. The position, however, is very different in a group of passages in which faith is described as 'reckoned for righteousness'. The phrase used is *λογίζεσθαι εἰς δικαιοσύνην*. The passages occupy a relatively small place in the Pauline writings, being found in Gal. iii. 6 and Rom. iv. 1-12 and 22. These passages have given rise to misunderstandings and misinterpretations of the doctrine of justification by providing shelter for unethical ideas of imputation. For this reason it will be of advantage to examine them separately in the next section.

(*e*) *St. Paul's Teaching concerning Imputation*

St. Paul's first use of the idea of imputation is in Gal. iii. 6: 'Even as Abraham believed God, and it was reckoned unto him for righteousness (*καὶ ἐλογίσθη αὐτῷ εἰς δικαιοσύνην*)'. This passage is a quotation of Gen. xv. 6, and it is used by St. Paul to illustrate the fact that God does not supply the Spirit and do mighty works among men 'by the works of the law', but 'by the hearing of faith' (Gal. iii. 5). His claim is that those who are 'of faith' are the true sons of Abraham (Gal. iii. 7-9). Beyond this he makes no further use of the quotation. His attention is occupied with the promise made to Abraham in Gen. xii. 3 (cf. Gen. xviii. 18): 'In thee shall all the nations be blessed' (Gal. iii. 8). When he refers expressly to justification (Gal. iii. 11), he dwells rather upon the words of Hab. ii. 4: 'The just shall live by his faith'.

These interests prevent him from making a further use of Gen. xv. 6; but in the interval before writing the Epistle to the Romans he has evidently reflected long on the exegetical possibilities of this passage. He sees that the statement regarding Abraham's faith in Gen. xv. 6 *precedes* the account of the instituting of circumcision in Gen. xvii. 10 f. Pursuing, therefore, a typically rabbinical argument, he claims that Abraham is the spiritual father of the Gentile as well as of the Jew, since it was while he was still uncircumcised that it was said of him that he believed God, 'and it was reckoned to him for righteousness'. That which Abraham believed was God's promise concerning his seed: 'Look now toward heaven, and tell the stars, if thou be able to tell them. . . . So shall thy seed be' (Gen. xv. 5). In the long section in Rom. iv. 3-12 he dwells upon the significance of Gen. xv. 6, and then, after describing Abraham's great faith, despite his advanced age and the barrenness of Sarah, he repeats the quotation: 'Wherefore also "it was reckoned unto him for righteousness"' (Rom. iv. 22). The section is of such importance that it should be read as a whole:

Rom. iv. 3-12, 22: 'For what saith the scripture? "And Abraham believed God, *and it was reckoned unto him for righteousness*" (Gen. xv. 6). Now to him that worketh, the reward is not *reckoned* as of grace, but as of debt. But to him that worketh not, but believeth on him that justifieth the ungodly, *his faith is reckoned for righteousness*. Even as David also pronounceth blessing upon the man, *unto whom God reckoneth righteousness* apart from works, saying,

> "Blessed are they whose iniquities are forgiven,
> And whose sins are covered.
> Blessed is the man to whom the Lord *will not reckon* sin"
> (Psa. xxxii. 1 f.).

Is this blessing then pronounced upon the circumcision, or upon the uncircumcision also? for we say, "To Abraham *his faith was reckoned for righteousness*" (Gen. xv. 6). How then was it *reckoned?* when he was in circumcision, or in uncircumcision? Not in circumcision, but in uncircumcision: and he received the sign of circumcision, a seal of the righteousness of the faith which he had while he was in uncircumcision: that he might be the father of all them that believe, though they be in uncircumcision, *that righteousness might be reckoned unto them;* and the father of circumcision to them who not only are of the circumcision, but who also walk in the steps of that faith of our father Abraham which he had in uncircumcision. . . . Wherefore also "*it was reckoned unto him for righteousness*".'

The argument is finally clinched in the passage:

> 'Now it was not written for his sake alone, that *it was reckoned unto him;* but for our sake also, *unto whom it shall be reckoned,* who believe on him that raised Jesus our Lord from the dead, who "was delivered up for our trespasses", and was raised for our justification' (Rom. iv. 23-5).

To those to whom it was originally addressed St. Paul's argument must have come with great force, since it provided a basis for the 'Not works, but faith' doctrine within the Old Testament itself. It traced the origins of the teaching to patriarchal times before the institution of the rite of circumcision, and supported it by an apt reference to the Psalter (Rom. iv. 7 f.; cf. Psa. xxxii. 1 f.). This example, however, is not the only instance, nor the last, of an argument, immediately successful, which ultimately has proved to be a liability. Whilst it is not fair to judge St. Paul by the exegetical canons of modern times, it is impossible not to see that his argument has seriously compromised the doctrine of justification by faith by suggesting objections to which it is not rightly exposed.

(1) In the first place, the use of the quotation from the Septuagint version of Gen. xv. 6 compelled St. Paul to employ the compromising expression, 'to reckon for righteousness'. To say the least, the associations of λογίζομαι are unfortunate; and whilst, in accordance with what has been said about words earlier, this is not necessarily a fatal objection, it cannot be said that it rises above these associations. The verb means 'to reckon, calculate, deem, consider', 'to reckon a person to be this or that', 'to account a thing as having a certain value'. As the evidence of the Papyri shows,[1] its atmosphere is commercial. Too easily it suggests the thought of a *quid pro quo*, or even a fictitious estimate. Most of the objections to the doctrine of justification by faith are probably strongly influenced by the passages in which it appears. Righteousness, it is held, is something imputed rather than real.

(2) Secondly, the parallel between Abraham's faith and the faith by which men are justified is far from being satisfactory. When it is said that 'Abraham believed God; and it was reckoned to him for righteousness', the meaning is that he accepted God's word as true, and thus was righteous. His faith revealed the kind of man he was. But, according to St. Paul's teaching, the faith by which a man is justified is not the acceptance of divine statements or promises, nor is it simply faith in God; it is personal reliance upon God's redemptive work in Christ; it is faith in Jesus Christ, the Redeemer. The use of the Old Testament quotation obscures this crux of Pauline teaching, and encourages the thought of belief as a requisite for justification. A man is justified because he believes some-

[1] Cf. Moulton and Milligan, *The Vocabulary of the Greek Testament*, 377 f.

thing! When we study Pauline teaching as a whole we see that this idea is a monstrous perversion of the truth, but there can be little doubt that it has found shelter under the wings of St. Paul's argument. The Apostle has suffered from his efforts to be convincing. Is there a half-conscious recognition of the inadequacy of the parallel in the marked stress he lays upon the quality of Abraham's faith, when he describes the patriarch contemplating his own body now 'as good as dead' and the deadness of Sarah's womb, and speaks of him as one who 'waxed strong through faith', giving glory to God and being fully assured that 'what he had promised, he was able to perform' (Rom. iv. 19-21)? The religious quality of the faith, indeed, is the one common element in the parallel; in the two cases the content of the faith is different. In the one case it is faith in God's promise; in the other faith in His redemptive activity and unfaltering reliance upon it.

The conclusion to be drawn from a study of the passages in question is clear. For the purpose of a historical study of the doctrine of justification, and especially the idea of imputation, their interest and importance are great; but for the understanding of the heart of St. Paul's teaching their significance is negligible. These passages should not be allowed to stand in the foreground when we think of justification. The passages of first importance are those in which he uses the verb δικαιόω, the adjective δίκαιος, the two nouns δικαίωμα and δικαίωσις, and the noun δικαιοσύνη when it is used in connexion with the idea of faith.

(f) Justification by Faith

We are now in a position to ask the question: What is justification by faith?

In the light of the preceding discussion we can see that by justification St. Paul means the gracious action of God in accepting men as righteous in consequence of faith resting upon His redemptive activity in Christ. Two things which can be distinguished in thought are here linked together in the closest relationship. The man has faith, and God is active in the atoning work of Christ; but neither of these in itself secures justification. The ground of the justifying act is God's redemptive work, and the conditioning cause is faith, but it is the interaction of both which brings a man into right relations with God. Unless this is perceived, it is misleading to say that we are justified by faith; for the faith in question is not faith in general, and not simply faith in God, but faith in God active in the redemptive ministry of Christ. It is equally misleading to say that we are justified by reason of the death of Christ; for whatever that death has achieved stands outside ourselves until there is a believing response which makes the achievement a vital element in our approach to God. We are justified when the soul breathes its deep Amen to all that God has accomplished on its behalf.

Such, then, in broad outline is justification as St. Paul understands it. This outline, however, raises many questions, and it is necessary to consider it more fully. It is also necessary to discuss aspects of the doctrine which St. Paul himself does not treat in his Epistles.

The roots of the doctrine are eschatological. Signs of this are visible in St. Paul's treatment, for, as we have seen, passages like Gal. v. 5, Rom. ii. 13, v. 19, viii. 33, and 1 Cor. iv. 4 suggest the idea of the Final Judgment. In thinking eschatologically man lifts his eyes beyond the evils of the present world to the End-time, when God's rule is finally established and His judgment is expressed upon nations and individuals. This conception is older than Israel and can be traced at least as far as the religious thought of Persia and Egypt. Its presence in the Old Testament, and, in particular, in the teaching of the prophets, does not need to be illustrated. In spite also of the distinctive changes characteristic of the teaching of Jesus, and clearly visible throughout the New Testament, it remains as a constituent element of Biblical thought. Even in the Fourth Gospel, the least eschatological of the New Testament writings, it lingers in passages like Jn. v. 28 f., vi. 40, 44, 54, xxi. 22, which not unnaturally, although without sufficient reason, have often been attributed to the hand of a redactor.

In St. Paul's mind the expectation of the Final Judgment is especially vivid. It is a small thing, he says, that he should be judged of man's judgment. He will not even presume to judge himself, since the verdict of his own conscience is not decisive. 'He that judgeth me', he affirms in moving words, 'is the Lord', and he warns his readers to judge nothing before the time 'until the Lord come, who will both bring to light the hidden things of darkness, and make manifest the counsels of the hearts' (1 Cor. iv. 5). In Rom. ii. 16 he speaks of the day 'when God shall judge the secrets of men, according to my gospel, by Jesus Christ', and in Rom. xiv. 10, as an argument against the evil of judging others, he affirms that 'we shall all stand before the judgment-seat of God'. 'So then', he adds, 'each one of us shall give account of himself to God' (Rom. xiv. 12; cf. also 2 Cor. v. 10).

This expectation is part of St. Paul's religious inheritance, as in some form or other it is an element in the belief of any one who takes the Christian religion seriously. It is not, however, the distinctive element in his thinking. That which stands out as both striking and significant is the manner in which eschatological ideas are transmuted and brought into the present. We cannot say that this process is new, since the original impulse is given in the teaching of Jesus when He interprets the Kingdom of God as a present reality visible in His Messianic Mission and Person (cf. Lk. iv. 21, xi. 20). But if it is not a new, it is certainly a parallel, development. Just as the Kingdom exists now in the Person of Jesus, so also, without losing the idea of a final consummation, the Judgment itself is carried into the present, as a fact of immediate significance. Man does not wait in trembling hope, with no prospect save that of a Final Assize. He is not left to await the last trump, but is confronted here and now with the mercy of God. In the twinkling of an eye the mind of God concerning him is made known; he is pronounced righteous, in virtue of his believing response to the redemptive work of God in Christ; and, although he receives no credential which automatically exempts him from further responsibility, he is introduced to a life of such intimate and growing fellowship with God that the Final Judgment is robbed of its terrors. We may, indeed, go further and say that, not only is the transmutation of the eschatological idea of the Judgment parallel with that of the Kingdom, but also that the two concepts stand in the closest possible relationship, since no man can enjoy the blessings of the Divine Rule until he fulfils, though not by his own power, the initial demand for righteousness. Thus it is that Jesus says: 'Seek ye first his kingdom, and his righteousness' (Mt. vi. 33). In its own idiom the Fourth Gospel interprets and associates the Kingdom and the Judgment in the words: 'Verily, verily, I say unto you, He that heareth my word, and believeth him that sent me, hath eternal life, and cometh not into judgment, but hath passed out of death into life' (Jn. v. 24). In this profound, but compressed, statement the suggestion is that, in consequence of a believing response to the activity of God in Christ, judgment is a fact of present experience, in virtue of which men enter here and now into 'eternal life', the Johannine counterpart to 'the Kingdom of God'. With this passage may be compared the sayings: 'He that believeth on him is not judged: he that believeth not hath been judged already, because he hath not believed on the name of the only begotten Son of God' (Jn. iii. 18); and: 'He that believeth on the Son hath eternal life' (Jn. iii. 36; cf. vi. 40, 47). From these sayings it is clear that, while justification is a distinctively Pauline doctrine, analogous ideas are found in the Gospels in close association with the thought of the Kingdom, and that, while both are eschatological in origin and retain elements from their original usage, both are reinterpreted in terms of the present experience of believers whose faith is based upon the work of God in Christ.

It is only in this wider context of thought that justification can be understood, but, for purposes of exposition, it is desirable to give further consideration to the doctrine in its Pauline setting.

The eschatological origins of the Pauline doctrine account for its terminology and its preoccupation with the idea of righteousness. The terms are those naturally used in connexion with the thought of a Final Judgment, springing as they do from the idea of δίκη 'custom' or 'right'. Equally natural is the emphasis upon righteousness. What must be determined at the Last Assize is whether nations and individuals are righteous or unrighteous. It is entirely congruous with eschatological thought that in the last chapter of the Apocalypse of St. John it is said: 'He that is unrighteous, let him do unrighteousness still . . . and he that is righteous, let him do righteousness still' (Apoc. xxii. 11). The time for amendment or otherwise is past when the judgment is given; what the man is now determines his final condition. This preoccupation with righteousness, however, had a deeper ground in the ethical character of Hebrew religion at its best. Thus, its truest notes are heard when, in reply to the Psalmist's question:

> 'Who shall ascend into the hill of the Lord?
> And who shall stand in his holy place?'

the answer is given:

> 'He that hath clean hands, and a pure heart;
> Who hath not lifted up his soul unto vanity,
> And hath not sworn deceitfully' (Psa. xxiv. 3 f.).

Righteousness is the primary demand of the God of Israel.

If such are the central conceptions associated with the Final Judgment, it is readily understandable that, when they are transmuted and carried over into the realms of present religious experience, changes of meaning and of reference are inevitable. It is impossible to borrow eschatological terms and ideas for new purposes and to leave them as they were. That is why, in the study of justification, a patient examination of *δικαιόω* and its cognates is necessary. It is for this reason also that purely lexical investigations carry us only to a certain point. The truth is, the terminology has to serve ends for which it was not originally intended. It creaks and groans in the process, concealing as well as revealing the truths it is forced to express. This fact is one of the causes of the long dispute between Protestant and Catholic theologians as to whether the verb means 'to deem righteous' or 'to make righteous'.

But if the transmutation affects the terminology, it also deeply influences the associated ideas. Righteousness, of course, can never be other than righteousness, but its special reference is determined by the circumstances in which the term is applied. With respect to the Last Judgment, when a man stands before the bar of God, it is used with reference to the sum of his deeds and the quality of his life. In the words of St. Paul the purpose of the Judgment is 'that each one may receive the things done in the body, according to what he hath done, whether it be good or bad' (2 Cor. v. 10). If, therefore, the man is 'justified', the things done in the body are acknowledged to be good; he is 'righteous' as having fulfilled, doubtless by the grace of God, the divinely appointed standards. It is obvious that once this eschatological scheme is dissolved, and its terminology is applied to the circumstances of present religious experience, 'righteousness' must acquire a new significance. It is still, as always, a valuation passed upon men by God, but it is no longer determined by things done, since past action is not under scrutiny. It is the present state of men that is at stake, their status as human beings before God, and this condition is determined by the response of faith to His redeeming activity. Whether terms like 'righteous' and 'righteousness' can be justly used in such a connexion, is a question for serious consideration. For the moment it is enough to determine the sense in which they are used in the Pauline doctrine of justification. In this doctrine, when it is said that God justifies men, the meaning is that he declares them to be righteous in His sight in virtue of spiritual conditions which to Him are valid, namely faith in Him as the Saviour and Redeemer of men.

Postponing for the moment further consideration of this righteousness in its positive aspects, we may with advantage note certain of its negative characteristics.

(1) First, it cannot, on any just estimate of Pauline thought, be regarded as fictitious. St. Paul would have

rejected any such suggestion with horror. 'God forbid', he would have said (cf. Rom. iii. 4, 5), and, in saying this he would have been consistent, since, as we have seen, he traces justification to the divine initiative.

(2) Second, the righteousness does not depend for its existence upon the mere *ipse dixit* of God; it is not a status or quality conferred upon man by the exercise of the Divine Will. Such a righteousness, even if it could be called righteousness at all, would be entirely devoid of ethical character; it could be no more than a permit to draw near, a right of entry to the celestial court.

(3) Thirdly, it is not simply a gift of divine grace. It is certainly a manifestation of grace, in the sense that it is initiated and made possible by the love of God; but it is not a mere pledge or token of love, since, if it is to be real, it must also be the righteousness of men, expressive of their mind, attitude, and purpose.

(4) Finally, as it is not a human achievement, so it cannot be claimed as a ground of merit. It is not something which man has won by his own effort and which therefore he can plead before God. St. Paul's polemic against the idea that justification can be 'by works' is a decisive battle in the history of Christian thinking. It is of the essence of the Gospel that, when a man draws near to God, he comes with nothing in his hands, casting himself completely upon the infinite grace of a loving but sovereign Lord.

The righteousness, then, which is implicit in the doctrine of justification is not fictitious, not arbitrary, not passive, not meritorious. On the contrary, and positively expressed, it is real, ethical, active, and binding in the sense that it is what God requires and makes possible.

The vital problem in justification is raised by the first of these characteristics. Is the righteousness implied real? In particular, as springing out of faith related to the redemptive activity of God, can it be truly called righteousness?

If the righteousness is real, it must have the positive notes of righteousness, that is to say, it must characterize a man standing in complete conformity with the will of God in thought and intention, in desire and purpose. As related to the doctrine of justification by faith, it need not, and indeed cannot connote ethical perfection, since the entire life of a man, or even his past life, is not in question. What is in question is the character of his life as he stands in the moment of a decision on which his future depends. What is his position in relation to God? Is he free to know Him and to enjoy Him for ever? Has he done with all pretences and evasions, with all claims to merit and favour? Does he cast himself wholly upon God, relying upon all that His grace has done for him in Christ and associating himself with all that redeeming activity is meant to express and do? When he so acts, he has stepped out of the category of the godless, and can be accepted by God as righteous, because, to the full extent of his present apprehension of the divine purpose for himself and the world, an apprehension ever growing from this focal moment in richness and insight, he has identified himself with that purpose. The sense of guilt and the inhibiting power of sin are taken away from him; he stands free to enter into abiding fellowship with God. The attitude of man to God which makes this relationship possible, according to St. Paul, is faith, and there is no better name by which to describe it. For the faith in question is not a mere trust in the truth of God's word or the acceptance of theological propositions concerning Him; it is reliance upon Him, dependence upon Him, self-committal to Him, as a redeeming and restoring God. It does not matter greatly whether we describe this attitude as faith in God, or in Christ, or in relation to the atonement, for in Pauline thought these three are one. To St. Paul faith in God is fundamentally faith in God as He is revealed in Christ; faith in Christ is faith in Him who is the 'image' of God; and faith related to the atonement is faith in God active to redeem men in Christ and His Cross. A faith of this kind cannot be a means to something fictitious; it is too rich and virile. Neither can it be a ground for merit, since it derives both its existence and its character from the personal object and the divine activity in which it rests. Justifying faith, then, is the conditioning cause of unmeritorious righteousness, a righteousness which is real, and not merely imputed. How this can be, and what is the actual relationship between faith and righteousness, are the questions which must be considered in the next section. These questions take us to the centre of the problem of justification.

(g) *Justifying Faith and Righteousness*

The question of the relation of justifying faith to righteousness takes us to the very heart of the Christian Gospel. Neither the Catholic nor the traditionally Protestant explanation is satisfactory to the modern mind, although each emphasizes important aspects of the truth.

The Catholic explanation is that man is made righteous by the infusion of divine grace. Influenced strongly by the teaching of Augustine[1] and Aquinas[2], the Council of Trent defined justification as 'not the remission of sins alone, but also the sanctification and renewal of the inner

[1]See the references given by Sanday and Headlam, *Romans*, 149 f., and R. S. Franks, *A History of the Doctrine of the Work of Christ*, i, 117ff.

[2]'Now the effect of the Divine love in us, which is taken away by sin, is grace, whereby a man is made worthy of eternal life, from which sin shuts him out. Hence we could not receive the remission of guilt, without the infusion of grace', *Summa Theologica*, Qu. cxiii. Art. 2.

man by the voluntary reception of the grace and gifts, by which man from unrighteous becomes righteous, and from being an enemy becomes a friend, that he may be an heir according to the hope of eternal life'.[1] It is the merit of this view that a real righteousness is contemplated; the believer is righteous, he is not merely accounted as such. None the less this explanation suffers fatally from the threefold objection that δικαιοῦν cannot be taken to mean 'to make just', that St. Paul does not speak of a divine gift of grace by which men are made righteous, and that justification is treated as if it were sanctification. In short, in this view the heart of the doctrine of justification is completely lost.

The Protestant solution escapes these perils. It treats the Pauline terminology with linguistic fidelity; it refrains from introducing non-Pauline elements into the doctrine; it does not confuse justification with sanctification. Its positive solution, however, in the form it commonly took in Reformation theology, bears the stamp of artificiality. By too rigid an adherence to the illustrative passages in which St. Paul uses λογίζεσθαι,[2] it taught a theory of imputation, according to which faith is accepted by God as an equivalent for righteousness. In much of the teaching of Luther himself, especially his earlier teaching, this idea is not central; for, in the ferment of his thought, justification by faith is not so much a single doctrine, but, as Harnack has observed, 'the fundamental form of the Christian's state'.[3] It is 'the beginning, middle, and end' of the believer's experience, and, in consequence, can be associated closely, and even identified, with regeneration and forgiveness. Justification is described by Luther both as a 'being righteous' and a 'be-

[1] *Conc. Trid.*, vi. 7. [2] See earlier, pp. 52-6.
[3] *History of Dogma*, vii. 207.

coming righteous'.[1] Faith justifies, in that it is the righteousness of Christ infused into the heart, and in so far is the ideal fulfilment of the law.[2] In his later teaching, however, the imputative view gains ground, and it became the official teaching of the Lutheran Church.[3] In the *Formula Concordiae* (1580), for example, it is explained that Christ's obedience is imputed to us for righteousness, and that this righteousness, offered to us through the Gospel and in the sacraments by the Holy Spirit, is applied and apprehended by faith.[4] The imperishable truth contained in this teaching is threatened by the doctrine of imputation which can never be anything else than an ethical fiction. Since it is not a commodity, but a personal state, righteousness cannot be transferred from the account of one person to another. Righteousness can no more be imputed to a sinner than bravery to a coward or wisdom to a fool. If through faith a man is accounted righteous, it must be because, in a reputable sense of the term, he is righteous, and not because another is righteous in his stead. Although, then, Reformation teaching is much nearer the Pauline doctrine than Catholic theology, it cannot be said to have been successful in surmounting

[1]'It is the former, inasmuch as by the faith which attains forgiveness man is really righteous before God; it is the latter, *inasmuch as the faith that has become certain of its God, can alone bring forth good works*,' Harnack, *op. cit.*, 208 f. The italics are Harnack's. Cf. H. R. Mackintosh, *The Christian Experience of Forgiveness*, 149. Dr. Mackintosh holds that justification, in the Lutheran sense, is 'effective as well as declaratory'.

[2]This opinion of O. Ritschl is quoted by R. S. Franks, *A History of the Doctrine of the Work of Christ*, i, 356.

[3]Cf. R. S. Franks, *op. cit.*, i. 356. Quoting from the *Formula Concordiae*, Dr. Franks writes of the classical passage in III. 10-5: 'It finally fixes the purely imputative view of justification adopted by Melanchthon as the only doctrine henceforward tenable in the Lutheran Church', *op. cit.*, i. 419.

[4]*Form. Conc.*, iii. 10-5.

the ethical difficulties of justification. What, then, is the relationship between faith and righteousness?

The connexion is sometimes explained by saying that, in virtue of faith, man possesses the germ or potency of righteousness. This view is satisfactory only if the germ or potency, however rudimentary it may be, is truly righteousness. It is entirely misleading if the germ is something other than righteousness; if it is some alternative or so-called equivalent, in the sense that faith is counted as righteousness. St. Paul himself seems to have been alive to this danger, for it is perhaps significant that only once does he speak of God justifying 'the ungodly' (Rom. iv. 5), and that he never describes Him as justifying 'sinners'. The absence of such phrases is surely remarkable, since his fervent belief is that justification is offered to the ungodly, to sinners. Why have we not many passages like Rom. iv. 5? The explanation can only be either that he saw the fatal ambiguity of such expressions or was half-consciously restrained by the positive aspects of justification. Sin alas! exists in believers; *simul justus et peccator* describes only too obviously the life of the Christian man. This aspect, however, of the Christian experience is not in St. Paul's mind when he speaks of justification. For him, terms like 'the ungodly' and 'sinners' describe men *before* justification. In Pauline thought, in the spiritual moment when a man is justified, he is no longer ungodly or a sinner; in a sense proper to the justifying act of God, he is truly righteous.

At its best, therefore, the germ illustration does not carry us very far in understanding justification. We have still to ask how the germ or potency, destined, as it is, to grow into perfect righteousness, comes into being. Is it the product of faith? Or is faith but one of the factors which bring it to life?

A satisfactory explanation can be reached only by considering how Christian faith is related to its object. Strictly speaking, apart from the object in which it rests, faith is not faith at all. Faith is always faith in something or in some one. Without this objective relationship, it is mere credulity or idle fancy. To a reflective mind this fact is perfectly clear, but in popular thought it is not recognized; faith is conceived as an independent principle self-operative in respect of righteousness. This fatal separation of faith from its object leads to confusion and error, especially as regards justification, as may be observed in the history of the doctrine.[1] As we have seen, 'justification by faith' is a counter-cry to 'justification by works'; this and nothing more. If, however, it is taken as a full statement of the doctrine, no satisfactory account can be given of the righteousness in question. The explanation is simple. *The righteousness springs from faith as it is related to its object; the object gives to it its character as the condition of righteousness.*

Now the object of justifying faith is not in dispute. In St. Paul's teaching it is the redemptive activity of God in Christ. We are justified freely by the blood of Him who died and rose because of our sins and our justification. It is upon this work of God in Christ that justifying faith rests and relies; it is because of a faith so constituted that men are justified. The believer is pronounced righteous because, in virtue of his faith resting upon the work of Christ, he really is righteous in mind and in purpose, although not yet in achievement.

[1] 'The unreal distinction of *fides informis* and *formata*, added to Luther's own extravagant language, produced a strong antinomian tendency. "Faith" almost comes to be looked upon as a meritorious cause of justification; an unreal faith is substituted for dead works; and faith becomes identified with "personal assurance" or "self-assurance" . . .', Sanday and Headlam, *Romans*, 152.

Calvin approaches a view of this kind when, in opposition to justification by works, he says: 'On the contrary a man will be justified by faith, when, excluded from the righteousness of works, he by faith lays hold of the righteousness of Christ, and *clothed in it* appears in the sight of God *not as a sinner but as righteous*.'[1] He weakens the statement, however, by the introduction of the idea of imputation. 'Thus we simply interpret justification as the acceptance with which God receives us into His favour and holds us for righteous, and say that this justification consists in the forgiveness of sins and *the imputation of the righteousness of Christ*.' This obvious reluctance to describe the justified man as righteous is due, partly to opposition to Roman teaching, and still more to the healthy desire to avoid language which might suggest a righteousness consisting in holiness and achieved excellence. In this sense, of course, the justified man is not righteous; he is righteous because, through faith in Christ the Redeemer, he gains a righteous mind.

Among modern writers C. H. Dodd has powerfully expressed this idea in his account of the state of mind of the justified man. 'In fact', he says, 'he is righteous, in a fresh sense of the word; in a sense in which righteousness is no longer, so to say, quantitative, but qualitative; in which it consists not in a preponderant balance of good deeds achieved, but in a comprehensive attitude of mind and will.'[2] He then goes on to urge that, if our highest values are personal, 'at bottom a man is right or wrong according to his relation with the personal centre of reality, which is God', and that a man who is in the relation of 'trusting surrender' to God is 'right'. 'He is justified, in no fictitious way, but by the verdict of

[1]*Institutes*, III. 11, 2. The italics are mine.

[2]*The Meaning of Paul for To-day*, 111.

particular, the liability of men to punishment.[1] Without doubt, this is too narrow and too negative an account of forgiveness, and it completely obscures the positive element in justification. The Reformed theologians and the later Lutherans effected a great improvement when they interpreted the punishment of sin as consisting in the separation of sinners from God, and, in consequence, as the suspension of fellowship with Him. Hence, forgiveness was held to be the restoration of sinners to His presence and to true fellowship with Him. Forgiveness, it was taught, consisted in the removal of spiritual and eternal death, and such earthly evils as remained in the experience of believers were explained as means of chastisement or trial.[2] It is clear from this account that there is much that is common to justification and forgiveness, but it is equally manifest that the tendency, in this account of forgiveness, is to stress its negative aspects without closing the door to its positive implications. In justification, on the other hand, the positive element is central; by the gracious act of God the believer is put into right relations with Himself and received into fellowship with Him. To identify justification, therefore, with forgiveness, at least in the sense of the term under immediate consideration, is to leave in the background the most distinctive features of justification; and, in point of fact, it is significant that many who have made the identification have felt compelled, at the cost of consistency, to go on to assert that justification is more than forgiveness.[3]

Thus far, however, we have been speaking of forgive-

[1]Cf. Ritschl, *Justification and Reconciliation*, Eng. tr., 40 ff.

[2]Cf. Ritschl, *op. cit.*, 44.

[3]For illustrations of this statement see the valuable account given by W. B. Pope of the teaching of John Wesley and later Methodist writers in his *Compendium of Christian Theology*, ii. 445-8.

ness in the narrower sense of the term. What must be said if forgiveness is understood, as in many modern discussions, as full restoration to fellowship with God? Obviously, on this view, the case for identification is very much more impressive. Its attractiveness, for example, is evident when Oman writes: 'It (justification) meant simply to be put right with God, as the prodigal was put right with his father when he came back into the security of his friendship and the blessedness of his family. In other words, it is truly to be forgiven.'[1] Simplifications of this kind, however, while attractive, are sometimes costly. 'To be put right with God' is an admirable phrase descriptive of justification; but to equate the latter with a forgiveness which is to be found in a return to the security of the divine friendship and of the blessedness of the filial relationship, is to make it synonymous with reconciliation and to lose the distinctive character of justification. This claim is not a mere battle about words. Definite religious interests are at stake. Once we interpret forgiveness as reconciliation and equate both with justification, we can describe their religious content only in terms of that which is common to them all; we lose the *differentia* of each. Some evidence of this can be seen in Oman's discussion. Having identified forgiveness with justification, he goes on to explain that we are justified by faith 'because faith is a discerning of God's mind'. 'We have forgiveness and all its fruits,' he says, 'because by faith we enter the world of a gracious God, out of which the old hard legal requirements, with the old hard boundaries of our personality and the old self-regarding claim of rights, have disappeared, a world which is the household of our Father where order and power and ultimate reality are of love and not of law.'[2] All this is very truly and beautifully

[1] *Grace and Personality*, 212. [2] *Op. cit.*, 213.

expressed; but is it justification by faith? What has happened to the idea of faith related to the redeeming work of God in Christ, by reason of which God brings us into right relations with Himself? In truth, it has disappeared, lost in the smoke of successive broadsides upon the evils of 'the legal principle'. The essence of God's pardon is said to be 'in showing Himself so gracious as to give us faith in His love', and 'in this sense we are justified by faith'. The truth is that in this description the language of justification is retained, but its substance is lost. What is set forth is forgiveness in the sense of reconciliation; the references to justification are decorative embroidery.

It appears, then, to be no more desirable to explain justification as forgiveness in the wider than in the narrower sense of the term. The price of the simplification effected is the deflation of our theological currency with the corresponding loss of definite religious values.

Much the same is true of other suggested identifications. In discussing the wider definitions of forgiveness we have already had occasion to speak of reconciliation. To identify justification with reconciliation, as Ritschl frequently does, is to conceal its character, as a part necessary to the whole. Justification is the act of God which makes reconciliation possible; it is the ethical condition of reconciliation, the gift to the sinner of that standing by which alone he can enter into fellowship with God. Similarly, nothing is gained by confusing justification with regeneration, conversion, adoption, or with sanctification. Regeneration is the work of the Spirit in the life of man, whereby his desires, motives, and hopes are cleansed and renewed; it is spiritual re-birth. This work of regeneration both precedes and follows justification; it antedates the moment when the soul enters into right relationships with God, and thereafter it continues in that process of sanctification which finds its goal in perfect love. Conversion is the work of the Spirit in drawing men to God as well as the experience, sudden or gradual, in which they turn to Him. Justification is the counterpart to this process, the divine act which gives it ethical meaning and spiritual validity: man surrenders, but God justifies. Adoption, while coincident with justification, is relatively its consequence; it is when, and because, men stand right with God that they know Him as Father and themselves as His sons. Finally, sanctification is the process in which the righteousness, present already in justification, finds its perfect expression in the moral and spiritual life. In a sense, the justified man is already sanctified, in that in justification the seal of God is set upon him; but we lose the immediacy of justification and its distinctive significance in the Christian experience unless we distinguish the initial act of God from the perfect fruition in which it is meant to issue.

These distinctions are tedious, but they are necessary to clear theological thinking. To no small degree it is because we tend to use four or five different terms as rough equivalents that our modern views regarding the problem of man's recovery and renewal are so confused and superficial. It is not suggested that we can separate in our consciousness and date these various aspects of the Christian experience. Some one or other of them may be so outstanding in our personal experience that we can link it with a definite time or place; but this is not to say that the rest are meaningless. Some of them, and, in particular, forgiveness, justification, and reconciliation, may be so vitally related that we cannot distinguish them in our consciousness at all; but this fact is no reason for refusing to recognize them as separate and essential aspects of God's dealing with the soul of man.

Our conclusion, then, is that justification is rightly distinguished from forgiveness, reconciliation, regeneration, conversion, adoption, and sanctification, and that it describes a vital element in the story of man's return to fellowship with God. It is the divine activity in which God gives effect to His redeeming work in Christ by making possible that righteous mind necessary to communion with Himself.

If this conclusion is sound, the theological importance of justification is undoubted. A theology which loses the idea of justification suffers grievous hurt, nor can it afford to dispense with the word unless it is fortunate enough to discover an equivalent; and of a satisfactory theological equivalent there is as yet no sign. It does not follow that the modern preacher is well advised to use the word 'justification'. And for two reasons. First, the word is not self-explanatory; it cannot be understood without a patient examination of Pauline teaching and an effort to think ourselves back into ancient modes of thought. Secondly, the word is encumbered with misconceptions. History has loaded it with doubtful legacies of debate; it means one thing to the Catholic, another to the Protestant, and nothing to the man in the street. In consequence, it is compromised by its fortunes almost beyond repair.

What is required in modern teaching, and few things are needed more, is a renewed emphasis on the truths for which justification stands. A generation of superficial theology has left many people with a sentimental belief in a good-natured and almost complacent God, a Buddha endowed with supplementary Christian attributes. Fellowship with God is conceived as a very simple and natural relationship which can be enterprised and taken in hand whenever we please and without onerous conditions. God has revealed His love in His Son: it is for us to respond to His gesture and to enjoy His friendship. So anxious have we been to exclude legal ideas from our thoughts of God that we have compromised the ethical foundations of our theology. We have created God in our own image and likeness.

Reflection reveals the futility of this situation. God is Love indeed, but just because of this fact His supreme care is for holiness, righteousness, and truth. He is light, and in Him is no darkness at all. He is 'the high and lofty One that inhabiteth eternity, whose name is Holy' (Isa. lvii. 15). Man, on the other hand, is a creature of time and space, frail in his purpose, divided in his loyalties, inclined to evil, and prone to sin. What fellowship can there be between light and darkness? How is communion with God conceivable? It is the merit of many outworn theological systems that, at least, they envisaged this problem; many Christian thinkers of to-day barely perceive it, or, if they perceive it, give it too little attention. But, however it is regarded, and even if it is ignored, it remains as the perennial problem of religion, threatening neglect and insistent upon solution. Far from being an easy assumption, fellowship with God is a desperate challenge to thought and belief.

It is, or should be, obvious that, so long as man loves evil, surrenders to its power, and manifests its fruits, fellowship with God is impossible. This impossibility is not merely an expression of the Divine Will, but is a necessity grounded in the nature of God, as the God of love, holiness, and truth. Before sinners can know God and experience His peace, they must cease to be sinners. Only the righteous, or those whom, in the ethical perfection of His Being, He can regard as such, can have fellowship with Him. And God can regard as righteous only those who are righteous, either because of attained ethical perfection, or by reason of a standing with Himself, in relation to sin, righteousness, and truth, which He alone can make possible. Such are the inalienable conditions of reconciliation with God.

Justification is a question first and last of man's *standing* with God, of his *mind* as a participant in the divine blessedness. How is this standing to be obtained, this mind to be acquired? Shallow indeed is a man's apprehension of human power if he imagines that he can claim this position or impart this character to himself. The instinctive language of the awakened soul is 'God be merciful to me a sinner'. We cannot submit our claims to the consideration of God. Silent before His mercy, we know that He alone can give effect to our standing before Him. And yet, even He cannot impart it by gift, by fiat, or by imputation, since righteousness is personal or nothing. We are faced, then, by a double dilemma. The righteousness must be our own, but we cannot create it; it must be of God, but He cannot confer it; it must be ours, and of Him, at one and the same time. The resolution of this dilemma is the problem of the Atonement, and the acid test of theories is the extent to which they can meet this moral and religious situation. There is good reason to think that the best solution of the problem is one which sees in God's redemptive activity in Christ the perfect revelation and embodiment of the highest ethical values, of love, righteousness, and truth; an affirmation made in the name of mankind, which individual men, through faith, can re-affirm and make their own, thus finding in it the avenue of their approach to God. In that focal moment when this relationship obtains, the sinner is no longer a sinner in the sight of God; righteous in mind, although not yet in achievement, he is given that standing with God which makes fellowship with Him ethically possible. Not merited by works, nor created by faith alone, this relationship is established by faith dependent upon, and vitalized by, that in which it rests, the astounding grace of God in Christ. Obviously a beginning, a decisive moment in the soul's approach to God, this relationship is either lost or is followed by that growth in righteousness which is the attainment of holiness, the path to perfect love.

Such is the meaning of justification by faith. The terminology and many of the associated ideas are those of St. Paul and of the Hebraic religion from which he drew them, but the inner meaning of the doctrine is the heart of the Gospel. For this reason it is *articulus stantis et cadentis ecclesiae*, the article by which a Church stands or falls;[1] and, with Luther, we may say of it, *articulus justificationis est magister et princeps, dominus, rector et judex super omnia genera doctrinarum, qui conservat et gubernat omnem doctrinam ecclesiasticam*, 'the article of justification is master and chief, lord, ruler and judge above every kind of doctrine, which preserves and directs every doctrine of the Church'.[2]

[1] *Art. Smalc.*, II, 1, EA² 25, 174, *Symbolische Bücher*, ed. J. T. Müller, 300, 5.

[2] *Disputation* d.d. 1, 6. 1537. Cf. F. Loofs, *Leitfaden zum Studium der Dogmengeschichte*, 4te Aufl., 1906, 741 f.

III

RECONCILIATION

FROM the discussion of forgiveness and of justification, we now turn to the subject of reconciliation. This inquiry brings us to the heart of our investigation, since, as we have seen, forgiveness and reconciliation are frequently identified in modern theology and defined broadly as restoration to fellowship with God. As before, the first step must be to examine New Testament teaching. In this matter our difficulty is the wealth of the material. How much of it illustrates the nature of reconciliation, and how much its fruits or consequences? It is perhaps impossible to draw a hard and fast line, and yet it seems obvious that some elements in the teaching belong to the one aspect more than to the other.

Our first task is to examine the Pauline use of the terminology of reconciliation, including the noun *καταλλαγή* and the verbs *καταλλάσσω* and *ἀποκαταλλάσσω*, since St. Paul alone among New Testament writers uses these words; but it will also be necessary to consider his teaching on congruous themes, such as peace with God, freedom, sonship, and fellowship with God; and, indeed, to study the witness of the New Testament wherever reconciliation is described, even though the Pauline terminology is not employed. Many difficult questions will naturally arise in the course of such an inquiry. Is reconciliation, for example, an act or a process; or, again, is it an act of God which inevitably issues in a process? Do peace, freedom, sonship, and fellowship belong to the essential content of reconciliation, or are they vital aspects of the life of the reconciled? So far as fellowship with God is concerned, it is clearly impossible to exclude it from the idea of reconciliation. How can we speak of reconciliation at all, if it does not include some experience of communion with God? On the other hand, New Testament teaching concerning fellowship with God is singularly rich and full; so much so, that to bring the whole of it within the range of the idea of reconciliation is actually to rob the latter of its distinctive content. While recognizing, therefore, that the two themes cannot be kept apart, we shall find it best to treat reconciliation and fellowship separately, as intimately related, but not identical, conceptions. A special chapter, in consequence, will be devoted to the subject of fellowship. Not even with this decision, however, are our problems of method at an end. What place in the discussion is to be given to such themes as the ethical life, life in the Spirit, and sanctification? What reconciliation can there be which does not end in the most perfect ethical life of the individual and of society and in the blessedness of the vision of God? None of the subjects mentioned can be omitted from consideration; and yet, even more than peace, freedom, sonship, and fellowship, they describe the life in which reconciliation issues and finds its consummation. For this reason they must be treated separately in a later chapter under the heading of Sanctification.

(*a*) *The Pauline Doctrine of Reconciliation*

The first thing which arrests attention is the extremely meagre use of the three Greek words which directly express the idea of reconciliation. They are found only in the Pauline Epistles, 1 and 2 Cor., Rom., Eph. and Col., and apart from 1 Cor. vii. 11, which refers to the reconciliation of a wife to her husband, there are only twelve examples of the use of the words in 2 Cor. v. 18-20, Rom. v. 10 f., Eph. ii. 16, and Col. i. 20 f.

1 Cor. vii. 11: 'or else be reconciled to her husband', is of interest because it illustrates the use of the passive form καταλλαγήτω of a relationship in which active participation or co-operation is implied. The woman is not expected to be quiescent in her attitude to the proposed reconciliation. This fact bears upon the use of the passive forms in 2 Cor. v. 20 and Rom. v. 10.[1]

(1) The earliest examples where the thought is that of reconciliation with God are those of 2 Cor. v. 18-20: 'But all things are of God, who *reconciled* us to himself through Christ, and gave unto us *the ministry of reconciliation*; to wit, that God *was* in Christ *reconciling* the world unto himself, not reckoning unto them their trespasses, and having committed unto us *the word of reconciliation*. We are ambassadors therefore on behalf of Christ, as though God were intreating by us: we beseech you on behalf of Christ, *be ye reconciled* to God'. Here the verb is used twice in the active, of the reconciling act of God which is explained in the words: 'God was in Christ reconciling the world to himself' (Θεὸς ἦν ἐν Χριστῷ κόσμον καταλλάσσων ἑαυτῷ). In this most important passage ἦν καταλλάσσων is a periphrastic imperfect.[2] The idea is not that of the A.V.: 'God was in Christ, reconciling the world to himself', as if the primary reference were to the Incarnation; and still less that the object of reconciliation was 'the world that is in Christ'; but that, in Christ, God was reconciling the world to Himself.[3] The significance of the historical revelation in Christ is

[1] Cf. F. Büchsel, *Theol. Wört.*, i. 256.

[2] Cf. J. H. Moulton, *Prolegomena*, 227. For the combination ὡς ὅτι ='that', cf. Moulton, *op. cit.*, 212.

[3] Cf. A. Plummer, *I.C.C.*, 2 *Cor.*, 183.

that it is God's reconciling action. Here, as always, God is the reconciler. The world, that is, the world of men, not the material universe, is the object of reconciliation. Never do we read of God being reconciled,[1] nor of man reconciling himself to God. How the reconciling of the world is effected, is brought out in the phrases: 'not reckoning unto them their trespasses' and 'having committed unto us the word of reconciliation'; it is accomplished by forgiveness and the proclamation of the Apostolic message.

In using the phrase, 'in Christ', St. Paul is thinking of Christ as the personal agent of reconciliation; but especially, as the context clearly shows, of His death and resurrection. The passage is preceded by the well-known reference to the constraining power of the love of Christ, by the plea that, since one died for all, therefore all died, and by the explanation that He died that men 'should no longer live unto themselves, but unto him who for their sakes died and rose again' (2 Cor. v. 14 f.). It is followed by the epigrammatic statement: 'Him who knew no sin he made to be sin on our behalf; that we might become the righteousness of God in him' (2 Cor. v. 21). In such a context it is beyond question that the reconciling work of God is conceived as accomplished in the death and resurrection of Christ.[2]

All through this section one cannot fail to be impressed with the immense importance St. Paul attaches to this message and to his sense of being divinely commissioned to declare it. Twice in the space of a few lines he speaks of the Apostolic commission: 'God . . . gave unto us the

[1]Cf. J. Denney, *The Death of Christ*, 143 f.

[2]Cf. Rom. v. 10: 'We were reconciled to God *through the death of his Son*'; Eph. ii. 16: '*through the cross*'; Col. i. 20: 'to reconcile all things unto himself, having made peace *through the blood of his cross*'.

is thinking, not simply of the final restitution of the universe, but of the supremacy of Christ's reconciling work to which he can set no bounds. No more than in 2 Cor. v. 19 is there any thought of a slowly ripening process, but of a decisive act of Christ the effects of which extend to earth and heaven itself.

How personal in its operation the work of reconciliation is conceived to be, is seen in the fact that the reference to the reconciling of 'all things' is followed immediately by the words: 'having made peace through the blood of his cross'. Peacemaking is essentially personal; it is a moral activity wrought by a person or persons upon persons; it is reconciliation in its most distinctive aspect. Such a phrase, in a context where 'all things' are in question, is highly significant for the trend of Pauline thought. In the sentence which follows, in the words: 'You . . . now hath he reconciled,'[1] this personal aspect is explicit. Here we have the same manward reference as in 2 Cor. v. 18-20 and Rom. v. 10 f.

The emphasis upon the death of Christ is equally marked. Peace has been made '*through the blood of his cross*'; the readers have been reconciled 'in the body of his flesh *through death*'. As in Rom. v. 9, the former phrase shows that St. Paul is thinking in sacrificial terms.[2] To explain it as suggesting only a violent death, comparable to that of a soldier on the battle-field,[3] is unsatisfactory. St. Paul knew his Old Testament and the vital significance of the term 'blood'; the precise sense in which he used the expression may not be known to us, but that he was

[1]The alternative readings, 'ye were reconciled' (B 33), and 'having been reconciled' (D G d g m), do not affect this argument.

[2]See earlier p. 46 f. See also the comments of Armitage Robinson on Eph. i. 7 and ii. 13.

[3]Cf. E. F. Scott, 26. See also C. A. Anderson Scott, *Christianity according to St. Paul*, 87.

thinking of life freely offered to God on behalf of men, is hardly open to dispute. In the second phrase the allusion to Christ's death is more general. The words 'in the body of his flesh' emphasize the reality of the humanity of Christ, culminating in death, in which the reconciliation was effected.[1] The word ἄμωμος in the phrase: 'to present you holy and without blemish (ἀμώμους) and unreproveable before him', confirms the view that St. Paul is using sacrificial ideas.[2]

The state preceding reconciliation is described in the words: 'You, being in time past *alienated* (ἀπηλλοτριωμένους) and *enemies* (ἐχθρούς) in your mind in your evil works'. The same participle is used in Eph. ii. 12 in the passage: 'alienated from the commonwealth of Israel, and strangers from the covenants of the promise, having no hope and without God in the world'.[3] The passage from Colossians lacks the references to Israel and is more broadly conceived; it describes the estranged and hostile attitude of men towards God, which is centred in the mind and expressed in deed. Whatever may be the meaning of ἐχθροί in Rom. v. 10 there can be no doubt that here it is used of man's hostility to God.[4] The phrases 'in your mind' and 'in your evil works' leave no other inference possible. Reconciliation is here conceived as a complete change from estrangement and hostility on the part of man to loving fellowship with God. Nothing is said in this passage of

[1]Lightfoot thinks that the words are added for greater clearness, to distinguish the natural body of Christ from the mystical body mentioned in verse 18, *Colossians*, 160. Many other commentators (cf. Abbott, 226) see a reference to the views of the false teachers regarding angels in connexion with the work of reconciliation.

[2]Cf. Lightfoot, 160; F. J. A. Hort, *The First Epistle of St. Peter*, 77. Note also παραστῆσαι in Rom. xii. 1, Lk. ii. 22.

[3]Cf. also Eph. iv. 18.

[4]Cf. Lightfoot, 159, T. K. Abbott, 225, E. F. Scott, 27.

the divine side of the relationship, but we ought not to assume that it can be ignored because God is not reconciled to man.

Finally, an important issue arises in the words: 'to present you holy and without blemish and unreproveable before him'. How does this phrase bear upon the Pauline conception of reconciliation as an immediate act of God? Unfortunately, this question is complicated by grammatical considerations. What is the subject of the infinitive? Are men 'presented' by God, or by Christ, or by the fulness of the Godhead which dwells in Christ; or do they present themselves before God? If, as we have suggested, 'God' or 'the Father' is the subject εὐδόκησεν ('it was the good pleasure of'), then it is God who reconciles and presents men to Himself—a difficult but not impossible interpretation. 'You . . . hath he reconciled . . . so as to present you . . .'.[1] The meaning is similar if 'all the fulness' is the subject.[2] Another possibility is to find the subject in a reference to the readers: 'So that ye should present yourselves (ὑμᾶς) . . . before him,'[3] but this view involves treating ὑμᾶς in a reflexive sense. Moreover, while Rom. xii. 1 illustrates this idea,[4] we should expect it to be expressed less ambiguously in the present passage

[1]Cf. Lightfoot, 159; C. H. Dodd: 'God has reconciled you . . . so as to give you an unimpeachable standing in his presence', *Abingdon Bible Commentary*, 1255. Lightfoot prefers the difficult reading 'ye were reconciled' and the view that παραστῆσαι is governed directly by εὐδόκησεν: 'And you who once were estranged . . . but now ye have been reconciled . . . to present you, I say, holy and without blemish'. In this case the second ὑμᾶς repeats the first. As T. K. Abbott, 226, says, this makes the sentence rather involved.

[2]The resulting interpretation, viz. that it is the totality of the Godhead dwelling in Christ which reconciles men and presents them to God, is much less probable.

[3]Cf. Meyer, *Colossians*, 312. See also the comments of Lightfoot, 160, and Abbott, 226.

[4]See also Rom. vi. 13: 'present yourselves (ἑαυτούς) unto God'.

if it were St. Paul's thought. There is least to be said for the view that it is Christ who presents men to God,[1] for there is nothing in the context to support it.

From the standpoint of careful exegesis it is necessary to make these subtle distinctions. We are compelled to recognize, however, that, no matter which of them is really implicit in St. Paul's language, he himself is not specially concerned to make any one of them, although most of them find expression elsewhere in his writings. It is best, therefore, not to press the question: Who presents men to God?, but to consider the presentation itself. It is, I think, conceived as a divine action, and the important questions are: What is its character? and: How is it related to reconciliation?

There can be little doubt that the reference is either to a present experience of the believer,[2] or, and more probably, to the Final Judgment. The former view is well expressed by C. H. Dodd. 'It is "justification by faith"', he says, 'of which St. Paul is speaking. It is not that the Colossians have attained, or are to attain in some remote future, a moral perfection which will secure their acceptance at the Last Judgment. It is that here and now, by the grace of God, who "justifieth the ungodly", they stand before him as his consecrated people, to whom he "imputes" no fault.'[3] This exegesis is most attractive and may be correct, but it is difficult to suppose that St. Paul is thinking of justification in this passage, a doctrine which he nowhere mentions in Colossians and Ephesians. It is much more probable that the thought is eschatological.[4]

[1]So Hofmann and Conybeare. See Meyer's discussion, 295.

[2]For the view that the thought is sacrificial see Lightfoot, 160 f. See the criticisms of T. K. Abbott, 227.

[3]*The Abingdon Bible Commentary*, 1256. Cf. Lightfoot, 160.

[4]Cf. Meyer, 313; Beet, 161; Scott, 28.

God;[1] hostility and estrangement are gone; we have entered into the enjoyment of fellowship with Him. If this is the argument, it is apparent once more that St. Paul is describing what elsewhere he calls reconciliation. It is significant that the characteristics of reconciliation reappear in the passage in his reference to peace with God. As in the case of the former, the peace is gained 'through our Lord Jesus Christ'. When, moreover, he goes on to say that through Him 'we have had our access by faith[2] into this grace wherein we stand' (Rom. v. 2), there is every reason to think that he has the work of Christ in mind. If justification and peace are causally related[3] in v. 1, the fact that he grounds justification in the work of Christ[4] carries with it the inference that he traces peace with God to the same source. Men have peace because God sees them as righteous, and he sees them as righteous because they trust in His salvation. Such appears to be St. Paul's belief. Like reconciliation,[5] therefore, peace with God is grounded in His redemptive work. Our conclusion, then, is as before: alike in character, and resting upon the same foundation, peace with God and reconciliation are one.

Now that we have examined New Testament teaching concerning peace, we can summarize its bearings upon the doctrine of reconciliation as follows. (1) Reconciliation is not only restoration to fellowship with God, but is also, and at the same time, the gift of His peace. (2) As such, it is a change in the disposition and experience of

[1]This is implicit if we read the subjunctive. Beet, 148, describes justification as the *means* to peace. See the comments of Sanday and Headlam, 120 f.

[2]'By faith' is omitted by B D F G and the Old Latin version. If the phrase is a gloss, it is thoroughly Pauline in character.

[3]Cf. Sanday and Headlam, 120.

[4]See earlier, pp. 45-7, 50, 71 f.

[5]See earlier, pp. 86-100.

men from frustration and defeat to a condition of harmonious adjustment to the will of God. (3) Reconciliation is a state of blessedness as well as an act of redeeming love. The words, 'Being therefore justified by faith, we have peace with God through our Lord Jesus Christ', irresistibly suggest a condition of integrated life into which the believer is introduced by the grace of God. (4) The view that reconciliation is the work of God is confirmed and strengthened, since inner peace cannot be obtained otherwise than as His free gift. (5) Lastly, the thought of salvation, as wrought by Christ in the power of His death, receives an added emphasis. He 'came and preached peace'; He made peace 'by the blood of His cross': these truths enlarge our apprehension of the reconciling work of God. In every respect, therefore, the teaching about peace includes the same notes as the doctrine of reconciliation, with the further advantage of a new emphasis upon a resultant condition of inner blessedness capable of endless development and enrichment.

(*c*) *Reconciliation and Freedom*

Unlike peace, freedom is not brought into direct association with reconciliation in the Pauline theology, and in the narrower sense it may be said to be the consequence or fruit of reconciliation. Because we have been reconciled we are free, and enjoy the liberty of the sons of God. Such, indeed, appears to be Pauline teaching. It is equally possible, however, to think of freedom and of sonship as belonging to the inner content of reconciliation, and, as in the case of peace with God, this possibility must influence our conception of what reconciliation means. New Testament teaching on each of these themes has inevitably made its contribution to that enlarged view of fellowship with God which is characteristic of modern theology.

Freedom is variously described as freedom 'from sin' (Rom. vi. 18, 22) and 'from the law of sin and death' (Rom. viii. 2). The noun can also be used summarily to describe Christ's work for men: 'For freedom did Christ set us free'; 'Ye, brethren, were called for freedom' (Gal. v. 1, 13). In James, Christianity is 'the perfect law, the law of liberty' (i. 25; cf. ii. 8: 'the royal law'), which also judges men (ii. 12: 'So speak ye, and so do, as men that are to be judged by a law of liberty'). The danger against which Christians are to guard is that of using freedom 'for an occasion to the flesh' (Gal. v. 13; cf. 1 Pet. ii. 16: 'as free, and not using your freedom for a cloke of wickedness'). Freedom, indeed, in one of its aspects, is a self-imposed bondage. 'When ye were bond-servants of sin, ye were free in regard of righteousness' (Rom. vi. 20); 'And being made free from sin, ye became *bond-servants of righteousness*' (Rom. vi. 18).

Especially is the gift of freedom associated with Christ. In the story of the Temple Tax Jesus Himself says in reply to Simon Peter 'Therefore the sons are free' (Mt. xvii. 26), a principle which covers much more than the paying of the half-shekel. In the Fourth Gospel He is represented as saying: 'If ye abide in my word, then are ye truly my disciples; and ye shall know the truth, and the truth shall make you free' (viii. 31 f.); and as declaring: 'If therefore the Son shall make you free, ye shall be free indeed' (viii. 36). In his own idiom St. Paul voices the same conviction when he says: 'Where the Spirit of the Lord is, there is liberty' (2 Cor. iii. 17). The widest prospects open out before him as he contemplates this freedom. Men who have been 'made free from sin', and have become 'servants to God', have their 'fruit unto sanctification, and the end eternal life' (Rom. vi. 22); whilst the divine goal of the creation is deliverance 'from the bondage of corruption into the liberty of the glory of the children of God' (Rom. viii. 21). The wide range of these quotations, found as they are in the Pauline, Petrine, and Johannine writings, as well as in the Epistle of James, is notable; it reveals the prominent place given to freedom in the experience and thought of primitive Christianity. The new faith was conceived, negatively, as involving deliverance from sin, corruption, and the Law, and positively, as bestowing a life of ethical and religious freedom issuing in service to God and man.

How can we do otherwise than think of this teaching when we contemplate the idea of reconciliation? A state or condition of freedom in itself, reconciliation as thus enjoyed becomes the inspiration of Christian thought and activity in respect of every aspect of the life of men. Freed from sin and spiritual death, and introduced into a life of inner peace and liberty, the reconciled man can tolerate no ideal less than that of the freedom of the spirit in man in every sphere, religious, social, and international. So closely is Christian service linked to its religious and doctrinal roots!

(*d*) *Reconciliation and Sonship*

If it is right to bring the idea of freedom within the content of reconciliation, it is still more justifiable to include sonship within its meaning, however true it may be that the progressive discovery of its illimitable significance belongs to the life of reconciled men. Once we allow that reconciliation is a state, and not only an act, this inference is inescapable; and all the more because sonship is a state which is brought into being by the sovereign act of God Himself.

Sonship is a word which describes similar aspects of the Christian life and experience to those of freedom, but in a warmer and more personal sense. The idea is prominent in the Gospels as well as in the Epistles. Jesus, for example, spoke of His disciples as the sons or the children of God. 'Blessed are the peacemakers', He said, 'for they shall be called sons of God' (Mt. v. 9). Men were to love their enemies, and pray for their persecutors, that they might be sons of their Father which is in heaven (Mt. v. 44 f.; cf. Lk. vi. 35: 'sons of the Most High'). In words quoted in Section (*c*), 'the sons', He said, 'are free' (Mt. xvii. 26).[1] In the saying from Q recorded in Lk. xi. 13 = Mt. vii. 11 τέκνα is used, probably because of its more intimate associations, of human relationships in an argument *a fortiori* which implies that men are τέκνα θεοῦ: 'If ye then, being evil, know how to give good gifts unto your children, how much more shall your Father which is in heaven give good things to them that ask him?'[2]

In the Johannine sayings men are never described as the sons, or children, of God, but the Evangelist uses τέκνα θεοῦ[3] in i. 12: 'but as many as received him, to them gave he power to become *children of God*, even to them that believe on his name', and xi. 52: 'that he might gather into one *the children of God* that are scattered abroad.' In 1 John it appears four times: iii. 1: 'that we should be called *children of God*'; iii. 2: 'Beloved, now are we *children of God*'; iii. 10: 'In this *the children of God* are manifest, and the children of the devil'; and v. 2: 'Hereby we know that we love *the children of God*.' In all these cases the term is used of believers, as it is also in the examples in the remaining Epistles yet to be considered; and the question arises whether sonship and the corresponding truth of the Father-

[1]In all the sayings quoted above the Greek word used is *υἱοί*.

[2]παῖς is not used in the sayings, and παιδίον only of children in general. In Jn. xxi. 5 the disciples are addressed as παιδία ('lads'). Cf. Bernard, *I.C.C., St. John*, 696.

[3]υἱοὶ θεοῦ is not found in the Johannine writings. Cf. Westcott, *The Epistles of St. John*, 123 f.

hood of God express a universal relationship, or one that is limited to the experience of those who believe in Christ.

The view that sonship and the doctrine of the Fatherhood of God are exclusively Christian in content, and are not universal in their scope, has often been advocated.[1] The argument probably gains its force from an illusion created by the not unnatural circumstance that the New Testament references to these ideas are related in an overwhelming degree to the situation of disciples and believers. Obviously, all that makes the filial relationship real and living can exist only where men truly believe in God and accept His unique gift of salvation. In the deepest sense of the words God cannot be our Father until we become His sons. But we are under no necessity to suppose that His Fatherhood depends on our faith and that His sons are created *ex nihilo.* The truth is that it is just because God is our Father while we are sinners, and because we are His sons, though disobedient, that the rich paternal and filial relationships described in the New Testament, and exemplified in present Christian experience, are possible.[2]

This doctrine of the universality of God's Fatherhood and, in consequence, of the filial relationship which at least in promise and potency exists before men truly become His sons, is entirely in harmony with the outlook of

[1]Cf. W. F. Lofthouse: 'To many, the statement that God is to be considered primarily as the Father of Jesus and not of men in general, save as they come to Him through Jesus, will be unwelcome and unreliable', *The Father and the Son* (1934), 67. 'Sonship', he observes, 'if we understand by it something more than what we share with the whole animal creation, is not an endowment of the human race; it is the gift of the Father, through the Son. It is not shared with the animals; it is shared with Christ', *op. cit.*, 79.

[2]Cf. J. S. Lidgett: 'The Fatherhood that is made completely manifest in redemptive and adopting grace must needs be creative and constitutive from the beginning. It must be universal in principle and power in order that it may become special and personal in realization and fulfilment,' *God in Christ Jesus*, 93.

Jesus and is implicit in His teaching. It is true most of His sayings relating to the Father and to sonship were spoken to His disciples;[1] and it may well be that His own intense appreciation of the depths of these relationships led to a disinclination to speak of these themes until the later stages of His ministry and in the hearing of a chosen circle;[2] yet, none the less, His words are too broad in their reference to be limited to believers. As we have seen, the implication of the saying: 'If ye then, being evil' (Mt. vii. 11), is that men, as such, are God's children; and the same is true of the words: 'Love your enemies . . . that ye may be *sons of your Father* which is in heaven: for he maketh his sun to rise on the evil and the good, and sendeth rain on the just and the unjust' (Mt. v. 44 f.). Can we suppose that Jesus was thinking only of believers when He pronounced peacemakers blessed, and declared that they should be called '*sons of God*' (Mt. v. 9), or when He taught men to pray, saying: '*Our Father*, which art in heaven' (Mt. vi. 9)? Moreover, however we interpret these sayings, the teaching of the parable of the Prodigal Son (Lk. xv. 11-32) is unmistakable. The suggestion that the prodigal is a son even while he wastes his substance in riotous living, and that the father is still the father although he is forgotten, is too clear to be ignored, and a theology which cannot find room for this interpretation is self-condemned.[3]

[1]Cf. T. W. Manson, *The Teaching of Jesus*, 96, 98.

[2]Cf. Manson, *op. cit.*, 101.

[3]It is therefore not a merit of the Fourth Gospel, but a severe limitation in its teaching, due to concentration upon a relatively few sublime themes, when it restricts the use of the name, Father, to Christ, uses the term τέκνα only of believers (Jn. i. 12, xi. 52, 1 Jn. iii. 1, 2, 10, v. 2), and by implication denies its relevancy to others (cf. viii. 42). In Jn. xi. 52 predestined, rather than potential (Bernard, 406), children of God are probably meant. On Fatherhood in the Fourth Gospel see W. F. Howard, *The Fourth Gospel in Recent Criticism and Interpretation*, 238.

Having said this, we must recognize that sonship attains its fulness of meaning only where there is a believing relationship between man and God, and that it is upon a sonship of this character that the New Testament concentrates its attention. In contrast with the filial state of the unregenerate this condition of sonship is so rich and full as to imply a miracle of spiritual transformation. It is not surprising, therefore, that St. Paul adopts the word *υἱοθεσία* ('adoption') from the vocabulary of contemporary social practice[1] in order to convey his sense of the dramatic change which follows upon faith in Christ the Redeemer. He sees it as an experience which was open to Israel (cf. Rom. ix. 4: 'whose is *the adoption*') and is now the possession of the Gentile believer. 'For ye received', he writes in words of exultation, 'not the spirit of bondage again unto fear; but ye received *the spirit of adoption* whereby we cry, Abba, Father' (Rom. viii. 15). The purpose of the sending forth of the Son in 'the fulness of the time' was that God 'might redeem them that were under the law, that *we might receive the adoption of sons* (τὴν υἱοθεσίαν) (Gal. iv. 5). This purpose indeed was eternal: 'having foreordained us *unto adoption as sons* through Jesus Christ unto himself' (Eph. i. 5); and, as in the case of justification, it is represented in the double aspect of a present experience (Rom. viii. 15) and an eschatological hope (Rom. viii. 23: 'waiting for our *adoption*, the redemption of our body').[2] To the modern reader 'adoption' has a colder and more formal connotation than it had for St. Paul. To us it tends to suggest the idea of treating a person as some one he is not, but to the Apostle, as in the usage of the ancient world, it meant entrance upon a

[1] Cf. Deissmann, *Bible Studies*, 239.

[2] I.e. for the redemption of the whole man. Cf. Anderson Scott, *Christianity according to St. Paul*, 238.

It is obvious that we shall be compelled to return to this challenging claim at a later stage. In the meantime it must be noted that, whilst Denney thinks of the work of Christ as a finished work, he is far from claiming that it is the only factor in the experience of reconciliation. Reconciliation avails and becomes effective through faith. If a man conscious of sin sees what Christ on His Cross means, there is only one thing for him to do, 'to abandon himself to the sin-bearing love which appeals to him in Christ, and to do so unreservedly, unconditionally, and for ever'.[1] 'This', he adds, 'is what the New Testament means by faith.' Once we begin to quote Denney it is difficult to stop. 'Every Christian experience whatsoever', he says, 'call it justification, adoption, or salvation—call it love, or repentance, or regeneration, or the Spirit—lies within faith and is dependent upon it. The virtue of all observances, sacramental or other, is conditioned by it.'[2] 'The feeble stream of our life, with all its aimless eddies and wanderings, is caught up and carried forward in the mighty stream of His eternal life.'[3] 'Faith freely and passionately identifies the sinner with the sin-bearer, absorbing into itself all His attitude in relation to sin: this is the only union with Christ of which experience has a word to say.'[4] On the wider aspects of reconciliation he says that the reconciled man is reconciled to love and the law of life. 'The love of God can only redeem those whom it inspires,' and 'the life of reconciliation is a life which itself exercises a reconciling power.'[5]

Turning from Denney, we may note two other discussions which also raise points of considerable interest and importance.

In *Grace and Personality* (1919) John Oman says that

[1]*Op. cit.*, 290. [2]*Op. cit.*, 291. [3]*Op. cit.*, 304.
[4]*Op. cit.*, 305. [5]*Op. cit.*, 328 f.

the distinctive element in the Christian religion is 'the kind of redemption it offers', and that, 'in contrast to all ways of renunciation, its way of being redeemed from the world is reconciliation'.[1] The issue is cleared, he maintains, if we consider what is meant by 'enmity against God'. 'The expression calls up the vague idea of a quarrel with a dim, vast figure in a remote Heaven, so utterly unconnected with our present doings that it is difficult to see how we ever could come into conflict with Him.'[2] Reality, however, is not one thing and God another. 'To be at enmity against God is neither more nor less than to be in bitter hostility to reality, with the sense that it is all against us.'[3] Hence, 'we are truly reconciled as we live, not as we profess, and we cannot be reconciled to God and be at enmity with what He appoints'.[4] Primarily, reconciliation to God is 'reconciliation to our lives by seeking in them only His ends'; it is '*reconciliation to the discipline He appoints and the duty He commands*'.[5] It is 'present fellowship with our Father in His Kingdom, as it is manifested through the world and in the midst of our brethren'.[6]

Oman's view is that we are reconciled to God by finding in our present life, and not merely hoping for it in another, that God's real meaning is a rule of love, by accepting which we discover an eternal purpose, for the realisation of which every event is working. The task, he says, is not to lay God open to us, but to lay us open to God. 'The difficulty to be overcome is primarily the manifold hypocrisies, springing, in the nature of the case, from all sin, which makes us pervert the witness of truth, and look in the world for love as mere goodness without

[1] *Op. cit.*, 118.
[2] *Op. cit.*, 122.
[3] *Op. cit.*, 123.
[4] *Op. cit.*, 124.
[5] *Op. cit.*, 126. The italics are Oman's.
[6] *Ibid.*

inward moral demand, and in our hearts for God's fellowship in the Spirit without application in any outward moral sphere.'[1] This is truly said; but how the difficulty is to be surmounted, we are not told. We are assured that 'to be reconciled is to be forgiven', and that 'we are forgiven when we know that He is waiting to be gracious'.[2] This teaching is perilously near the suggestion that the absence of reconciliation is due to a kind of spiritual myopia: we have merely to see God and to respond to His revelation. A deeper note is struck when Oman speaks of reconciliation as the bearing of any cross which is God's will, and is of God's working, not of man's achieving. What is required is 'a resolutely veracious will, which is neither to be attracted by the pleasant ways of evil nor dismayed by its threats'. 'As that is how God seeks peace, that is how we are His sons.'[3] The beauty of such thoughts must be gratefully acknowledged, but their adequacy to the depth of New Testament teaching must be doubted. Perhaps the tenuousness of the exposition is most apparent when Oman equates reconciliation with revelation. In this context alone he refers to Christ who is 'the supreme revelation only as He is the supreme reconciliation';[4] and Christ is the supreme reconciliation because He accepts all life's discipline and 'makes peace by obedience to righteousness even to death'.[5] The greatest thing Oman says about reconciliation is that its practical issue is 'to find ourselves in an order of love which is our succour, so far beyond our own contriving and for ends so far above our own conceiving, that we have no concern except to serve in it'.[6] 'A saved soul . . . is a soul true to itself because, with its mind on God's will of love and not on itself, it stands in God's world unbribable and

[1] *Op. cit.*, 167. [2] *Op. cit.*, 226. [3] *Op. cit.*, 108.
[4] *Op. cit.*, 166. [5] *Op cit.*, 153. [6] *Op: cit.*, 251.

undismayed, having freedom as it has piety and piety as it is free.'[1]

A greater contrast with the theology of Denney could hardly be imagined, and for this reason it may be well, in conclusion, to describe the treatment of reconciliation of a living scholar who is strongly influenced by the teaching of Oman but strikes a fuller evangelical note. In *The World and God* (1935) Professor H. H. Farmer urges that God's saving revelation of Himself in Christ, at one and the same time, shows man the truth and enables him sincerely to face and accept it. 'It does this', he says, 'because it is a revelation of God as holy love.'[2] To apprehend this revelation is to be truly and deeply penitent. 'But it is also to be forgiven, to be reconciled, to be aware that the fundamental alienation of the whole being from God is overcome.'[3] The two experiences are not successive. 'It is not possible to be truly penitent in the presence of the love of God revealed in Christ without experiencing forgiveness and reconciliation.'[4] Again, the saving revelation is given through a historical personality 'completely surrendered to, at one with, indwelt by, that divine holy will of love by which man, in his darkness, needs to be confronted'.[5] Further, the revelation is given through the Church. 'Reconciliation to God through Jesus Christ is not, and never can be, apart from the fellowship of those in whom that reconciling work is also being wrought out. From this point of view, the statement that outside the Church there is no salvation is unexceptionable. . . .'[6] The man who is being reconciled to God through Christ grows more and more aware that his life rests on a personal order determined by the holy love of God; that he is called upon to serve that love in his deal-

[1] *Ibid.* [2] *Op. cit.*, 197. [3] *Op. cit.*, 197 f.
[4] *Op. cit.*, 198. [5] *Ibid.* [6] *Op. cit.*, 200.

ings with men; and that he must and can commit himself to it at whatever risk or cost 'or, even more, when, with increasing knowledge of God, there comes an increasing sense of disloyalty and sin both in himself and in his fellows'. 'This', says Professor Farmer, 'is the life of faith, sustained day by day by the vision of God given through Christ, and supremely through His Cross.'[1]

It will be noticed that in this stimulating presentation reconciliation is conceived as a process rather than, as in the New Testament, as an act or state. Indeed, Professor Farmer has a valuable chapter on the eschatological aspect of reconciliation.[2] In this treatment there is both gain and loss: gain, as showing the experiences in which reconciliation issues, and without which it is vain; loss, in that attention is deflected from its decisive character and the act of God in Christ on which it depends. As is inevitable, Professor Farmer's view of the death of Christ is closely connected with his account of reconciliation. Fundamentally, the death is an act of revelation, of objective revelation, wrought in flesh and blood and on the plane of history. It breaks upon us as light out of the darkness and evil of existence. 'The discernment is given that as the holy love of Jesus is in the midst of all this evil, so also is that on which it rests and by which it is sustained, namely the holy love of God.'[3] How the consummation of the life of Jesus in the crucifixion should mediate the assurance of a divine love, he declares, 'it is in the nature of the case impossible to say'. Later, however, he claims that in the Cross are discerned 'a righteousness which

[1] *Op. cit.*, 201.

[2] *Op. cit.*, 204-29. How far its content is extended is seen in the statement: 'Reconciliation thus has at its heart a present possession and an as yet unrealised hope; and each of these requires and strengthens the other' (222).

[3] *Op. cit.*, 243.

finally breaks through the categories of distributive justice', and 'a complete self-commitment . . . to a divine overshadowing providence whose purpose of love, though it is being wrought out through the obedience of His suffering servant in this present awful scene of history, none the less transcends history altogether'.[1]

The four discussions outlined above have been selected because they are representative. Many other examples could be given;[2] but enough has been said to show how central reconciliation is in modern theology, how frequently it is described as restoration to fellowship with God, and how closely it is connected with the work of Christ. Of current interpretations the one most widely held is probably the view that reconciliation depends upon man's humble acceptance of the revelation of God made in Christ. This view, we have seen, can find noble and moving expression; but from these heights, with varying degrees of adequacy, it shades down to the opinion that reconciliation is due to a change of mind when the sinner sees the Crucified. We are redeemed, it is even said, not by the sufferings of Christ, but by the sympathy, desire, and love of the Sufferer. In this presentation, as it seems to the present writer, modern theology is seen in its decline, as compared with the more robust, if offensive, theology of the past. In view of the place assigned to the Person of Christ, it is unjust to say that the death of Christ is barely distinguished from that of Socrates. The real gravamen of the charge is that the attempt to say what the love of Christ does, as distinct from what it reveals, is largely abandoned. Attention is concentrated upon the psychology of man's response to that which, happily, he

[1] *Op. cit.*, 246.

[2] Cf. my article on 'The Best Books on the Atonement', *Expository Times*, xlviii, 267-73.

has observed, rather than upon a work of God in Christ which is wrought on his behalf. Doubtless there are many causes for this tendency, and not least a reaction and recoil from traditional theories; but an important part of the explanation is the fact that the idea of reconciliation is unduly restricted. It is cut off from its historical connexion with the remission of sins and with justification; and it is not sufficiently articulated with its results, in a growing fellowship with God and in sanctification. In Chapter VI it will be argued that full justice to the implications of reconciliation can be done only if it is seen in this large complex of ideas, and that the Atonement must be studied in relation to the Christian experience as a whole.

IV

FELLOWSHIP

We have already seen that the idea of fellowship with God is singularly rich and full. In the New Testament, fellowship includes, not only the idea of communion, or fellowship proper, but also the Pauline doctrine of mystical union with Christ, the Johannine teaching about 'abiding in' and 'being in' Christ, and the testimony of the Gospels and Epistles in general concerning seeing and knowing God. Whilst none of these ideas need be excluded from the Biblical conception of reconciliation, it is manifest that they include vital processes in the growth of reconciled men in association one with another within the Christian Church. Fellowship, in short, describes both reconciliation itself and its fruits, and it does this to a greater degree than is true of peace with God, freedom, and sonship.

The truth of this claim must now be examined, and for this purpose it is necessary to consider (*a*) New Testament teaching concerning Fellowship or κοινωνία; (*b*) The Pauline phrase 'in Christ'; (*c*) The Pauline idea of living, dying, and rising with Christ; (*d*) The Johannine teaching about 'abiding in' and 'being in' Christ; (*e*) The New Testament teaching on seeing and knowing God; (*f*) Fellowship in the Christian Community. As arising out of these studies it will be natural, finally, to discuss (*g*) The Origins of New Testament Teaching concerning fellowship with God; and (*h*) The place of the idea of fellowship in modern theology.

(a) *Fellowship or Κοινωνία*

Among the words which call for special notice under this head are the two adjectives, which are also used as nouns, *κοινωνός* and *συγκοινωνός*; the two verbs *κοινωνέω* and *συγκοινωνέω*; and, above all, the noun *κοινωνία*.

(i) *Κοινωνός* (10 times) and *συγκοινωνός* (4 times) are practically indistinguishable,[1] and are used to describe partners in common enterprises, such as Christian work (2 Cor. viii. 23) or even business (Lk. v. 10); sharers in common experiences, as, for example, persecution (Heb. x. 33, Apoc. i. 9), suffering (2 Cor. i. 7), sacrificial worship (1 Cor. x. 18), murder (Mt. xxiii. 30), and contact with devils (1 Cor. x. 20); and men who enjoy common privileges, the divine favour (Rom. xi. 17: 'the root of the fatness of the olive tree'), and 'the gospel' (1 Cor. ix. 23). Out of fourteen examples only three[2] suggest a common religious experience: Phil. i. 7: 'Ye are all *partakers with me of grace*'; 1 Pet. v. 1: 'I . . . who am also *a partaker of the glory that shall be revealed*'; and 2 Pet. i. 4: 'that through these ye may become *partakers of the divine nature*'. It cannot be said, therefore, that these are words of a distinctively religious content.

(ii) Even more remarkable is the use of the verbs *κοινωνέω* and *συγκοινωνέω*. In eleven passages there is only a single case where a distinctively spiritual experience is in question, namely, 1 Pet. iv. 13: 'Insomuch as ye are *partakers of Christ's sufferings*, rejoice'; and here the reference is concrete and practical rather than mystical[3] (cf.

[1]For the perfective use of *σύν* in compounds see W. F. Howard, *Grammar*, ii. 324 f.

[2]Possibly there is a fourth example in Philm. 17: 'If then thou countest me a partner.' Cf. M. R. Vincent, *I.C.C.*, *Philippians and Philemon*, 189. 'In the faith', however, does not seem a probable explanation.

[3]Cf. *The Atonement in New Testament Teaching*, 44.

Rom. xv. 27). The remaining ten examples refer to such actions as the rendering of financial aid (Rom. xii. 13, Gal. vi. 6, Phil. iv. 15) or sharing in spiritual blessings (Rom. xv. 27), in sins (1 Tim. v. 22, Apoc. xviii. 4), in evil works (2 Jn. 11), in 'the unfruitful works of darkness' (Eph. v. 11), in flesh and blood (Heb. ii. 14), and in physical afflictions (Phil. iv. 14). Out of twenty-five passages, therefore, thus far we have found only four which are directly relevant for our discussion, and it is noteworthy that three of these are from the Petrine Epistles. The one certain Pauline instance speaks of a common sharing of the divine grace (Phil. i. 7) rather than of fellowship with God.

(iii) The passages in which κοινωνία is used supply a much higher proportion of religious examples; although here out of eighteen instances, ten and perhaps twelve describe the corporate fellowship of Christians or their association in definite activities. Thus, it is used of the community-life of believers (Acts ii. 42,[1] and 1 Jn. i. 3a and 7), of co-operation or partnership in respect of the Gospel (Phil. i. 5, Gal. ii. 9), and of contributions or alms-giving (Rom. xv. 26, 2 Cor. viii. 4, ix. 13, Heb. xiii. 16, Philm. 6).[2] It is possible also that 2 Cor. xiii. 13 and Phil. ii. 1 should be interpreted of the fellowship within the community which is created by the Spirit.[3] In the

[1]C. A. Anderson Scott, *Expository Times*, xxxv, 567, interprets 'the fellowship' as that of the Community. See F. Hauck, *Theol. Wört.*, iii, 809. Lake's rendering is 'their fellowship', i.e. with the Apostles, *The Beginnings of Christianity*, iv. 27.

[2]Philm. 6 is difficult to interpret. Lightfoot, 333, paraphrases it: 'Your kindly deeds of charity, which spring from your faith'; Vincent, 180: 'the communication of thy faith'; Scott, 105: 'the faith which unites you with Christ.' Dibelius, *H.Z.N.T.*, 79, also explains it of faith-communion with Christ.

[3]So Anderson Scott, *Christianity according to St. Paul*, 160 f. Lightfoot, 107, and Vincent, 7, support the view that fellowship with the Spirit is meant.

following six passages, however, a definite Christian experience of fellowship with God or with Christ is implied:

1 Cor. i. 9: 'God is faithful, through whom ye were called into *the fellowship of his Son Jesus Christ our Lord.*'

1 Cor. x. 16a: 'The cup of blessing which we bless, is it not *a communion of the blood of Christ?*'

1 Cor. x. 16b: 'The bread which we break, is it not *a communion of the body of Christ?*'

Phil. iii. 10: 'that I may know him, and the power of his resurrection, and *the fellowship of his sufferings*, becoming conformed unto his death.'

1 Jn. i. 3b: 'Yea, and *our fellowship is with the Father, and with his Son Jesus Christ.*'

1 Jn. i. 6: 'If we say that *we have fellowship with him* (God), and walk in darkness, we lie, and do not the truth.'

Summarizing our results, we see that in forty-three passages only nine, or at most twelve,[1] use the words in question of a distinctively religious or mystical experience. Of these, four speak of fellowship with Christ or with His sufferings (1 Cor. i. 9, x. 16 (*bis*), and Phil. iii. 10; cf. 1 Jn. i. 3b), while two only, both in 1 John (i. 3b, 6), mention fellowship with God. The remaining three refer to sharing in grace (Phil. i. 7), future glory (1 Pet. v. 1), and the divine nature itself (2 Pet. i. 4). None of the five Greek words is found in the Fourth Gospel or in the sayings of Jesus, and in the Synoptics κοινωνός alone appears twice only (Mt. xxiii. 30, Lk. v. 10) in a purely secular sense. St. John is the only writer who speaks explicitly of fellowship with God or with the Father. St.

[1]The more doubtful cases are 2 Cor. xiii. 13, Phil. ii. 1 and 1 Pet. iv. 13.

Paul prefers to speak of fellowship with Christ, with His sufferings, or with His body and blood, and for these purposes employs these words sparingly. The facts, to say the least, are surprising, since these are the terms we might expect to find in the Greek New Testament to express the idea of fellowship with God or with Christ. Nothing perhaps could show more clearly how sporadically the term 'fellowship', so popular in modern religious writings and in 'Group' discussions, appears in the primitive Christian documents. The idea, of course, is present in many variant forms which delineate more sharply its character; but the modern terminology, perhaps because of its vague and general content, is seen in the Epistles only in its beginnings.

There is, however, another and important side. Besides using these words of mystical experiences of communion with God, the New Testament writers use them to describe the association of Christians within the community, in respect of work (1 Cor. ix. 23, 2 Cor. viii. 23, Philm. 17), of suffering (1 Pet. iv. 13), and especially of almsgiving (Rom. xii. 13, xv. 26, 2 Cor. viii. 4, ix. 13, Gal. vi. 6, Phil. iv. 15, Heb. xiii. 16). The same vocabulary, that is to say, is used of the relationships of men with God and of men with men, and for this purpose it is borrowed, not from distinctively religious sources, but from general usage[1] in which it describes partners in business and in marriage and sometimes in the rites of pagan worship. In the New Testament it attains a new glory and a new depth of meaning which fit it for that wide currency which it has gained in modern theology and in popular Christian movements.

[1]Cf. Moulton and Milligan, *The Vocabulary of the Greek Testament*, 350 f.; J. Armitage Robinson, *H.D.B.*, 460 ff.; D. S. Sharp, *Epictetus and the New Testament* 111.

(*b*) *The Pauline Phrase 'In Christ'*

We now turn to the phrase 'In Christ' or 'In the Lord' which is found in the Pauline Epistles at least 164 times.[1] Unfortunately, the phrase is not capable of a certain and demonstrable explanation; it does not always convey one and the same meaning. It appears to be a kind of shorthand which summarizes much that St. Paul expresses in other ways.

Under the influence of ideas suggested by the Mystery-religions, the phrase has often been interpreted of absorption into, or fusion with, the divine; but this interpretation is not true of St. Paul's usage. Deissmann, who in 1892 wrote a valuable monograph on the formula,[2] holds that it describes a fellowship-mysticism. 'Just as the air of life which we breathe is "in" us and fills us, and yet we at the same time live and breathe "in" this air, so it is with St. Paul's fellowship of Christ: Christ in him, he in Christ.'[3] Often wrongly applied to the 'historic' Jesus, the formula 'must be conceived as the peculiarly Pauline expression of the most intimate fellowship imaginable of the Christian with the living, spiritual Christ'.[4] As Johannes Weiss has pointed out,[5] Deissmann is mistaken in assuming that in all passages the phrase carries the same emphasis. Sometimes it indicates that salvation is present in the person of Christ (Rom. iii. 24, 2 Cor. v. 19); at other times it describes the act of a representative (1 Cor. xv. 22: 'so also *in Christ* shall all be made alive'): in some cases the

[1] So Deissmann, excluding Colossians, Ephesians, and the Pastoral Epistles.

[2] *Die neutestamentliche Formel 'in Christo Jesu'*.

[3] *St. Paul*, 128.

[4] *Ibid.*

[5] *The History of Primitive Christianity*, 468 f.

words depend on verbs of praising (1 Cor. i. 31, etc.), hoping (Phil. ii. 19), and trusting (Phil. ii. 24); and in others again the 'in' is instrumental or is used in the sense of 'through' (1 Thess. iv. 1: 'We beseech and exhort you *in the Lord Jesus*'). Weiss, however, recognizes the full mystical sense in such passages as 1 Cor. i. 30, 2 Cor. v. 17, Phil. iv. 1, cf. iv. 13, 1 Thess. iii. 8; and to these may be added other examples like Rom. vi. 11, viii. 1, 1 Thess. i. 1, as well as parallel passages in which the phrase 'in the Spirit' appears.[1] It will be useful to supply a representative list of these passages:

Rom. vi. 11: 'Even so reckon ye also yourselves to be dead unto sin, but alive unto God *in Christ Jesus*.'

Rom. viii. 1: 'There is therefore now no condemnation to them that are *in Christ Jesus*.'

1 Cor. i. 30: 'But of him are ye *in Christ Jesus*.'

2 Cor. v. 17: 'Wherefore if any man is *in Christ*, he is a new creature.'

Phil. iv. 1: 'So stand fast *in the Lord*, my beloved.'

Phil. iv. 13: 'I can do all things *in him* that strengtheneth me.'

1 Thess. i. 1: 'Paul, and Silvanus, and Timothy, unto the church of the Thessalonians *in God the Father and the Lord Jesus Christ*.'

1 Thess. iii. 8: 'For now we live, if ye stand fast *in the Lord*.'

Rom. xiv. 17: 'For the kingdom of God is not eating and drinking, but righteousness and peace and joy *in the Holy Spirit*.'

1 Cor. xii. 3: 'No man speaking *in the Spirit of God* saith, Jesus is anathema; and no man can say, Jesus is Lord, but *in the Holy Spirit*.'

It will be seen how strongly these passages support Deissmann's interpretation.

Sanday and Headlam take a very similar view. They hold that 'in Christ' and 'in Christ Jesus' always relate to

[1] Rom. viii. 9, xiv. 17, 1 Cor. xii. 3, etc.

the glorified Christ, not to the historic Jesus, and they interpret the formula as the summary expression of the doctrine of the mystical union of the Christian with Christ which underlies Rom. vi. 1-14.[1] In opposition to Deissmann, who explains the phrase as a Pauline formation, they think that it 'came in some way ultimately from our Lord Himself'.[2] In agreement with them and with Deissmann, Anderson Scott holds that in such cases as 1 Cor. i. 30, Rom. viii. 1, Phil. iv. 1, 1 Thess. i. 1 and Philm. 16 the significance of the preposition 'in' is local. 'Christ is conceived of as in some sense the habitation or dwelling-place of the Christian. Like the Spirit He is conceived of as a Sphere or Atmosphere within which men may live and move.'[3] He thinks that, while it would be incorrect to say that St. Paul 'identifies' Christ and the Spirit, they are treated in Rom. viii. 9-11, in respect of the experience of Salvation on its positive side, as 'interchangeable'. The same is true, he contends, of the relation between Christ and the Church (cf. Eph. i. 22 f.), the Fellowship or Divine Society of Redeemed Men; and he interprets the experience of 'being in Christ' as mediated through 'being in the Fellowship'. 'The Society represented the Saviour in such a way and to such a degree that the faith-union with Christ which was the key to salvation found perpetual expression and illustration in the fellowship of the Church.'[4] There does not seem to be any necessary antagonism between this communal interpretation, which is favoured also by R. N. Flew,[5] and

[1] *I.C.C., Romans*, 86 f., 160 f. [2] *Op. cit.*, 161.

[3] *Christianity according to St. Paul*, 153. [4] *Op. cit.*, 158.

[5] *Jesus and His Church*, 212-4. Flew maintains that, for St. Paul, communion with Christ was not 'a mere individual possession or private privilege'. 'It was inseparable from the thought of membership in the Ecclesia. Indeed it was the characteristic mark of the Ecclesia,' *op. cit.*, 213.

the view of Deissmann; but, as between the two explanations, the emphasis upon personal faith-union or fellowship with Christ Himself marks the more fundamental element in the experience.

This conclusion would need to be greatly modified if Schweitzer's interpretation of 'being in Christ' could be accepted.[1] Schweitzer explains the phrase in a quasi-physical sense as signifying a sharing of, or being grafted into, 'the corporeity of Christ'. This difficult conception is determined by eschatological considerations. By dying, he argues, Jesus passed into the mode of existence appropriate to the conditions of the Messianic Kingdom to be inaugurated at the General Resurrection. Into the self-same mode of being believers must enter, and they are brought into it by baptism, in virtue of which they participate in the Mystical Body of Christ, and by the Eucharist whereby they are assured of a part in the future Messianic Feast. What St. Paul means by 'being in Christ' is 'the predestined solidarity of the Elect with one another and with the Messiah', participation in 'the corporeity of Christ'. The merit of this construction, which is worked out by Schweitzer with a wealth of detailed argument which cannot here be described, is that it establishes a lineal connexion between a 'Christ-mysticism' taught by Jesus Himself (cf. Mt. v. 11 f., x. 40, Mk. viii. 35, 38), and the 'Christ-mysticism' of St. Paul; its weakness, apart even from the necessarily speculative character of the eschatological doctrine with which it is associated, is the abstract character of its account of union with Christ. What is described by Schweitzer is not personal communion conditioned by faith,[2] but a mode of being

[1]Cf. *The Mysticism of St. Paul*, 52 ff., 227 ff. See W. F. Howard, *The Fourth Gospel in Recent Criticism and Interpretation*, 165.

[2]*Op. cit.*, 116.

effected by eschatological rites. Nothing could show more clearly the schematic character of the formula 'in Christ', and the necessity of interpreting it by what St. Paul says elsewhere, and in more definite terms, concerning communion with Christ.[1] For this purpose we must consider more closely his teaching about dying, rising, living, being glorified, and reigning with Christ; and, most of all, his greatest mystical utterance in Gal. ii. 20: 'I have been crucified with Christ; and it is no longer I that live, but Christ liveth in me: and the life that I now live in the flesh, I live in faith, the faith which is in the Son of God, who loved me and gave himself up for me.' These passages must be examined separately in the next section, where it will be found that the kind of spiritual relationship which they presuppose is precisely that which is implied by the more distinctive examples of the phrase 'in Christ' in the list printed above.

(c) *The Pauline Idea of Dying, Rising, and Living with Christ*

At first sight it might appear that these ideas are more mysterious than that of being 'in Christ'; and certainly their meaning is luminous, and their content real, only to those who know in their personal experience the truths they represent. And yet the general character of these ideas is clear from the terms in which they are described. St. Paul, in mentioning them, is not speaking of experiences which are peculiar to himself. His use of the plural shows that there is no question of any secret or esoteric doctrine. He is thinking of a spiritual relationship to Christ which he believed was as much open to the Christians of Corinth, Rome, Galatia, and the Roman province of Asia as it was to himself. This fact, as well as the nature of the

[1] This necessity is recognized by Schweitzer, *op. cit.*, 122.

experiences in question, may be seen from the following list of representative passages:

συζῆν: 'But if we died with Christ, we believe that *we shall also live with him*' (Rom. vi. 8).

συμπάσχειν: 'if so be that *we suffer with him*, that we may be also glorified with him' (Rom. viii. 17).

συσταυροῦσθαι: 'knowing this, that our old man *was crucified with him*' (Rom. vi. 6); 'I have been *crucified with Christ*' (Gal. ii. 20).

συναποθανεῖν: 'Ye are in our hearts *to die together* and live together' (2 Cor. vii. 3); 'For if *we died with him*, we shall also live with him' (2 Tim. ii. 11).

συνθάπτειν: '*We were buried therefore with him* through baptism into death' (Rom. vi. 4); '*having been buried with him* in baptism' (Col. ii. 12).

συνεγείρειν: '(baptism), wherein *ye were also raised with him* through faith in the working of God, who raised him from the dead' (Col. ii. 12); 'If then *ye were raised together with Christ*, seek the things that are above, where Christ is, seated on the right hand of God' (Col. iii. 1); 'and *raised us up with him*, and made us to sit with him in the heavenly places, in Christ Jesus' (Eph. ii. 6).

συζωοποιεῖν: '*You did he quicken together with him*' (Col. ii. 13); 'but God . . . *quickened us together with Christ*, and raised us up with him . . . ' (Eph. ii. 4 ff.).

συνδοξάζειν: 'if so be that we suffer with him, *that we may be also glorified with him*' (Rom. viii. 17).

συγκληρονόμοι: 'and if children, then heirs; heirs of God, and *joint-heirs with Christ*' (Rom. viii. 17).

συμβασιλεύειν: 'if we endure, *we shall also reign with him*' (2 Tim. ii. 12).

There is an advantage in surveying these passages as a whole because they show that the relationship described is one of mystical fellowship with Christ so personal and intimate that the believer enters into, and shares in, the experiences of Christ, His life, suffering, crucifixion, death, burial, resurrection, quickening, glorification, heirship, and kingship. These are not simply external events, contemplated from without, but experiences in which he participates in virtue of the faith-relationship between himself and the Exalted Christ. They are made possible, within the fellowship of the Church, by faith and by common acts of worship, including baptism and sacramental devotion, directed to the Living Lord; but, fundamentally, they are personal experiences of the believer which, as an individual, he knows, or may know, for himself. Their character is indicated best by the words of Gal. ii. 20, quoted above, which indeed can rightly be extended to all the allied experiences of suffering, resurrection, and exaltation already named. The essential condition is that the old selfish ego is dethroned, and is replaced by the Christ-self, the personality in which Christ 'lives'. No loss of personal identity is implied by St. Paul's words;[1] for, after saying: 'I no longer live, but Christ liveth in me', he immediately adds: 'and the life that I now live in the flesh, I live in faith, the faith which is in the Son of God, who loved me and gave himself up for me.' The mysticism which is described in these words is a 'fellowship-mysticism', which, far from meaning absorption into the divine, carries with it an enhanced and enriched personality, with increased powers and possibilities of life. The area of moral and religious experience is widened; the mind, the feelings, and the will are stimulated and engaged, no longer at the behest of purely self-regarding purposes, but in obedience to motives which are 'bap-

[1]On this passage J. Weiss observes: 'It will always remain suggestive that the most impressive statement upon which, as a matter of fact, all our knowledge of his mysticism is based, is at once interrupted or qualified by a confession entirely in the spirit of the I-and-thou-religion,' *The History of Primitive Christianity*, 470.

tized into Christ' and are associated with His work for men in dying, rising, living, and interceding on their behalf. This redemptive ministry is unquestionably His, wrought upon the Cross and incapable of receiving addition in its positive content, but, none the less, within the limit of his powers the believer shares in it and enters into its meaning, because the love, implicit in his faith, breaks down the barriers which so often enclose men within egoistic ways of thinking and living. The experience is one in which personal interests and the purposes of God are no longer separate realms, but superimposed circles with a common centre, however incomparable in radius. The Christian dies, is buried, rises, lives, and is glorified with Christ, and waits to reign with Him when His victory shall be complete. Released from the limitations which cabin and confine his existence, he is brought into an ampler form of life, with increased possibilities of pain and joy. In virtue of his fellowship with Christ, he too feels the crushing weight of the world's sin and bears it upon his heart, so that for him also there is a Gethsemane and a Golgotha; but, with Christ again, he rises from death and despair in an Easter morning which sets the tone and temper of his life, fixing his hope in imperishable faith upon an End-time when God shall be all and in all and His will be done on earth as it is in heaven. The foundation of these experiences, which belong to the very meaning of the believer's life, is faith in, and mystical fellowship with, Christ as Redeemer, Saviour, and King. Far from causing him to neglect the hard facts of existence by reason of ineffable spiritual experiences, this fellowship impels him to face the starkest realities of life with an enlarged knowledge, a deeper understanding, and an untiring love. Already, in this present world, he lives with Christ, sustained by the victorious powers of the Age to Come. It is in the same context of thought that the formula 'in Christ' must be understood. When it is used in a mystical sense, it expresses in brief what St. Paul means by dying, rising, and living with Christ; it denotes union with Him in the realities of His saving ministry.

(d) *Johannine Teaching about 'Abiding' and 'Being in Christ'*

In the last two sections we have been concerned exclusively with Pauline teaching, and it now remains for us to examine the Johannine passages which speak of 'abiding in' and 'being in' Christ or the Father, and also of their 'abiding' or 'being' in men. In section (*a*) we have already noticed those passages in 1 John in which κοινωνία is used, and we have seen that they describe, not only a fellowship with Christ, but also one with God. The statements now to be considered, in the Fourth Gospel as well as in 1 John, are those in which μένειν ἐν and εἶναι ἐν are used with the dative of the person. Once more it will be advantageous to supply a representative list of these passages, and first those in which the writer speaks of 'abiding':

Jn. vi. 56: 'He that eateth my flesh and drinketh my blood *abideth in me*, and *I in him*.'

Jn. xv. 4: '*Abide in me*, and *I in you*. As the branch cannot bear fruit of itself, except it abide in the vine; so neither can ye, except *ye abide in me*.'

Jn. xv. 5: 'I am the vine, ye are the branches: He that *abideth in me*, and *I in him*, the same beareth much fruit.'

Jn. xv. 6: 'If a man *abide not in me*, he is cast forth as a branch, and is withered.'

Jn. xv. 7: 'If *ye abide in me*, and my words abide in you, ask whatsoever ye will, and it shall be done unto you.'

1 Jn. ii. 6: 'He that saith he *abideth in him* ought himself also to walk even as he walked.'

1 Jn. ii. 24: 'If that which ye heard from the beginning abide in you, *ye shall also abide in the Son*, and *in the Father*.'

1 Jn. ii. 27: '*Ye abide in him*' (mg., 'abide ye').

1 Jn. ii. 28: 'And now, my little children, *abide in him*.'

1 Jn. iii. 6: 'Whosoever *abideth in him* sinneth not.'

1 Jn. iii. 24: 'And he that keepeth his commandments *abideth in him*, and *he in him*. And hereby we know that *he abideth in us*, by the Spirit which he gave us.'

1 Jn. iv. 12: 'If we love one another, *God abideth in us*, and his love is perfected in us.'

1 Jn. iv. 13: 'Hereby know we that we *abide in him*, and *he in us*, because he hath given us of his Spirit.'

1 Jn. iv. 15: 'Whosoever shall confess that Jesus is the Son of God, *God abideth in him*, and *he in God*.'

1 Jn. iv. 16: 'God is love; and he that abideth in love *abideth in God*, and *God abideth in him*.'

The greater frequency of this teaching in 1 John is noteworthy. In the Gospel it appears only in the allegory of the Vine, and once in the Eucharistic Discourse of Jn. vi. In the Gospel it is used only of Christ, but in 1 John of Christ and of God. In both writings the relationship is mutual: Christ or God abides in man, and man abides in Christ or God. We should note, further, that in passages not quoted above the same language is used of God's word (v. 38, 1 Jn. ii. 14), of Christ's words (xv. 7), of the presence of the Father in the Son (xiv. 10b), the message of the Gospel (1 Jn. ii. 24), the anointing from God (1 Jn. ii. 27), the divine seed (1 Jn. iii. 9), eternal life (1 Jn. iii. 15), and of the love of God (1 Jn. iii. 17);[1] and it is also used of abiding in Christ's word (viii. 31), in His

[1]Cf. also 2 Jn. 2 (the truth) and 9 (abiding in the teaching).

love (xv. 9 f.), in the vine (xv. 4), and in love (1 Jn. iv. 16). *Μένειν ἐν* is distinctively a Johannine usage.

The passages in which *εἶναι ἐν* appears are less numerous and there does not seem to be any difference of meaning:

Jn. xiv. 10: 'Believest thou not that *I am in the Father, and the Father in me?*'

Jn. xiv. 20: 'In that day ye shall know that *I am in my Father*, and *ye in me*, and *I in you.*'

Jn. xvii. 21: 'That they may all be one; even as *thou, Father, art in me*, and *I in thee*, that *they also may be in us:* that the world may believe that thou didst send me.'

Jn. xvii. 23: '*I in them*, and *thou in me*, that they may be perfected into one; that the world may know that thou didst send me, and lovedst them, even as thou lovedst me.'

Jn. xvii. 26: 'And I made known unto them thy name, and will make it known; that the love wherewith thou lovedst me may be in them, and *I in them.*'

1 Jn. ii. 5 f.: 'Hereby know we that *we are in him:* he that saith he abideth in him ought himself also to walk even as he walked.'

1 Jn. v. 20: 'And *we are in him that is true, even in his Son Jesus Christ.*'

These passages clearly show that the terminology in question is merely an abbreviated form of the use of *μένειν ἐν*, resembling in this respect the Pauline use of the formula *ἐν Χριστῷ*.

In substance, the Johannine mysticism closely resembles the Pauline mysticism, the principal differences being that the former also discloses itself as a God-mysticism and does not make use of the Pauline idea of dying and rising with Christ. Like the Pauline mysticism, that found in the Johannine writings is a 'fellowship-mysticism' in which the personal relationship is so reciprocal in character that, alternatively, it can be described by saying that God or Christ 'abides in' the believer or that the believer 'abides in' God or 'in' Christ. In this respect also the Pauline use of the phrases 'Christ in you' and 'You in Christ' supplies a close parallel. More important still is the strong ethical note which so decisively distinguishes this teaching from the characteristic utterances of Hellenistic piety. Less varied in range than in the Pauline Epistles, this ethical emphasis is clearly marked in the Johannine passages quoted above. To profess fellowship with God, and to walk in darkness, is to lie, and to fail in doing the truth[1] (1 Jn. i. 6); to be in union with Christ is to prove to the world that God has sent Him (Jn. xvii. 23, 26); the mark of its reality is to 'walk' 'even as he walked' (1 Jn. ii. 5 f.). The essential condition of abiding in Christ is the keeping of the commandments (1 Jn. iii. 24), and abiding in God is also abiding in love (1 Jn. iv. 16).

(e) *New Testament Teaching on Seeing and Knowing God*

Closely connected with the subjects discussed in the preceding sections is the teaching of the New Testament concerning seeing and knowing God.

The greatest utterance upon this theme is, of course, the saying of Jesus in the Matthaean Beatitudes: 'Blessed are the pure in heart: for *they shall see God*' (v. 8). If this saying appears to stand apart in the Synoptic tradition, it is connected in the closest possible manner with all that Jesus taught about God.[2] Jewish teachers, as well as Jesus, taught the Fatherhood of God,[3] but it is the characteristic mark of His teaching that He brings God inti-

[1] Cf. Hoskyns and Davey, *The Riddle of the New Testament*, 40.

[2] Cf. K. E. Kirk, *The Vision of God*, 94-7.

[3] Cf. C. G. Montefiore, *The Old Testament and After*, 201-6, *The Beginnings of Christianity*, Part I, Vol. I, 47-50; R. Bultmann, *Jesus and the Word*, 191-4; G. Dalman, *The Words of Jesus*, 189-94.

mately near to man, and so provides the necessary basis for the idea of fellowship with Him. The God who feeds the ravens (Lk. xii. 24), clothes the lilies (Lk. xii. 27), marks the sparrow's fall (Lk. xii. 6 f.), makes His sun to rise on the evil and the good, and sends rain on the just and the unjust (Mt. v. 45), and who receives men as His sons (cf. Mt. v. 9, 45, Lk. xv. 11-32), is the near and approachable God whom men can see and know. The central idea of the Kingdom as the Rule or Reign of God implies a fellowship of men to whom He is known as the living and gracious God.

It is characteristic of St. Paul that he speaks of knowing rather than of seeing God and especially of knowing Christ. In unforgettable words he declares that in comparison with 'the excellency of the knowledge of Christ Jesus', he counts everything else as refuse (Phil. iii. 8), and describes as the object of his longing the desire to know Him in the power of His resurrection and the fellowship of His sufferings (Phil. iii. 10).[1] Knowledge of Christ, however, is not for St. Paul something other and distinct from the knowledge of God. On the contrary, it is 'in the face of Jesus Christ' that He who said: 'Light shall shine out of darkness', has shined in our hearts 'to give the light (R.V. mg. 'illumination') of the knowledge of the glory of God' (2 Cor. iv. 6). This glory we behold as in a mirror,[2] and 'are transformed into the same image from glory to glory' (2 Cor. iii. 18). St. Paul is keenly conscious of the contrast between our present

[1]Cf. Moffatt's translation and the comments of J. H. Michael, *The Moffatt N.T. Commentary*, *The Epistle to the Philippians*, 150 f.

[2]κατοπτριζόμενοι can equally well be rendered 'beholding as in a mirror' (cf. A.V. and R.V. mg.) or 'reflecting as a mirror', (R.V.). Plummer, *I.C.C.*, 2 *Cor.*, 105, supports the latter; so also R. H. Strachan, *The Moffatt N.T. Commentary*, 2 *Cor.*, 90. K. E. Kirk, *The Vision of God*, 103, supports the former interpretation.

knowledge and that of the End-time. 'Now we see in a mirror, darkly; but then face to face.' 'Now', he adds, 'I know in part; but then shall I know *even as also I have been known*' (1 Cor. xiii. 12). This thought of being known by God is one to which he refers in two other passages: in 1 Cor. viii. 1-3: 'Knowledge puffeth up, but love edifieth. If any man thinketh that he knoweth anything, he knoweth not yet as he ought to know; but if any man loveth God, *the same is known of him*,' and in Gal. iv. 9: 'Now that ye have come to know God, *or rather to be known of God*, how turn ye back again to the weak and beggarly elements . . .?' It would seem that to St. Paul the thought of being known by God was as wonderful as, if not more wonderful than, that of knowing God.[1] In any case, we must add both these themes to our account of his teaching concerning fellowship with God.

Mention must also be made of the Apostle's great mystical utterance in Col. iii. 3, which is second in importance only to Gal. ii. 20. 'Ye died,' he says, 'and *your life is hid with Christ in God*.' If, as many commentators think, he is referring in the words 'Ye died' to baptism,[2] it is of the spiritual experience of dying to sin that he is thinking and not simply of the rite itself. When he speaks of the new life to which the believer in Christ is introduced as 'hid in God', he does not for a moment mean that it is concealed from the world, but that it is a life rooted within the being of God Himself (cf. ii. 7). To some extent his thought is similar to that of Phil. iii. 20: 'For our citizenship is in heaven';[3] the believer lives on earth, but already here and now his true life is that of the

[1]Cf. K. E. Kirk, *op. cit.*, 105.

[2]Cf. Lightfoot, 207; A. E. J. Rawlinson, Peake's *Commentary*, 870; E. F. Scott, 63.

[3]Cf. Dibelius, *H.Z.N.T.*, *An die Kolosser Epheser an Philemon*, 30.

Age to Come.[1] In Col. iii. 3, however, the still richer thought is present, that through Christ his life is one of abiding fellowship with God. In themselves, the words 'hid with Christ in God' might appear to suggest an extreme type of mysticism, in which the human is lost in the divine, as drops of water are merged in the ocean; but the phrase 'with Christ' forbids such an interpretation, not to speak of St. Paul's consistent teaching elsewhere. We must therefore conclude that, although here St. Paul does not speak of the knowledge of God, it is precisely of an experience of fellowship that he is thinking, and that the figure of hiding is used in order to suggest that, like a buried treasure or a deep-rooted tree, the new life is founded within the riches of the being of God.

In the light of these further aspects of St. Paul's teaching it is clear that too much can be made of the claim that his mysticism is a 'Christ-mysticism' while that of St. John is a 'God-mysticism'.[2] As we have seen, this distinction rests upon a broad basis of fact and, as we shall find subsequently, there are good reasons for making it. Nevertheless, the antithesis is misleading if it obscures the truth that fellowship with God is a cardinal element in St. Paul's teaching. The passages cited above have shown this. It is illustrated further in the salutation of both letters to the Thessalonians, in which he speaks of his readers as 'the church of the Thessalonians *in God the Father* (2 Thess. i. 1: '*our Father*') and the Lord Jesus Christ'. It is implicit also in his description of Christ as 'the image (εἰκών) of God' (2 Cor. iv. 4, Col. i. 15) and as 'the mystery of God . . . in whom are all the treasures of wisdom and knowledge hidden' (Col. ii. 2 f.), and in his declaration that 'in him dwelleth all the fulness of the Godhead

[1] Cf. Heb. iv. 3, vi. 5, 18-20.

[2] Cf. Schweitzer, *The Mysticism of St. Paul*, 5.

bodily' (Col. ii. 9; cf. i. 19). Most of all is it evident in the Epistle to the Ephesians in which he speaks of 'the dispensation of the mystery which from all ages hath been hid in God who created all things' (Eph. iii. 9) and prays that his readers 'may be strong to apprehend with all the saints what is the breadth and length and height and depth, and to know the love of Christ which passeth knowledge, *that ye may be filled unto all the fulness of God'* (Eph. iii. 18 f.). The thought of Christ as God's 'open secret' (μυστήριον) recurs in his writings (cf. 1 Cor. ii. 1, Col. i. 26 f., ii. 2),[1] and its implication is that of a God who welcomes and receives men into abiding fellowship with Himself.

Like St. Paul, St. John also speaks of knowing and seeing God, but, in contrast with St. Paul, he makes a greater use of the idea of seeing, or beholding, God. It is true that he says explicitly: 'No man hath seen God at any time' (i. 18; cf. v. 37, vi. 46, 1 Jn. iv. 12, 20), but in this assertion he is simply denying that God is visible to the bodily eye (cf. Ex. xxxiii. 20, Deut. iv. 12, Ecclus. xliii. 31) or can be perceived apart from the revelation of God in Christ. His deepest conviction is that God is made known, and can be seen, in Christ. 'The only begotten Son', he asserts, 'which is in the bosom of the Father, *he hath declared him*' (i. 18). Of the Word who became flesh, he says: '*We beheld his glory*', and the glory is interpreted as that of 'the only begotten from the Father, full of grace and truth' (i. 14). This emphasis is maintained throughout the Gospel in the 'Christ-testimonies' of xiv. 7: 'If ye had known me, ye would have known my Father also: from henceforth *ye know him, and have seen him*'; xiv. 9: 'He that hath seen me *hath seen the Father*': and

[1] Cf. also 'the mystery of Christ' (Eph. iii. 4, Col. iv. 3) and 'the mystery of the gospel' (Eph. vi. 19.).

xii. 45: 'He that beholdeth me *beholdeth him that sent me*.' With even added force it is insisted in 1 John that the revelation in the Word is that which the Church has 'heard', 'seen', 'beheld', and 'handled', and that the reality which was manifested was 'the life, the eternal life, which was with the Father' (1 Jn. i. 1-4), and there is held out to the believer the promise of the perfect vision of God: '*We shall see him even as he is*' (1 Jn. iii. 2).

From these passages it is evident that it may be just as wrong to describe the Johannine teaching as 'God-mysticism' as it is to distinguish the Pauline doctrine as 'Christ-mysticism'. St. John is no less emphatic than St. Paul that it is through Christ that the believer comes to know God and to have fellowship with Him. As a matter of fact, the passages listed in Section (*d*), in which fellowship with Christ is mentioned, are more numerous than those which speak of fellowship with God or with the Father; whilst, as we have seen, in the passages under review it is clearly taught that in Christ men know and see the Father. This truth is the common element in the teaching of St. Paul and St. John, however true it is that the latter affirms more distinctly the possibility of fellowship with God. The evidence studied in the present section shows that there is a broad basis of primitive Christian teaching behind the special terms and expressions in which it is crystallized.

(*f*) *Fellowship in the Christian Community*

We have found so many references to fellowship within the Christian community that it is necessary to present this teaching more fully, together with other New Testament ideas which are naturally associated with it.

Without attempting to survey in detail the words and phrases examined in Sections (*a*) to (*e*), we may recall the fact that in very few of the examples is the experience or activity of an individual solely in question. Even in a case like Phil. iv. 13: 'I can do all things *in him* that strengtheneth me', it is evident that not for a moment is St. Paul thinking of a fact which is peculiar to himself. In the passages in which *κοινωνία* and allied words are employed the overwhelming number of examples refer to experiences and activities which Christians share one with another. The same is true of the many cases where the phrases 'in Christ', 'in the Lord', and 'in Him' are found; and a glance at the list of verbs compounded with *σύν*, set out in Section (*c*), is sufficient to show that almost all of them are used in the plural. Equally notable is the communal emphasis in the Johannine use of the idea of 'abiding' and 'being in Christ', and in the passages, Pauline and Johannine, which speak of knowing and seeing God. It is not the individual alone who is pronounced 'blessed' because he shall 'see God', but 'the pure in heart', and it is to the Christian community that St. John speaks when he holds out the promise: 'We shall see him even as he is.'

Remarkable, however, as these facts are, they do not convey the full force of New Testament testimony. In addition to them its teaching concerning the Kingdom as the Rule of God must be remembered, its references to the Church as the Body of Christ,[1] its allusions to the New Covenant established by Him,[2] its doctrine of the Holy Spirit in the life and worship of believers.[3] In all these cases men living, suffering, and triumphing together are contemplated. The believer lives, endures, and conquers in association with other believers, and in a common

[1]Cf. 1 Cor. xii. 27, Eph. iv. 12. See also Eph. i. 23, v. 30, Col. i. 18, 24.

[2]Cf. Mk. xiv. 24, 1 Cor. xi. 25. [3]See later, pp. 180-5.

allegiance to, and dependence upon, the Exalted Lord. This communal interest is present in the New Testament even where none of the express terms mentioned above is employed. In the Fourth Gospel, for example, where neither the Ecclesia nor the Body of Christ is named as such, this interest is especially marked,[1] in the allegories of the Shepherd (x. 1-16) and the Vine (xv. 1-8), the Supper-discourses of xiii-xvi, and the great High-priestly Prayer of xvii. 'Abide in me, and I in you. As the branch cannot bear fruit of itself, except it abide in the vine; so neither can ye, except ye abide in me.' 'Neither for these only do I pray, but for them also that believe on me through their word; that they may all be one; even as thou, Father, art in me, and I in thee, that they also may be in us: that the world may believe that thou didst send me.' The individual believer has every right to apply the spiritual message of these words to himself, but if he has regard to them as they stand in the Fourth Gospel, he will hear them as a member of the Christian community, living in fellowship with others in the communion to which he belongs and longing for the healing of the broken Body of Christ. The same communal reference is manifest also in the Apocalypse in the words: 'Behold, I stand at the door and knock: if any man hear my voice and open the door, I will come in to him, and will sup with him, and he with me' (iii. 20). The words are addressed to the individual, not as an isolated person, but to each man as a member of the community, and, originally, of all communities, the Church in Laodicea! The truth is, of course, that 'the individual' is an abstraction unless he lives in fellowship with others, and only in the community

[1]Cf. E. F. Scott, *The Fourth Gospel: its Purpose and Theology*, 104-44; G. Gloege, *Reich Gottes und Kirche*, 229-32; R. N. Flew, *Jesus and His Church*, 239-51.

can he gain his individuality. Religion, as Ritschl has reminded us, is always social;[1] and it is necessarily so, in so far as it is Christian. More than anywhere else is this truth apparent in the Epistle to the Ephesians,[2] where it is taught that, as reconciled men, Christians are 'fellow-citizens with the saints, and of the household of God, being built upon the foundation of the apostles and prophets, Christ Jesus himself being the chief corner stone' (ii. 19 f.; cf. 21 f.).

The question arises why the New Testament does not carry this conception of fellowship further still, in respect of nations and of peoples. Virtually, it sanctions the widest manifestations of fellowship in its teaching about the reconciliation of Jew and Gentile, in its superiority to the distinctions of bond and free, barbarian and Scythian, male and female (Gal. iii. 28, Col. iii. 11), and, above all, in the universalism of its Gospel and the broad sweep of its ethical teaching. Nevertheless, in questions of war and peace, social institutions, economic problems, and international relationships there is a want of explicit teaching which is often a ground of perplexity to social workers and internationalists with Christian sympathies. There is an obvious answer to these difficulties in the fact that the New Testament contains the Christian literature of the formative period before many of the practical problems of social life emerged, and still more in the truth that Christianity is a spirit and not a law. But the best answer of all is that the New Testament affirms the vital principle, upon which all schemes of social and international betterment depend, when it insists, first and foremost, that men must enter

[1] *Justification and Reconciliation*, 578.

[2] Cf. J. Scott Lidgett: 'If it is in one aspect the Epistle of personality, quickened and satisfied in Christ, it is equally and concurrently the Epistle of the Christian commonwealth, the Catholic Church,' *God in Christ Jesus*, 246.

into fellowship with God, in association with others, before further expressions of fellowship can offer more than a delusive promise.

How vital, in its bearings upon personal reconciliation and fellowship, is the work of God in Christ, we have already seen; but here we may note also that the same truth is taught in the New Testament in respect of the Church, and that it extends to all types of fellowship. The Church of God is that which He purchased 'with the blood of One who was His own' (Acts xx. 28); it is the Bride of the Lamb (Apoc. xxi. 2, 9, xxii. 17), the object of the love of Him who 'gave himself up for it; that he might sanctify it, having cleansed it by the washing of water with the word', that He might present it to Himself 'a glorious church, not having spot or wrinkle or any such thing' (Eph. v. 25-7). If fellowship within the Church depends upon the work of God in Christ, we may be sure also that the same is true of the fellowship of nations and peoples. The history of our time reveals the vanity of schemes of international co-operation which are based on no deeper foundation than kindly feeling and the sense of decency; the New Testament teaches that the one true hope of communal fellowship bears, and must bear, the sign of the Cross.

It cannot be too strongly emphasized, however, that, while this communal aspect is of the greatest importance, fellowship does not automatically follow from the bare fact of inclusion within the Christian Society. There is no guarantee that simply by becoming part of the visible Church and sharing in its rites and worship we have communion with God and fellowship with men. Fellowship is a sacred flame kindled at the altar fires of God, and, while it burns at its steadiest and best within the Society, it cannot burn at all unless first the fire is sent from God.

(g) *The Origins of New Testament Teaching concerning Fellowship with God*

The evidence assembled in Sections (*a*) to (*f*) shows convincingly the wealth and fulness of the New Testament teaching concerning communion with Christ and with God. Before examining its importance for modern theology, it is necessary to consider the problem of its origins. Is it a genuine product of the religious movement which begins with Jesus, or is it due to infiltration from non-Christian sources? Are we to find its foundation in the Old Testament and in the teaching of Jesus, or is its character determined by the contemporary forms and expressions of Hellenistic piety?

There can be no doubt at all that one of the formative factors which have contributed to shape the teaching we have examined is the Old Testament revelation concerning the knowledge of God. It is true that in the Old Testament the knowledge of God is often primarily 'an ethical relation to Him', and that 'when it says that God knows man, it means that He has sympathy and fellowship with him';[1] but in the higher flights of prophetic revelation, and sometimes in the Psalms, a distinctively religious relationship is described. Among the prophets, Hosea traces the controversy of Yahweh with the people of Israel to the fact that 'there is no truth, nor mercy, nor *knowledge of God* in the land' (iv. 1). 'My people', he cries, 'are destroyed for lack of *knowledge*' (iv. 6); and the God he proclaims is One whose word is: 'I desire mercy, and not sacrifice; and *the knowledge of God* more than[2] burnt-offerings' (vi. 6). In the Psalms stand the

[1] A. B. Davidson, *The Theology of the Old Testament*, 78.

[2] Or 'apart from'. Cf. J. Skinner, *Prophecy and Religion*, 179; R. H. Kennett, *The Church of Israel*, 121 n.

great exhortation: 'Be still, and *know* that I am God' (xlvi. 10), and the haunting prayer: 'Search me, O God, and *know my heart*: Try me, and *know my thoughts*' (cxxxix. 23); and in the New Covenant announced by Jeremiah are emblazoned the words: 'They shall teach no more every man his neighbour, and every man his brother, saying, Know the Lord: for *they shall all know me*, from the least of them unto the greatest of them, saith the Lord: for I will forgive their iniquity, and their sin will I remember no more' (xxxi. 34). With these words may be compared that radiant vision of the future in Isa. xi. 9, in which the prophet looks forward to the time when 'the earth shall be full of *the knowledge of the Lord*, as the waters cover the sea'.

Besides these passages those must be recalled which speak of God as *satisfying* man in the deepest needs of his spirit, as, for example, in Psa. xvii. 15, Psa. cvii. 9, and Psa. cxlv. 16:

> 'As for me, I shall behold thy face in righteousness:
> I shall be *satisfied*, when I awake, with thy likeness.'
>
> 'For he *satisfieth* the longing soul,
> And the hungry soul he filleth with good.'
>
> 'Thou openest thine hand,
> And *satisfieth* the desire of every living thing.'

More important still are the references in the Old Testament to those who in some measure saw God, Jacob at Penuel (cf. Gen. xxxii. 30: 'I have seen God face to face, and my life is preserved'); Moses, of whom it was said: 'And the Lord spake unto Moses face to face, as a man speaketh unto his friend' (Ex. xxxiii. 11; cf. Num. xii. 6-8, Deut. xxxiv. 10), and who was traditionally said to have seen the back of Yahweh from a cleft in the rock (Ex. xxxiii. 17-23); Micaiah who 'saw the Lord sitting on his throne' (1 Kings xxii. 19); Amos, who saw Him 'standing beside the altar' (ix. 1; cf. vii. 7); Isaiah, who beheld Him in the Temple (vi. 1); and Ezekiel, who saw 'visions of God' by the river Chebar (i. 1 ff.).[1] It is true that in the Old Testament and in later rabbinic discussions there was a certain reluctance to speak of 'seeing God', but it was due mainly to the fear of crude and literal interpretations. C. G. Montefiore quotes Mr. H. Loewe as saying: 'The phrase "to see God" was always altered by the Massorites to the passive, even when the sentence was wrested and grammar strained. They anticipated our objection to the use of such a phrase as "seeing God" literally.'[2] Emphasis was laid on the necessity of the study and observance of the Law, upon the condition of righteousness, and upon the fact that the vision would be corporate. K. E. Kirk observes that, while there are traces in rabbinic literature of visionary experiences, as in the case of Rabbi Akiba, in general 'the Rabbis deferred the full beatific vision to the days of the Messiah, or at all events to the hour of death'.[3]

Even from this necessarily brief survey it is evident that the New Testament teaching concerning fellowship with God rests upon an Old Testament foundation. Nevertheless, the wealth of the New Testament teaching is so great, and its distinctiveness in certain features is so marked, that it is impossible to account for it on this basis alone. At one with the Old Testament in the stress it lays upon the knowledge of God, the fulness of His self-giving, and the possibility of seeing Him face to face, the New Testament presents the idea of fellowship with an added depth and intimacy and is distinguished above all by its unwavering conviction that this fellowship is gained in and through Christ.

[1]These examples are those cited by K. E. Kirk in *The Vision of God*, 11.
[2]*Rabbinic Literature and Gospel Teachings*, 26 f. [3]*Op. cit.*, 19.

We have seen that for the most part this teaching is found in 1 and 2 Peter, the Pauline Epistles, the Fourth Gospel, and 1 John. It cannot occasion surprise that it is given mainly by St. Paul and St. John, for these are the writers who, while resting firmly upon primitive tradition and belief, develop the implications of the κήρυγμα in the light of the death and resurrection of Christ. The question inevitably arises whether this claim of fidelity to the primitive tradition is true of the idea of fellowship with God. Does this teaching stand in lineal succession with the mind and thought of Jesus, or is it an infiltration into Christianity from Greek religious circles?

It is, I think, reasonable enough to assert that St. Paul and St. John were responsive to the religious philosophy inherent in Greek religion,[1] and that elements in their terminology are derived from current usage,[2] but to go further, and to claim direct borrowing, so that the primitive Christian faith was transformed, cannot be proved or even shown to be probable. The attempts of Reitzenstein[3] and Bousset[4] to explain the mysticism of St. Paul and St. John as the product of Hellenic influences have failed on three grounds: the late date of the Hellenic sources to which appeal is made, the marked ethical character of Pauline and Johannine teaching, and the greater probability that its foundation is to be traced in the teaching of Jesus. So far as the mysticism of St. Paul is concerned, this conclusion is strongly supported by Schweitzer.[5] The Johannine theology he explains as a Hellenization

[1]Among other discussions of this question see S. Angus, *The Mystery-Religions and Christianity*; C. Clemen, *Primitive Christianity and its Non-Jewish Sources*; T. Wilson, *St. Paul and Paganism*; W. L. Knox, *St. Paul and the Church of the Gentiles*.

[2]Cf. H. A. A. Kennedy, *St. Paul and the Mystery-Religions*.

[3]*Die hellenistischen Mysterienreligionen*, 3rd ed., 1927.

[4]*Kyrios Christos*, 2nd ed., 1921.

[5]*The Mysticism of St. Paul*, 26-33.

of St. Paul's teaching.[1] This latter view can be rendered plausible only by neglecting the Jewish elements in the Fourth Gospel and by exaggerating the Evangelist's interest in the sacraments.[2] There is, I believe, a definite Greek strain in the Gospel, in the Logos doctrine, the attitude taken to eschatology, and the preference it shows for terms like light, truth, and eternal life; but the deeper notes are Jewish, especially in its doctrines of God and of sin, and the longer it is studied the more fully its connexion with Synoptic sayings is appreciated. Our earlier investigation does not support the claim that the Johannine mysticism is a development of Pauline teaching. On the one hand, the vocabulary is different. St. John uses none of the striking verbs compounded with *σύν* set out in Section (*c*) which are so characteristic of St. Paul; he shows a marked preference for *μένειν ἐν* which St. Paul does not use; and, while both writers employ the construction *εἶναι ἐν*, St. John never has the formula *ἐν Χριστῷ* in 1 John. On the other hand, although the idea of communion with the Living Christ is distinctive in both Pauline and Johannine teaching, St. John has no parallel to St. Paul's conception of dying, rising, and suffering with Christ. Since a generation separates the two writers, it is highly probable that, like Ignatius,[3] the Fourth Evangelist knew the major Pauline Epistles and was deeply influenced by their teaching. To assert, however, that the Johannine theology is a Hel-

[1] *Ibid.*, 334-75.

[2] Schweitzer writes: 'The sacramental stands for so much, in the Johannine mysticism of union with Christ, that the main significance of the death of Jesus is, according to it, the provision of the sacraments,' *op. cit.*, 364. For a sounder study of Johannine sacramental teaching, see W. F. Howard, *The Fourth Gospel in Recent Criticism and Interpretation*, 163-73.

[3] Cf. *The New Testament in the Apostolic Fathers* (Oxford Society of Historical Theology), 63 ff.

lenization of St. Paul's teaching, is to make a claim which lacks adequate basis. It is much more satisfactory to explain the two as related, but substantially independent, developments of ideas implicit in the sayings of Jesus, enriched by Hellenic sympathies, but determined by belief in the religious significance of His death and resurrection as it was appreciated in the primitive Christian communities.

In the Synoptic tradition there are undoubtedly sayings[1] of Jesus which provide the starting-point for the New Testament emphasis upon fellowship with Christ. When Jesus pronounced blessed those who were reproached and persecuted for His sake (Mt. v. 11), and when He spoke of those who should lose their lives for His sake (Mk. viii. 35) or fail to show loyalty to Him in His humiliation (Mk. viii. 38), He presented the suggestion of a personal relationship to Himself which could hardly fail to become the nucleus of a fellowship-mysticism after His resurrection. Even more is this claim true of His declaration: 'He that receiveth you receiveth me, and he that receiveth me receiveth him that sent me' (Mt. x. 40), His statement that those who do the will of God are His brother, sister, and mother (Mk. iii. 35), His affirmation that to receive a little child in His name is to receive Himself (Mt. xviii. 5), His words in the Parable of the Sheep and the Goats: 'I was an hungred, and ye gave me meat: I was thirsty, and ye gave me drink' (Mt. xxv. 35), and His claim: 'He that loveth father or mother more than me is not worthy of me; and he that loveth son or daughter more than me is not worthy of me' (Mt. x. 37).

[1]The sayings instanced below are those cited by Schweitzer as evidence for the basis of the Pauline mysticism in the teaching of Jesus, *op. cit.*, 105-9.

In themselves, these sayings are not a sufficient basis for the teaching we have examined so long as they are considered apart from the death and resurrection of Jesus. When, however, they are read in the light of these events, and of the significance which primitive Christianity found in them, their importance is very great. It is no wonder that currency was soon given within the Christian community to sayings like Mt. xviii. 20: 'Where two or three are gathered together in my name, there am I in the midst of them,' and xxviii. 20: 'And lo, I am with you alway, even unto the end of the world', words which are rightly explained by modern critics as 'Christian formations'. The significant thing is that the first believers, as indeed is true of most Christians down to the present day, found it quite natural to believe that Jesus had said these things, since the sayings expressed in direct speech truths which corresponded so closely with their religious experience. Many of the Johannine sayings must be understood in the same way. To the first believers the Christ who had conquered death and was now the Risen Lord, although triumphant and at the right hand of God, was felt to be still present in the fellowship of the Church; with Him they enjoyed a union which actually gave them the consciousness of communion with God.

This religious conviction was not simply due to inferences prompted by reflection upon sayings and events in the life of Jesus on the part of individuals; it was deepened and enriched by the corporate life and worship of the primitive Church. Baptism, for example, must have contributed powerfully to the idea of fellowship with Christ. When the catechumen descended into the waters, he must have reflected that Jesus Himself had been baptized; and this fact alone would suggest a point of association. Moreover, he had already made a confession of his faith, in which emphasis was laid on the fact that Christ died for sins and was raised according to the Scriptures, and that afterwards He had been seen by the first disciples (1 Cor. xv. 3-5). With this confession ringing in his ears it was not difficult for him to relate the stages in the act of baptism to the events recalled in the primitive Christian creed. Entrance into the waters reminded him of the dying of Christ, immersion of His burial, and emergence of His resurrection; and in an hour of intense spiritual emotion he would feel that, spiritually, he was dying, being buried, and rising with Christ. It may be that in Rom. vi. 3-11 St. Paul is introducing these ideas for the first time when he asks: 'Are ye ignorant that all we who were baptized into Christ Jesus were baptized into his death?', when he asserts that 'we were buried therefore with him through baptism into death', and continues the parallelism in the words: 'that like as Christ was raised from the dead through the glory of the Father, so we also might walk in newness of life'. On the other hand, it may be that the Apostle is simply reminding new readers of truths which he had already taught in other Churches, and with which he might suppose them to be familiar.[1] In any case, once expressed, these ideas would immediately be intelligible to the first Christians who had a much better acquaintance with adult baptism than is possessed by the Church of to-day. Among Baptists and in Christian Missions beyond the seas there is naturally a much closer modern parallel. The interaction of thought would be mutual. Fellowship with Christ gave a deeper meaning to Baptism, and Baptism imparted a deeper understanding of fellowship with Christ.

As in the case of Baptism, so also the experiences associated with the primitive Christian Eucharist helped

[1]Note, in particular, 'Are ye ignorant that . . .' (Rom. vi. 3).

to shape, and in turn were shaped by, the New Testament idea of fellowship. From the beginning the Eucharist was intimately connected with the events and sayings of the Ministry of Jesus; with the Last Supper, and probably also with the earlier Galilean fellowship-meals, reflected in the stories of miraculous feeding in Mk. vi. 35-44 and viii. 1-9, which He had celebrated with His followers in anticipation of the great Messianic Feast.[1] Believers who participated in the primitive Eucharist, now doubly eloquent of the sacrificial death of Jesus and of the perfecting of the Kingdom, felt, and could not fail to feel, that they had communion with the One who had first broken the loaves in the wilderness near Bethsaida and finally on the last night in which He was betrayed. They did not think of Him as a dead prophet or a departed teacher, but as One who though glorified and exalted was with them here and now. On him they fed, in the power of His death and of His risen life they participated, and they looked forward to a still closer fellowship when they should be glorified with Him and reign with Him in the perfected Kingdom of God. Thus the Eucharist was a powerful formative factor in the New Testament experience of fellowship with Christ, and through Him with God.

To the influences already mentioned must be added those exerted by the praise and collective worship of the primitive communities. Following methods already familiar to them in the worship of the synagogue and the Temple,[2] the first Christians must have discovered the great influence of liturgical worship and of the singing of hymns upon the formation of belief. In the references to 'psalms and hymns and spiritual songs' in Col. iii. 16

[1]Cf. Schweitzer, *The Quest of the Historical Jesus*, 374-80.

[2]Cf. A. B. Macdonald, *Christian Worship in the Primitive Church*, 112.

and Eph. v. 19 (cf. 1 Cor. xiv. 26) we have direct evidence of the practice of hymn-singing in the primitive Church, and scholars have pointed to what are probably fragments of early hymns in Lk. i and ii, the Apocalypse, and the Pauline and Pastoral Epistles.[1] In this matter the history of later religious movements in the life of the Church, as, for example, in the story of Methodism,[2] throws light upon the conditions of primitive Christianity; and it can hardly be doubted that the idea of fellowship with Christ was among the experimental truths which gained force and depth by the singing of psalms and hymns.

These, then, are some of the factors, historical and religious, out of which the Pauline and Johannine teaching concerning fellowship with Christ emerged—the Old Testament religious tradition, the sayings of Jesus, the events of His ministry, especially His death and resurrection, reflection on the part of individual teachers and preachers, the sacraments of Baptism and the Eucharist, and the adoration and collective worship of the primitive Christian communities. To neglect these factors, and to explain the teaching of St. Paul and St. John as an addition to the primitive faith under the influence of Hellenistic religious life and practice, is to forsake the immediate for the remote, the certain for the possible but speculative, probable as it is that the ideas connected with the Mystery-religions made it easy to commend the Gospel to the

[1]Cf. A. M. Hunter, *Paul and His Predecessors*, 41-51. Among the passages mentioned by Dr. Hunter are Apoc. iv. 11, v. 9 f., 12 f., xi. 17 f., xv. 3 f., xix. 6-8; in the Pastoral Epistles, 1 Tim. iii. 16, 2 Tim. ii. 11-3, and Tit. iii. 4-7; and in the Pauline Epistles, Eph. v. 14 and Phil. ii. 6-11.

[2]Cf. S. G. Dimond, *The Psychology of the Methodist Revival*, 119-24. 'The themes of the hymns were doctrinal and experimental, and thus their educational value was considerable. Singing these songs frequently gave definition to the various phases of religious experience, and the repetition provided the new converts with a range of religious ideas which formed a basis for theological construction,' *op. cit.*, 122.

Gentile world and provided in some cases useful terms for its expression. Fellowship with Christ, and through Him with God, are not extraneous ideas imported from without, but are doctrines, with a deep experimental root, integral to Christianity, closely linked with its history and continuous with its vital tradition.

(*h*) *The Place of the Idea of Fellowship in Modern Theology*

It is not necessary to illustrate at any length the place given to the idea of fellowship in modern theology, for it would be difficult to name a recent work concerned in any important degree with the relationships of God with men, or with those of men with men, which fails to make full use of this idea. In theological articles also, in the discussions of retreats and fraternals, and in sermons and popular lectures no idea is so common. To such a degree is this the case that there is a real danger lest the word 'fellowship' should become vague in content and misleading in its relation to other Christian ideas.

In a well known and widely esteemed work Wilhelm Herrmann has defined 'personal Christianity' as 'a communion of the soul with the living God through the mediation of Christ', and he describes this as a conception about the general meaning of which Christians are fully agreed.[1] 'Herein', he says, 'is really included all that belongs to the characteristic life of Christendom—revelation and faith, conversion and the comfort of forgiveness, the joy of faith, and the service of love, lonely communion with God, and life in Christian fellowship.'[2] 'All this', he maintains, is 'only truly Christian when it is experienced as communion with the living God through the

[1] *The Communion of the Christian with God* (Eng. tr. of the 4th German ed. by R. W. Stewart), 9.

[2] *Ibid.*

mediation of Christ. When we believe in a man's personal Christianity we are convinced that he stands in that relation to God in which all this takes place.'[1] Elsewhere he describes in moving words what it is to meet with God in Christ. 'We know that in Christ we meet with God, and we know what sort of a meeting this is; we know that this God gives us comfort and courage to face the world, joy in facing the demands of duty, and with all this eternal life in our hearts.'[2] In these words we have a classical description of a conception of the Christian life which happily is very widely accepted in all parts of the Church to-day.

Just because this conception of fellowship or communion with God is so widely accepted it is necessary that we should consider how it is related to other Christian ideas, to forgiveness, reconciliation, and sanctification, and how it depends upon the historical foundations of Christianity, the life, death, and resurrection of Christ, together with their religious corollary, the fact of an abiding and living Lord. Failure to apprehend these various relationships can only lead to a misty conception of fellowship which either means very little indeed or degenerates into an unhealthy type of mystical piety.

So far as forgiveness is the remission of sins, its relation to fellowship is easy to determine. Forgiveness, in this sense, is the necessary condition of fellowship; for there can be no communion with God so long as sins are unrecognized, unconfessed, and unannulled. Sin bars the way to fellowship; its removal, therefore, is the *sine qua non* of reconciliation. This does not mean, of course, that sin must first be completely annihilated, since in fact it is through fellowship with God that it is burnt out and finally destroyed. To think otherwise is to make com-

[1] *Ibid.* [2] *Op. cit.*, 173.

munion with God the goal and consummation of the Christian hope, whereas in reality it is the Christian experience itself. What is required, if fellowship is to be possible, is that in the mercy of God sins which have been confessed should be known as barriers rolled away. To the Christian man this deliverance is always a miracle; as Herrmann has said, it is 'utterly marvellous'.[1] Like faith,[2] it is an anticipatory experience of communion with God; for, in forgiveness, the soul receives a warm and living sense of the nearness of God, of His astounding love as made known to sinners. So little can we map out and completely isolate the dealings of a loving God with men! Communion, however, in the full meaning of the word, is known only when the burden of sin falls from our back and is seen no more. Then only do we truly live, at peace with God and knowing the blessings of freedom and sonship.

Justification, in like manner, is antecedent to fellowship. In the greatness of His love, God receives as righteous the utterly contrite who, making no claim to merit, rest in His redeeming love, and thus reveal a mind responsive to the goodness, righteousness, and truth which come to them in Christ. As the work of God, justification is the sign of His reconciling love, whether we perceive its nature, as indeed we may, or whether it remains hidden from us in an unanalysed experience of forgiving love. Both these divine works, the remission of sins and the new status which God gives on the ground of faith, are foretastes and intimations of fellowship; but, in the fulness of its meaning, fellowship, as an ever growing and deepening life of mutual love, follows and is dependent upon them.

Reconciliation, or forgiveness in the wider sense of the term, as the restoration of the soul to fellowship with God, already includes within itself the remission of sins and

[1] *Op. cit.*, 131. [2] Herrmann, *op. cit.*, 241 f.

justification, and is at one and the same time fellowship with God and the introduction to fellowship. Each of these points is important. On the one hand, reconciliation is meaningless if it does not include fellowship with God. Through this experience unreality in our thoughts of Him, and the sense of alienation from Him, are gone. As reconciled men, we know that He is our Father and that we are His children; we receive His peace and the freedom He bestows. The reconciliation, indeed, is not established unless we have a true knowledge of these things. On the other hand, reconciliation is our introduction to fellowship with God. In our study of New Testament teaching we have seen how rich are the possibilities of fellowship, the heights and depths, the length and breadth, of its privileges. Reconciled with God, we are offered these treasures. With open hands, we stand before the unsearchable riches of Christ. We can abide in Him, die with Him, rise with Him, and, through Him, we can know and see God more and more completely. Our life 'is hid with Christ in God'. Moreover, and in consequence of this divine communion, a richer and deeper fellowship with men is open to us. Members of the Ecclesia of God, the present manifestation of His Rule and the prophecy of its final consummation, we enter upon a life in which the barriers of nationality and of class are submerged. There are, indeed, no boundaries to this fellowship; it is eternal life itself in a Kingdom without frontiers, including men 'of every tribe, and tongue, and people, and nation'.

Sanctification, as we shall see, is the fruition and the climax of this fellowship with God and men; it is perfect love, beatitude, and the final gift of the vision of God.

In a measure, these distinctions are logical rather than experimental, but they are not any the less important on that account. Within the Christian life the forgiveness of sins may be experienced more fully, and its wonder appreciated far more deeply, as fellowship with God grows and increases. Equally justification may be recognized, as a fact of God's gracious dealing with us, as we look back from mountains of Beulah; and it may, or may not, be totally impossible for us to distinguish the spiritual moment when reconciliation as the act of God issues in the life of fellowship. Ritschl has admirably shown that faith itself is subject to the same principle of development. If it is attained through sudden conversion, it marks the beginning of the Christian life 'in the full compass of its characteristics'. 'But if, amid the surroundings of Church life, education is the normal form in which individuals attain to faith in Christ, it is not to be expected that faith should be called forth in its definite peculiar character, in the totality of its characteristics, prior to the operations of God's grace in the sphere of moral discipline and action.'[1] All this must be freely recognized as a true description of the Christian experience. None the less, in the interests of the idea of fellowship with God, theology is compelled to distinguish the elements it contains and their mutual relationships one to another. Only so can we perceive how utterly marvellous fellowship is, and is capable of becoming.

The crowning value of a true understanding of fellowship with God is that thereby we see unmistakably its vital dependence upon the work of Christ in all its fulness. As rooted in faith, and including the forgiveness of sins, justification, and reconciliation, it requires for its birth and its vitality all that is necessary to each. If pardon, acceptance with God, and the gift of peace and of son-

[1] *Justification and Reconciliation*, 598. His further observation: 'Faith in Christ can be expected only in maturer life,' is an exaggeration.

ship are made possible and assured to the believer by the redemptive work of Christ, trebly so must this be true of fellowship with God. In consequence, all thought of communion with God which ignores the Cross of Christ is theological lightmindedness. Herein, too, is the reason why the various aspects of fellowship, set forth in New Testament teaching, are all associated, directly or indirectly, with the work of Christ for men. *Κοινωνία*, in one of its most distinctive expressions, is 'the fellowship of his sufferings'. To be 'in Christ', in the richest form of that Pauline experience, is to have fellowship with Him who died and rose again, a fellowship so close that the believer lives, dies, and rises together with Him. This relationship extends even to the rites of the Christian Society. To be baptized, in the Pauline theology, is to be baptized into Christ's death; to share in the Supper is to receive the cup of the new covenant sealed by His blood. Different in emphasis, the Johannine teaching about 'abiding in' and 'being in Christ' refers primarily to fellowship with the Risen and Exalted Lord, but He, no less, is the One who laid down His life that He might take it again, the Lamb of God, our Advocate with the Father, the *ἱλασμός* for the sins of the world. Both as a possibility and an experience, fellowship depends upon the work of Christ.

Finally, we must add a point of special importance which emerges as we consider the richer aspects of fellowship with God and with men, and which is still more manifest when we think of sanctification. As a continuous and growing experience, fellowship requires, as its foundation, a continuous redeeming and restoring ministry of Christ. Based on all that was accomplished on Calvary, it depends in all its heights and depths upon the work of Him who ever liveth to make intercession for us.

V

SANCTIFICATION

IN our study of the Christian experience we must now consider the work of sanctification in which reconciliation and fellowship find their goal and consummation. The term 'sanctification', which is not necessarily the best word to describe the Christian ideal, is here used because of its traditional association with the great words investigated in the earlier chapters. Among other expressions used to describe this ideal are perfection, Christian perfection, sinless perfection, beatitude, *unio mystica*, *via unitiva*, the vision of God, and perfect love; and each of these is important as describing a particular aspect of the goal. Perhaps the least satisfactory terms are those which include the word 'perfection', since they imply the idea of a standard which it is difficult to dissociate from the suggestion of something fixed and static; whereas the Christian ideal, if it is to find a worthy expression, must be conceived as capable of endless enrichment. The term 'beatitude' concentrates attention unduly upon the felicity or blessedness of the believer, without suggesting adequately the essential character of the work of God in the process of attainment. The Latin phrases are too exclusively mystical and all that is valuable in their meaning is included in the phrase 'the vision of God'. Of the various expressions open to us the best are 'the vision of God', 'sanctification', and 'perfect love'. In the sequel it will be argued that 'perfect love' is the most satisfactory of all, inasmuch as it suggests the highest quality of life, akin to the life of God Himself, sustained and perfected by Him alone.

These distinctions will assist us in deciding the best method of treatment, but other considerations also need to be taken into account. The reconciling work of God, we have seen, is itself a sanctifying activity, in the sense that the believer is set apart and consecrated to holy ends and purposes; but in the Christian experience, both in its individual and communal aspects, this divine hallowing needs to be worked out in a life of ethical and spiritual progress. In this development the ethical and the spiritual cannot be separated; in Christianity there are no ethical aims which are not at the same time spiritual, and there are no spiritual ideals which are not also ethical. It follows, therefore, that we must consider: (*a*) Sanctification and the Ethical Life; and, since spiritual growth is especially the work of the Spirit, (*b*) Sanctification and Life in the Spirit. At this point it will be necessary to examine New Testament teaching concerning (*c*) Sanctification and the Christian Ideal. Further, inasmuch as sin is incompatible with sanctification, we must discuss (*d*) Sanctification and Sinless Perfection. Other themes which also demand attention are: (*e*) Sanctification and the Vision of God; (*f*) Sanctification and Perfect Love; (*g*) Sanctification and the Community; and, finally, (*h*) The Place of Sanctification in Modern Theology.

(*a*) *Sanctification and the Ethical Life*

St. Paul's denial that justification is 'by works' carries with it the same conclusion in the case of reconciliation. Reconciliation is the work of God; to it man contributes nothing save his willingness to be reconciled; he cannot win it, establish his claim to it, or make it the reward of his aspirations. As a little child, he receives it as the gift of God, made possible by the work of Christ.

The possibility of interpreting this circumstance in an

antinomian direction is only too obvious, and the New Testament reveals how quickly libertarian inferences were drawn and with what vehemence they were repudiated. 'Works' are not the ground of reconciliation, but unquestionably they are its fruits. On this point St. Paul is just as emphatic as, and much more informative than, St. James; he stands close to the teaching of Jesus: 'By their fruits ye shall know them' (Mt. vii. 20). It is only against the background of this strong ethical emphasis that New Testament teaching on sanctification can be understood.

For our purpose, it is not necessary to treat the ethical teaching of the New Testament in detail. On this subject the standard works should be consulted.[1] All that we need consider are the outlines of the teaching.

In the Gospels it is noteworthy that the 'paradigms' or 'pronouncement-stories', which belong to the earliest strata of the tradition, deal frequently with moral questions.[2] Forgiveness, table-fellowship, wealth, charity, adultery, clean and unclean things, conduct on the Sabbath, the question of the payment of tribute-money, the nature of the great commandment, are some of the problems treated. Again, the early collections of the sayings, in Q, M, and the source presupposed by St. Mark's Gospel, together with many of the Lukan parables, are predominantly ethical in character. The inference, that the primitive communities were deeply interested in questions of conduct, is certain; and, that the teaching of Jesus Himself possessed a marked ethical tone, is beyond question.

[1]Cf. H. Rashdall, *Conscience and Christ*; E. F. Scott, *The Ethical Teaching of Jesus*; C. A. Anderson Scott, *New Testament Ethics*; J. Moffatt, *Love in the New Testament*; Newman Smyth, *Christian Ethics*.

[2]Cf. M. Dibelius, *From Tradition to Gospel*, *The Message of Jesus*; E. B. Redlich, *Form Criticism*; V. Taylor, *The Formation of the Gospel Tradition*.

It is, of course, true that Jesus had no ethical system. In His teaching there is no discussion of 'the good', no definition of the moral idea, no theory of evil. What we find are aphorisms and religious principles of life and action. The outstanding character of the sayings is not their originality, since parallels of one kind or another can be found to most of them,[1] but the power inherent in them, due in part to their unforgettable form and beauty, but still more to the personal authentication which He gives to them. They have wings because they come from Him.[2] His achievement, as a religious teacher, is that the qualities He commends have come to be known as 'Christian virtues', despite the Greek and oriental parallels. Among these qualities are sincerity, purity, humility, compassion, obedience, meekness, the forgiving spirit, love for enemies, and self-sacrifice.[3] On the other hand, the evils He repudiates are insincerity, hypocrisy, over-anxious care, retaliation, and the judging of others;[4] and among the things which defile a man are 'evil thoughts, fornications, thefts, murders, adulteries, covetings, wickednesses, deceit, lasciviousness, an evil eye, railing, pride, foolishness' (Mk. vii. 21f.). If, in the teaching of Jesus, there is no theory of the ideal, there are acute ethical judgments. For example, the catalogue of evils given above is preceded by the penetrating word: 'There is nothing from

[1]Cf. Strack-Billerbeck, *Kommentar zum Neuen Testament aus Talmud und Midrasch*; Montefiore, *The Synoptic Gospels*.

[2]Cf. J. Weiss: 'So with Jesus; His ideals as such are neither so novel nor so revolutionary as to create a new world; they derive their procreative virtue solely from the fact that He made them *His own*, *lived* them, and *died* for them,' *Hastings' D.C.G.*, i. 544.

[3]Cf. Mt. v. 5-8, 33-7, 44, vi. 1, xviii. 4, 21f.; Mk. x. 15; Lk. vi. 27f., 33, 35, xiv. 8-11, xvii. 7-10; Jn. xv. 13.

[4]Cf. Mt. v. 39-42, vi. 25-34, vii. 1-5, 15-23, x. 31, xxiii. 2-36; Lk. vi. 29 f., 37 f., 41 f., xi. 39-52, xii. 22-31.

without the man, that going into him can defile him: but the things which proceed out of the man are those which defile him' (Mk. vii. 15); and, as a practical principle of conduct, nothing surpasses the Golden Rule: 'All things therefore whatsoever ye would that men should do unto you, even so do ye also unto them: for this is the law and the prophets' (Mt. vii. 12 = Lk. vi. 31). The recognition that the great commandments are those which commend love to God and love to one's neighbour illustrates the inwardness of the teaching of Jesus; and His acceptance of a completely altruistic ideal is implicit in His words about cross-bearing (Mk. viii. 34), on drinking the cup of suffering (Mk. x. 38), and on the necessity of dying in order to live (Mk. viii. 35-7). These sayings have an unmistakably ethical tone, but nowhere is there any suggestion of a morality which exists in and for itself. His ethical teaching is rooted deeply in His religious convictions, and, indeed, is the expression of these convictions in relation to conduct and action; more characteristically still, it bears the impress of His authority and carries with it insistent claims on the allegiance of men.

It is important to recall these aspects of the teaching of Jesus because the main question we have to consider is whether the same practical emphasis is maintained in primitive Christianity. Does St. Paul attach the same importance to conduct in personal and social relationships in spite of his absorbing interest in justification and reconciliation? His attitude to the Law[1] supplies an affirmative answer, since, while he denies that believers are 'under the law' (Rom. vi. 14), while he speaks of it as an 'attendant' to bring men to Christ (Gal. iii. 24), and declares that He was sent to redeem men subject to its yoke (Gal. iv. 5), he

[1]I have treated this point fully in *The Atonement in New Testament Teaching*, 112-5.

also characterizes it as 'holy' and 'spiritual' (Rom. vii. 12, 14), and affirms that the end in view in the sending of Christ was 'that the ordinance of the law might be fulfilled in us, who walk not after the flesh, but after the spirit' (Rom. viii. 4). The same answer is also fully sustained by the ethical exhortations with which his Epistles abound.

Not infrequently St. Paul refers to the example of Christ who 'pleased not himself' (Rom. xv. 3), and indeed makes this appeal the foundation of some of his greatest doctrinal statements, as in 2 Cor. viii. 9: 'Ye know the grace of our Lord Jesus Christ . . .,' and Phil. ii. 5-11: 'Have this mind in you which was also in Christ Jesus. . . .'[1] If he asks his converts to imitate himself, it is only in so far as he imitates Christ (1 Cor. xi. 1; cf. 1 Thess. i. 6). His writings often echo Christ's ethical teaching,[2] and he is never tired of exhorting his readers, not to seek their own, but each his neighbour's good (1 Cor. x. 24).[3] The supreme motive is love. 'Through love', he writes, 'be servants one to another' (Gal. v. 13); 'Above all these things put on love, which is the bond of perfectness' (Col. iii. 14). So marked is this emphasis that his 'Hymn to Love', in 1 Cor. xiii, is as characteristic of his teaching as his doctrine concerning justification, reconciliation, and adoption. Among the qualities which he longs to see in the lives of his converts are gentleness, goodness, and noble-mindedness (cf. Rom. xv. 14, Gal. v. 22 f.),[4] and, along with injunctions to this end he lays a notable stress upon that which is 'seemly' in conduct 'toward them that

[1]Cf. also Rom. xv. 7, Eph. v. 2, 25, Col. iii. 13.

[2]Especially in Rom. xii. Cf. C. A. Anderson Scott, *Christianity according to St. Paul*, 215.

[3]Cf. also 1 Cor. x. 32 f., Rom. xv. 2, Phil. ii. 4.

[4]Cf. also Gal. vi. 1, Col. iii. 12.

are without' (1 Thess. iv. 12).[1] The greatest sympathy for positive virtues, many of which were prized in the Gentile world,[2] is shown in Phil. iv. 8, where things true, honourable, just, pure, lovely, and of good report are mentioned in a list which ends in the words: 'if there be any virtue, and if there be any praise, think on these things.' Besides these exhortations are those which, in the opinion of some, are based on moral codes[3] current in Gentile circles, in which duties to husbands, wives, children, fathers, slaves, and masters are set forth and commended (Col. iii. 18–iv. 1, Eph. v. 22–vi. 9).[4] There are limitations in the Pauline ethical teaching, particularly in relation to slavery, marriage, war, and the State, but far more is given than it is reasonable to expect in pioneer writings, intended to deal with immediate and pressing problems in an atmosphere charged with eschatological hopes and aspirations.

In any attempt to detach the Pauline ethic from its doctrinal foundations there is a certain artificiality which can be defended only on the ground that it throws into relief the ethical background of St. Paul's teaching concerning justification, reconciliation, and, above all, sanctification. The Christian ideal is nowhere divorced from ethical principles; on the contrary, the two stand together in the closest possible connexion. In the New Testament this union is assumed rather than debated, except in so far as St. Paul strongly denies that the Christian can continue

[1]Cf. also Rom. xiii. 13, 1 Cor. vii. 35, xiv. 40.

[2]Cf. J. H. Michael, *The Moffatt New Testament Commentary*, *The Epistle to the Philippians*, 200-8.

[3]Cf. J. W. C. Wand, *Westminster Commentaries*, *The General Epistles of St. Peter and St. Jude*, 3-9.

[4]For other possible examples of the use of moral codes, extended in Christian usage, in 1 Pet. ii. 11–iii. 12, v. 1-5, 1 Tim. ii. 1–vi. 19, and Tit. ii. 1–iii. 2; cf. Wand, *op. cit.*, 7.

in sin and Jesus maintains that the tree is known by its fruits. If, in practice, this fact has often been ignored, the fault cannot be laid at the door of the classical Christian documents.

Although ethical teaching is especially prominent in the Pauline Epistles, it is distinctive also in other New Testament writings. St. John describes Christ's friends (φίλοι) as those who do the things which He commands them (Jn. xv. 14; cf. xiv. 15, 21), and sets forth, as the 'new commandment' which He gives to us, that we love one another, even as He has loved us (Jn. xiii. 34; cf. xv. 12). The same teaching is given in a series of passages in 1 John, in ii. 3, 7, iii. 22, iv. 21, v. 2 f. In ii. 4 it is laid down that 'he that saith, I know him, and keepeth not his commandments, is a liar, and the truth is not in him'; and in iii. 7 f. the importance of righteousness is taught in the words: 'He that doeth righteousness is righteous, even as he is righteous: he that doeth sin is of the devil.' The strongly ethical tone of the Epistle of St. James is well known, and its teaching about respect of persons (ii. 1-9), works (ii. 14-26), the tongue (iii. 1-12), and wealth (iv. 1-6), is felt to recall the sayings of Jesus. Of the moral codes already mentioned a further use appears to be made in 1 Peter ii. 13–iii. 9, and in 1 Tim. ii. 1-11 and Tit. ii. 1-10. In the Epistle to the Hebrews love to the brethren, hospitality to strangers, the care of prisoners, the honour of marriage, freedom from the love of money, and contentment with the possessions we have, are enjoined (xiii. 1-6).

This brief summary would require to be supplemented if our intention were to give a full account of the ethical teaching of the New Testament, but, as illustrating the strong ethical tone of the writings which teach the need for sanctification and the attainment of the Christian ideal, it is adequate for the end we have in view. Sanctification is enjoined by writers whose interests are fully ethical.

(*b*) *Sanctification and Life in the Spirit*

Sanctification not only has a strong ethical foundation, but also stands in the closest relation to New Testament teaching concerning Life in the Spirit. In almost all its aspects the Christian experience is directly related to the work of the Spirit of God. All growth and discovery, every aspiration and achievement both in its beginning and its end, are due to His inspiration. Such is the teaching of the New Testament. It follows, therefore, that, if we are to understand sanctification aright, we must consider, not indeed this teaching as a whole,[1] but as much of it as is relevant to the discussion.

The originating impulse of the New Testament doctrine of the Spirit was the teaching of Jesus and those new and surprising facts of the Christian experience which cried out for an explanation. This explanation was found in the Old Testament prophets. The action of Peter on the Day of Pentecost in citing Joel ii. 28-32: 'And it shall come to pass afterward, that I will pour out my spirit upon all flesh...', is characteristic of primitive Christianity. The first Christians believed that they were living in a day of fulfilment; they also treasured the words of Jesus about the Spirit's guidance in the hour of trial (Mk. xiii. 11; Lk. xii. 12 = Mt. x. 20), His warning concerning the danger of blasphemy against the Holy Spirit (Mk. iii. 29; Lk. xii. 10 = Mt. xii. 32), His claim that the Spirit of the Lord rested upon Himself (Lk. iv. 18), and His promise that His disciples should be clothed with power from on

[1] I have discussed this teaching more fully in my Lecture on 'The Spirit in the New Testament' in *The Doctrine of the Holy Spirit* (by members of the staff of Wesley College, Headingley, 1937), 41-68.

high (Lk. xxiv. 49).[1] In such circumstances it is not remarkable that the Acts and the Epistles should so frequently describe the Christian experience as a life moulded and directed by the power of the Spirit.

In the Acts emphasis is laid upon the endowment of the Spirit as the necessary equipment for Apostolic service (i. 8), including even the serving of tables (vi. 3) as well as guidance in perplexity (xi. 12, 17) and fidelity in the face of danger (xx. 22 f.). The reception of the Spirit is the mark of the believer (xix. 2; cf. Gal. iii. 2, Heb. vi. 4), sometimes preceding (x. 44, 47) and sometimes following upon (ii. 38) baptism.

St. Paul brings the work of the Spirit into intimate relationship with the life of the believer and the fellowship of the Church. The Spirit, he insists, is not to be quenched (1 Thess. v. 19) or grieved (Eph. iv. 30); and his reason for these and other exhortations is his fervent belief that the Spirit is the source of true life and conduct. 'If we live by the Spirit', he writes, 'by the Spirit let us also walk' (Gal. v. 25). How ethical his conception is, appears in the words which follow the passage just cited: 'Let us not be vainglorious, provoking one another, envying one another' (Gal. v. 26), and even more in his description of 'the fruit of the Spirit' as 'love, joy, peace, longsuffering, kindness, goodness, faithfulness, meekness, self-control' (Gal. v. 22). Especially important is the place he gives to the Spirit in his account of the new life which follows justification in the experience of believers. If the Spirit dwells in them, they are not 'in the flesh', but 'in the spirit' (Rom. viii. 9, 11); He bears witness to their sonship (Rom. viii. 16), assists them in their prayers

[1]For explanations of the limited number of such sayings in the Synoptic tradition, see R. N. Flew, *Jesus and His Church*, 69-71; also *The Doctrine of the Holy Spirit*, 53 f.

and makes intercession for them 'with groanings which cannot be uttered' (Rom. viii. 26). In the Corinthian Epistles he speaks of them as having been justified 'in the name of the Lord Jesus Christ, and in the Spirit of our God' (1 Cor. vi. 11). He reminds them that, as individuals, their body is 'a sanctuary of the Holy Spirit' (1 Cor. vi. 19), and that, collectively, they are 'God's sanctuary' and that 'the Spirit of God' dwells in them (1 Cor. iii. 16).[1] The Spirit both restrains and prompts them in their religious affirmations. It is not possible for them, 'speaking in the Spirit of God', to say, 'Jesus is anathema', while the confession of the Lordship of Jesus can be made only 'in the Holy Spirit' (1 Cor. xii. 3). God has 'sealed' them, and has given to them 'the earnest of the Spirit' in their hearts (2 Cor. i. 22; cf. v. 5). In Ephesians also he reminds his readers that, 'having believed', they were 'sealed with the Holy Spirit of promise' (i. 13), and that 'in one Spirit' they have 'access . . . unto the Father' through Christ (ii. 18). He prays that they may be 'strengthened with power through his Spirit in the inward man' (iii. 16), and speaks of 'the unity of the Spirit in the bond of peace' (iv. 3). Just as there is 'one Body', the Church, so there is 'one Spirit, even as also ye were called in one hope of your calling' (iv. 4).

In the Johannine writings the Spirit is also freely mentioned. In the Apocalypse the references are reminiscent mainly of Old Testament usage, while those in 1 John are concerned with the idea of knowledge (iii. 24, iv. 2, 6, 13, v. 6) and with witness-bearing (v. 6, 8). In the Fourth Gospel the Spirit is the source of the New Birth (iii. 5-8). 'It is the Spirit that quickeneth' (vi. 63), and God does not give Him 'by measure' (iii. 34). In vii. 39 this gift is connected with the glorifying of Jesus. 'The Spirit', the

[1]Cf. Robertson and Plummer, *I.C.C.*, 1 *Corinthians*, 66, 128.

Evangelist explains, 'was not yet given; because Jesus was not yet glorified.' In the Farewell Discourses the Spirit is 'the Paraclete', whose function is to teach the disciples (xiv. 26, xvi. 13), to bear witness to Christ (xv. 26), and to convict the world of sin, of righteousness, and of judgment (xvi. 8).[1] Finally, the disciples receive their Apostolic commission in the words: 'Receive ye the Holy Spirit: whose soever sins ye forgive, they are forgiven unto them; whose soever sins ye retain, they are retained. (xx. 22 f.).[2]

In the rest of the New Testament similar teaching, while less prominent, is widely represented. In Hebrews, Old Testament quotations are introduced by the phrase, 'the Holy Spirit saith' (iii. 7), or 'beareth witness' (x. 15);[3] His gifts or 'distributions' (ii. 4) are mentioned; and those who were once enlightened are described as those who were made 'partakers of the Holy Spirit' (vi. 4). With these passages may be compared 1 Pet. i. 2, 12, and iv. 14, 2 Pet. i. 21, Jude 19 f., 2 Tim. i. 14, and Tit. iii. 5.[4]

It is impossible to dissociate this rich and many-sided work of the Spirit from the thought of spiritual attainment, although it is only to a surprisingly small extent that a direct connexion is established in the New Testament.[5] In the main, the passages relating to sanctification, which we have yet to examine, lie apart from those which describe life in the Spirit, reconciliation, and fellowship with God. None the less, just as in the case of the ethical

[1]Cf. *The Doctrine of the Holy Spirit*, 60-7. [2]See earlier, p. 13.

[3]Cf. ix. 8.

[4]The references to the Spirit in 1 Tim. iii. 16 and Jas. iv. 5 are uncertain.

[5]1 Pet. i. 2 speaks of 'sanctification of the Spirit'. Wand, *op. cit.*, 39, suggests that introduction to the 'royal priesthood', which is the Christian Church, is meant, but he recognizes that moral character is also probably in view to some extent. The qualification seems strange. Cf. Bigg, *I.C.C.*, *St. Peter and St. Jude*, 92.

teaching of the New Testament, it is of supreme importance to give attention first to all that is taught concerning the origin and development of the Christian experience, if only to rebut the suggestion that the doctrine of sanctification is magical and irrational. The significant fact to remember is that sanctification, as a process and an ideal, is taught by the same New Testament writers who describe fellowship with God and the operations of the Spirit in the Christian experience. Sanctification, therefore, may be described as the flowering of Christian growth and development. Indeed, we may go so far as to say that, if the New Testament made no explicit references to the Christian ideal, and to the obligation of men to seek its attainment, we should be compelled to infer, from its teaching concerning the spiritual life, that such an ideal exists and is binding. A life nourished by the love of God, and sustained by the Spirit, is meant to unfold into the beauty of the perfect flower.

One point is of special importance: there is no support in New Testament teaching for the view that sanctification is a sudden and miraculous gift of the Spirit in response to importunate prayer. Pentecost, to which, in this connexion, reference is often made (cf. Acts ii. 1-13; cf. iv. 31), was the endowment of the primitive Church with power; there is no indication that it entailed complete victory over sin and the attainment of ethical and spiritual perfection.[1] Similarly, in New Testament usage, the phrase, 'filled with the Spirit', does not connote the fulfilment of the Christian ideal, but the bestowal of new energy,[2] and of charismatic gifts such as prophecy, administrative capacity, teaching, exhorting, and even liberality

[1]From the Acts we should infer the contrary. Cf. v. 1-11, vi. 1; also Gal. ii. 11-8.

[2]Cf. Acts vi. 5, vii. 55, xi. 24, xiii. 52.

(cf. Rom. xii. 6-8). In Corinth it meant the glossolalia, the gift of ecstatic speech (cf. 1 Cor. xiv.). Sanctification of life is undoubtedly growth in holiness, through the love of God shed abroad in the heart by the Holy Spirit (cf. Rom. v. 5); but of any short cut to the attainment of the ideal by a special endowment of the Spirit the New Testament knows nothing.

(c) *Sanctification and the Christian Ideal*

Against the background of the ethical and religious teaching we have described, the New Testament statements with reference to the Christian ideal stand out as a startling challenge. In the light of them it will be seen that the Christian life is not meant simply to be one of high moral tone, nor even a supernatural life in which the power of the Spirit is manifestly operative. The New Testament plainly teaches that, while it is all this, and more, the life to which we are called is a life moving towards ethical and spiritual perfection.

In order to establish this claim, it will be best, with a minimum of comment, to set out this teaching, leaving aside for the moment for subsequent discussion the difficult passages which present the ideal as one of sinless perfection, and reserving for later sections those statements which describe the ideal more fully, as the vision of God or as perfect love.

An important feature of New Testament teaching is that the Christian ideal is already implicit in the sayings of Jesus as they were remembered by the earliest communities. From the M source comes the well-known saying recorded in Mt. v. 48: 'Ye therefore shall be *perfect* (τέλειοι), as your heavenly Father is perfect', to which there is a parallel, drawn probably from Q, in Lk. vi. 36: 'Be ye merciful, even as your Father is merciful.'

If these are different forms of the same saying, there is good reason to prefer the Lukan form,[1] but it is also possible that the two are different sayings. If the Matthaean form is not original, it describes an ideal which the Jerusalem community found it natural to associate with the teaching of Jesus; and this view is strongly supported by the only other instance of τέλειος in the Gospels, in St. Matthew's addition to the saying addressed to the young man who went away sorrowful: 'If thou wouldest be *perfect* (τέλειος), go, sell that thou hast, and give to the poor . . .' (Mt. xix. 21). Whatever the difficulties of these sayings may be, teaching regarding the Christian ideal is clearly present in other sayings of Jesus, in particular in Mt. v. 8: 'Blessed are the pure in heart: for *they shall see God*,' and in the saying on the Great Commandment in Mk. xii. 29-31: 'The first is, Hear, O Israel; The Lord our God, the Lord is one: and thou shalt love the Lord thy God *with all thy heart*, and *with all thy soul*, and *with all thy mind*, and *with all thy strength*. The second is this, Thou shalt love thy neighbour *as thyself*. *There is no other commandment greater than these*.' The last sentence St. Matthew replaces by the saying: 'On these two commandments hangeth the whole law, and the prophets' (xxii. 40).

There can be no doubt, therefore, that Jesus set forth a lofty ideal of ethical and spiritual attainment. This fact, indeed, is evident in all that He says concerning 'eternal life'[2] and in His indication of the possibilities of sonship

[1]Cf. T. W. Manson, *The Mission and Message of Jesus*, 347. But see also R. N. Flew, *The Idea of Perfection in Christian Theology*, 4.

[2]Cf. Jn. iv. 14, 36, v. 24, 39, vi. 27, 40, 47, 54, x. 28, xii. 25, 50, xvii. 2, 3. In the Synoptic Gospels, however, the idea is eschatological. Cf. Mk. x. 30 (and parallels), Mt. xxv. 46, Lk. xvi. 9 ('the eternal tabernacles'). The reply to the young man's question (Mk. x. 17) is the point of transition to Johannine teaching.

in such a saying as: 'Love your enemies, and do them good, and lend, never despairing; and your reward shall be great, and *ye shall be sons of the Most High*' (Lk. vi. 35).

In the teaching of St. Paul a similar emphasis, expressed in a variety of ways, appears in his letters from first to last. The end that he has in view in his prayers for the Thessalonians is that God may stablish their hearts '*unblameable in holiness* (ἀμέμπτους ἐν ἁγιωσύνῃ) before our God and Father, at the coming of our Lord Jesus Christ with all his saints' (1 Thess. iii. 13). 'This is the will of God,' he writes, 'even *your sanctification*' (ὁ ἁγιασμὸς ὑμῶν) (1 Thess. iv. 3); and his prayer for them is: 'The God of peace himself *sanctify you wholly* (ἁγιάσαι ὑμᾶς ὁλοτελεῖς); and may your spirit and soul and body be preserved *entire* (ὁλόκληρον), *without blame* (ἀμέμπτως) at the coming of our Lord Jesus Christ' (1 Thess. v. 23). In 2 Cor. vii. 1, he says: 'Let us cleanse ourselves from all defilement of flesh and spirit, *perfecting holiness* (ἐπιτελοῦντες ἁγιωσύνην) in the fear of God';[1] and in Rom. vi. 19: 'Present your members as servants to righteousness *unto sanctification*' (εἰς ἁγιασμόν). In Colossians and Ephesians we find the same teaching. To the Colossians he declares that the object of his apostolic labours is that he may present 'every man *perfect* (τέλειον) *in Christ*' (i. 28; cf. i. 22);[2] and in Ephesians he explains the purpose of the ministry as '*the perfecting* (καταρτισμός) *of the saints*', 'the building up of the body of Christ,' 'till we all attain (καταντάω) unto the unity of the faith, and of the knowledge of the Son of God, *unto a full-grown man* (τέλειον), unto the measure of the stature of the fulness of Christ' (iv. 12 f.).

[1]For the claim that ἁγιασμός and ἁγιωσύνη describe an ethical process, see O. Procksch, *Theol. Wört.*, i. 114-6.

[2]St. Paul also says that Epaphras always strives for the Colossians in his prayers that they may stand 'perfect and fully assured (τέλειοι καὶ πεπληροφορημένοι) in all the will of God' (Col. iv. 12).

In addition to the Pauline Epistles, the Johannine writings, the Epistle of St. James, and the Epistle to the Hebrews have much to say concerning the attainment of the Christian ideal.

In the Fourth Gospel Jesus declares that He sanctifies Himself for the sake of His disciples, 'that they themselves also may be *sanctified* (ἡγιασμένοι) in truth' (xvii. 19); and in the allegory of the Vine He develops the thought of spiritual growth in the words: 'Every branch that beareth fruit, he *cleanseth* (καθαίρει) it, that it may bear more fruit' (xv. 2). In his First Epistle, St. John cherishes the hope that we shall be like the Father, 'for', he says, 'we shall see him even as he is' (iii. 2). 'Every one that hath this hope set on him', he writes, '*purifieth* (ἁγνίζει) himself, even as he is pure' (iii. 3); and in iii. 6, 9, and v. 18, which must be considered in the next section, he speaks of complete victory over sin. In iv. 12, he mentions the love of God as '*perfected*' (τετελειωμένη) in us, and in iv. 18 writes of '*the perfect love*' (ἡ τελεία ἀγάπη) which casts out fear.

The author of the Epistle of James urges his readers to let patience have its '*perfect work*', that they may be '*perfect and entire* (τέλειοι καὶ ὁλόκληροι), lacking in nothing' (i. 4), where, however, the ideal of 'a perfect and complete character' appears to be the principal thought in mind.[1]

Finally, the writer of the Epistle to the Hebrews constantly uses this vocabulary of perfection, with reference to the person and work of Christ and the intellectual, moral, and spiritual growth of his readers. Jesus is 'the author and *perfecter* (τελειωτής) of our faith' (xii. 2). Having been '*made perfect*' (τελειωθείς), 'he became unto all them that obey him *the author* (αἴτιος) *of eternal salvation*' (v. 9; cf. ii. 10, vii. 28), and is able 'to save *to the*

[1]Cf. J. H. Ropes, *I.C.C.*, *St. James*, 138.

uttermost (εἰς τὸ παντελές)' those who draw near to God through Him, 'seeing he ever liveth to make intercession for them' (vii. 25). Sometimes the reference is intellectual, as, for example, when the writer exhorts his readers to seek fuller truth concerning Christ in the words: 'Let us press on *unto perfection* (τελειότης),'[1] or when he affirms the complete efficacy of the sacrifice of Christ in the claim: 'By one offering he hath *perfected* (τελειόω) for ever them that are sanctified (τοὺς ἁγιαζομένους)' (x. 14). Moral and spiritual attainment of the Christian ideal, however, are clearly in mind in xii. 23 when he speaks of 'the spirits of just men *made perfect*' (τετελειωμένων), and, above all, in the sonorous benediction towards the close of the Epistle:

> 'Now the God of peace, who brought again from the dead the great shepherd of the sheep with the blood of the eternal covenant, even our Lord Jesus, *make you perfect* (καταρτίζειν) *in every good thing to do his will*, working in us that which is well-pleasing in his sight, through Jesus Christ; to whom be the glory for ever and ever' (xiii. 20).

Other aspects of New Testament teaching, including the nature of the Christian ideal, have yet to be considered, but enough has been said already to render one conclusion certain. Beyond doubt the New Testament teaches the absolute necessity of ethical and spiritual perfection, or, if we prefer the word, attainment. It knows nothing of a reconciliation with God which does not make this goal the object of passionate desire. Not only is this teaching explicit, but also it is, as we have seen, most widely represented, being found in the sayings of Jesus and the Epistles of St. Paul, St. John, St. James, the writer of the Epistle to the Hebrews, and, as we shall see, St. Peter. It would, indeed, be difficult to find any important

[1] vi. 1.

doctrinal theme which is more broadly based or more urgently presented. Moreover, as we have argued, the pursuit of the ideal is implicit in every Christian truth of an experimental kind, whether it be eternal life, fellowship with God, union with Christ, or life in the Spirit.

Why, then, it must be asked, is this teaching so frequently neglected, so much so that one of its best exponents is compelled to speak of it as 'a bypath in Christian theological systems'?[1]

So far as this neglect is not due to historical causes, it is largely a reaction against the presumptuous claims of fanatical sects and the antinomianism which often followed in their train. Recoiling from such exhibitions of moral laxity, and keenly conscious of failure in themselves and the Church at large, many theologians have sought refuge in silence. The neglect is also fostered by the serious exegetical difficulties in the interpretation of such New Testament passages as Rom. vi. 2, 6, 11, 14, 22, and 1 Jn. iii. 6, 9, and v. 18, which appear to teach the necessity of sinless perfection, within the compass of the present life, as part of the Christian ideal. Thus far, in our treatment of New Testament teaching, we have postponed the discussion of these passages, in order to throw into relief the positive aspects of the doctrine. A point, however, has now been reached when they must be examined, and to this inquiry we now turn.

(*d*) *Sanctification and Sinless Perfection*

Every one must recognize that known and deliberate sin is incompatible with the attainment of the Christian ideal, and that its rejection and conquest, in the power of

[1]An opinion of Dr. F. Platt (cf. the article on 'Perfection (Christian)', *E.R.E.*, ix. 728-37) quoted by H. W. Perkins, *The Doctrine of Christian Perfection*, viii.

divine grace, is an obligation resting upon the Christian man. Is it possible, however, for sin to be entirely destroyed and rooted out within the bounds of his present earthly life; and if it is not, can a worthy account be given of sanctification? The consequences either of affirming or of denying this possibility appear to be equally serious. On the one hand, if we assert that the ideal is one of sinless perfection here and now, in the opinion of many Christian thinkers, and these not the least spiritually minded, we demand a degree of attainment which cannot be achieved. On the other hand, if we deny this possibility, we seem to compromise the Christian ideal, and thus to fall short of those tremendous exhortations to seek holiness of life we have examined in the last section. In either case, the neglect of the doctrine, to which we have referred, appears natural, if not inevitable. In these circumstances, the passages in Rom. vi and in 1 John, which speak of the conquest of sin, call for study, in order that we may see what the teaching of the New Testament actually is.

The Pauline passages in Rom. vi are as follows:

vi. 2: 'We who died to sin, how shall we any longer live therein?'

vi. 6: 'Our old man was crucified with him, that the body of sin might be done away, that so we should no longer be in bondage to sin; for he that hath died is justified from sin.'

vi. 11: 'Reckon ye yourselves also to be dead unto sin, but alive unto God in Christ Jesus.'

vi. 14: 'For sin shall not have dominion over you.'

vi. 22: 'But now being made free from sin, and become servants to God, ye have your fruit unto sanctification, and the end eternal life.'

These haunting passages sound the death knell of sin; but there is no reason to suppose that St. Paul is describing a state of Christian perfection in which sin is completely destroyed. The reference to 'having died to sin' is ambiguous, and its meaning must be considered later. Otherwise the prevailing thought is that, as an emancipated man, the believer has no need to fall under the power of sin. Sin is no longer lord. How far St. Paul is from thinking of sinless perfection, is seen in the fact that, in the very midst of these passages, he inserts the exhortation: 'Let not sin therefore reign in your mortal body, that ye should obey the lusts thereof' (vi. 12). The implication is that the believer must not, and need not, give place to sin, but that he is still exposed to its assaults and to the peril of defeat. And this is the constant presupposition of his exhortations, and in particular of his solemn words in 1 Cor. ix. 27: 'I buffet my body, and bring it into bondage: lest by any means, after I have preached to others, I myself should be rejected.' Moreover, one cannot forget his confession in Phil. iii. 12 f., which proves clearly that, for himself, the attainment of the Christian ideal still lay ahead: 'Not that I have already obtained, or am already made perfect: but I press on, if so be that I may apprehend that for which also I was apprehended by Christ Jesus. Brethren, I count not myself yet to have apprehended.'[1] These considerations make it impossible to suppose that in Rom. vi he is describing a condition of sinless perfection.

And yet, the true meaning of St. Paul's words in this chapter still remains to be determined, and especially his question: 'We who died to sin, how shall we any

[1]It is of interest to recall that John Wesley, who claimed that God appeared to have raised up Methodists chiefly to preach full sanctification, never claimed to have attained to it. Cf. R. N. Flew: 'Was it some fastidiousness, some half-unconscious suspicion that avowal would be perilous to the health of his soul?', *op. cit.*, 330.

longer live therein?' (vi. 2). As is so often the case, the context in which these words, and the other passages in the list printed above, appear, provides the clue to his meaning. This fact will be illustrated if, by way of example, we set down the section vi. 1-7 as a whole, placing in italics the key sentences which determine the meaning.

'What shall we say then? *Shall we continue in sin, that grace may abound? God forbid.* We who died to sin, how shall we any longer live therein? *Or are ye ignorant that all we who were baptized into Christ Jesus were baptized into his death? We were buried therefore with him through baptism into death: that like as Christ was raised from the dead through the glory of the Father, so we also might walk in newness of life.* For if we have become united with him by the likeness of his death, we shall be also by the likeness of his resurrection; knowing this, that our old man was crucified with him, that the body of sin might be done away, that so we should no longer be in bondage to sin; for he that hath died is justified from sin.'

The issue, it will be seen, is not sinless perfection, but whether it is open to the believer to continue to sin in order that the grace of God may more fully be displayed. St. Paul indignantly rejects this inference, and reminds his readers of what their baptism meant to them. It was a mystical experience in which, as they plunged into the waters, they shared in their Lord's conquest over sin and all its powers. At an earlier point in our discussion we have observed how important this estimate of baptism was to St. Paul and the Churches to which he ministered, and that, through the infrequency of adult baptism in the modern Church, it has become strange to us.[1] In Rom. vi. 1-7 it is the centre of the argument. St. Paul says, in effect, 'Remember what your baptism meant. There you renounced sin. It was a baptism into the death of sin

[1] See earlier, p. 162 f.

through union with Christ.'[1] No doubt in his account of this experience the actual and the ideal are not distinguished, as a less ardent teacher might have distinguished them. The initial experience needed to be reaffirmed and deepened through continued faith, watchfulness, and worship; but it was initial, not final. St. Paul's plea was that his readers should live in the power of this experience. 'Reckon yourselves dead unto sin', did not mean that they had finished with the enemy, but that it was a broken and discomfited foe. They were to live in the atmosphere of victory: 'Sin shall not have dominion over you.' Whether in the course of our earthly life a point can be reached when the conquest is complete, is a question still open for our consideration. St. Paul's words encourage the hope, but they do not affirm its actual fulfilment.

So much must we say so long as Rom. vi. is in question. When, however, the Christian ideal in its totality is before his mind, he refuses to be bound by the limits dictated by theological prudence. Thus, he can make it the subject of his prayers that the spirit, soul, and body of his converts may be 'preserved entire, without blame at the coming of our Lord Jesus Christ' (1 Thess. v. 23); and it is clear that, while these words have an eschatological ring, they do not speak of a perfection imparted at the Parousia, but of a state already reached when Christ comes with His saints (cf. 1 Thess. iii. 13). The prayer shows that he

[1] 'And just as Christ summed up His attitude towards the world by His death upon the cross, so the Christian's attitude to the world was summed up in his baptism. At that moment he died to the world of sin. This state of deadness to sin has to be constantly renewed, or again and again recovered. But it was in that sacramental moment realized in principle and symbolically represented', C. Gore, *The Epistle to the Romans*, 214. Cf. Sanday and Headlam, 162 f. 'The paradox runs through Paul, as it runs through Christian experience, peace and struggle, victory and temptation, hope and questioning. The Christian is one who is becoming what he is', C. A. Anderson Scott, *Foot-Notes to St. Paul*, 40.

saw no reason why the victory over sin, implicit already in baptism, should not be consummated; and this belief is in harmony with his conception of sanctification as the ultimate purpose of reconciliation (Col. i. 21 f.).[1] His words, however, are a prayer, not an express statement of fact; and the passage just mentioned: 'You . . . hath he reconciled . . . to present you holy and without blemish and unreproveable before him,' describes an end contemplated, but not yet achieved. The evidence suggests that St. Paul had not reached a hard and fast conclusion; that, while he did think of freedom from sin and the perfecting of holiness as possible within the present life, he was unable to insist upon sinlessness as an essential element in the Christian ideal here and now.

The Johannine passages, in 1 John, while apparently more rigorous in expression, represent the same point of view. These passages are as follows:

iii. 6: 'Whosoever abideth in him sinneth not: whosoever sinneth hath not seen him, neither knoweth him.'

iii. 9: 'Whosoever is begotten of God doeth no sin, because his seed abideth in him: and he cannot sin, because he is begotten of God.'

v. 18: 'We know that whosoever is begotten of God sinneth not; but he that was begotten of God keepeth him, and the evil one toucheth him not.'

In themselves, these passages seem to describe, and to require, a standard of sinless perfection, but when we read them in the light of the Epistle as a whole, we see that this is a hasty conclusion. Immediately before the last passage quoted above is a statement which, in spite of its obscurity, recognizes the possibility of sin in believers: 'If any man see his brother sinning a sin not unto death, he shall ask, and God will give him life for them that sin not

[1] See the earlier discussion on pp. 97-9.

unto death' (v. 16a). 'There is a sin unto death,' the writer explains, and adds, 'not concerning this do I say that he should make request' (v. 16b).[1] This inference is confirmed by ii. 1: 'My little children, these things I write unto you, that ye may not sin. And if any man sin, we have an Advocate with the Father, Jesus Christ the righteous.' It is rendered certain by the solemn words of i. 8f.: 'If we say that we have no sin, we deceive ourselves, and the truth is not in us. If we confess our sins, he is faithful and righteous to forgive us our sins, and to cleanse us from all unrighteousness.' In the light of these words we must conclude that, in the strongly worded passages quoted above, St. John is thinking of deliberate and voluntary transgressions, not of sin in its finer and more subtle forms. And he is justified in speaking so decisively, because, so long as we 'abide in Christ', and truly experience the miracle of the New Birth, temptation recedes from the soul like hungry waves which fall back battered and defeated from the protecting rocks.

The conclusion to be drawn is that, so long as we rely steadily upon the grace of God, the possibility of sinless perfection cannot be denied; and that, as regards open transgressions, freedom from sin is meant to be the mark of the Christian. 'A Christian is so far perfect, as not to commit sin,' wrote John Wesley;[2] but he also wrote: 'Absolute or infallible perfection I never contended for. Sinless perfection I do not contend for, seeing it is not scriptural.'[3] If his statements upon this question cannot always be reconciled, this fact is not surprising in view of the complexity of the question. It is, however, impor-

[1] What the 'sin unto death' may be is uncertain. Possibly it is apostasy (cf. Heb. vi. 4-6), possibly blasphemy against the Holy Spirit; but we do not know.

[2] *Works*, xi. 376. [3] *Works*, xii. 257.

tant that we should ask why we are compelled to hesitate in affirming sinless perfection here and now as essential to the Christian ideal. This hesitation does not spring from any doubt about the power of divine grace, or from any desire to accommodate the ideal to a less exacting standard suitable to the frailty of man; it arises from our knowledge of the subtle and penetrating nature of evil, which may cause a man to be guilty of sins of the spirit, of pride, vanity, and self-complacency, of which he may not be even conscious.[1] Only richer and fuller experiences of union with Christ and of fellowship with God, in company with other Christians in the Christian Society, the Church, can create that degree of spiritual sensitiveness and of moral illumination whereby complete victory is won; and, whilst in some cases the revealing hour of death may perfect the education of the soul,[2] it is probable that for most men the discipline and insight of life beyond the grave are needed before we receive that sanctification without which no man shall see the Lord (Heb. xii. 14).

It is not a matter for regret that the New Testament does not dwell on the possibilities of perfection in the Hereafter, but concentrates the urgency of its appeal upon the issues of life and death here and now; for, thereby, no excuse is left for spiritual sloth. It also makes greatly for spiritual health that the emphasis lies, not upon scrupulous concern for subtle sin, but upon the attainment of a positive ideal, the vision of God and the life of perfect love. The true Christian is not a man tortured by painful anxiety

[1]See the illuminating discussion of R. N. Flew, *op. cit.*, 332 f., who reminds us of the words of Martineau: 'Moral evil is the only thing in the creation of which it is decreed that the more we are familiar with it, the less we know of it,' *Endeavours After the Christian Life*.

[2]This theory, held by Calvinists and the early Methodists, was, in part, a reaction against the doctrine of Purgatory. Cf. H. W. Perkins, *The Doctrine of Christian Perfection*, 273.

whether he has reached a sinless state; he is rather a pilgrim whose heart is filled with divine love, and whose eyes await the fuller coming of the glory of God. If this is so, the difficulties of the idea of sinless perfection ought not to deflect our interest from the study of the Christian ideal. Rather must we examine the more eagerly its positive nature and content.

(*e*) *Sanctification and the Vision of God*

The relevant New Testament statements descriptive of the idea of the vision of God have already been considered in the chapter on Fellowship, in Section (*e*), which treats the experience of Seeing and Knowing God. To this stage of the discussion they rightly belong, since the life of fellowship with God is certainly one in which God is seen and known. But no less certainly does this teaching bear upon the question of the nature of the Christian ideal. St. Paul writes: 'Now we see in a mirror, darkly; but then face to face' (1 Cor. xiii. 12), and throughout its long history, as unfolded, for example, in the great work of the Bishop of Oxford, *The Vision of God*,[1] the pursuit of the Christian ideal has been upheld by the belief that 'the glory of God is a living man; and the life of man is the vision of God'.[2] The story of monasticism[3] is the story of this unceasing pursuit, and the great saints of Catholic Christianity, including St. Augustine, St. Benedict, St. Francis of Assisi, St. Dominic, St. Bernard of Clairvaux, St. Thomas Aquinas, and St. Ignatius of Loyola are the great torch-bearers in the onward race.

[1]K. E. Kirk, *The Vision of God: The Christian Doctrine of the Summum Bonum* (1931).

[2]Iren., *Adv. Haer.*, iv. 20. 7: gloria enim Dei vivens homo; vita autem hominis visio Dei; cited by Dr. Kirk, *op. cit.*, 1, 313.

[3]Cf. H. B. Workman, *The Evolution of the Monastic Ideal*; K. E. Kirk, *op. cit.*, 174 ff.

The peculiar claim of the idea of the Vision of God to describe the Christian ideal is that it is strongly based in the teaching of Scripture, that it has fully authenticated itself in the history of the Church, and that it commends itself to Christian reflection and judgment as a worthy presentation of the goal. It has the supreme advantage of resting upon the words of Jesus: 'Blessed are the pure in heart: for they shall see God' (Mt. v. 8). It is implicit also in the Pauline affirmation that God 'shined in our hearts, to give the light of the knowledge of the glory of God in the face of Jesus Christ' (2 Cor. iv. 6), and that, beholding this glory with unveiled face, we all 'are transformed into the same image from glory to glory' (2 Cor. iii. 18). It is even more fundamental to Johannine thought, in that St. John declares that in Christ the Church has already seen the glory of the Father (Jn. i. 14; cf. i. 18, xii. 45, xiv. 7, 9), and that to its members the certainty is given: 'We know that, if he shall be manifested, we shall be like him; for we shall see him even as he is' (1 Jn. iii. 2; cf. Apoc. xxii. 4). The hope of attaining this vision is expressed continually in the writings of Christian saints and teachers, in the greatest of Christian poetry, as, for example, in Dante's *Divina Commedia* and Milton's *Paradise Lost*, in Christian art, worship, praise, and prayer. If we have regard to the longings of the Church as a whole, we cannot but recognize how deeply rooted is the feeling which F. W. Faber describes when he writes:

> 'Father of Jesus, love's reward,
> What rapture will it be
> Prostrate before Thy throne to lie,
> And gaze, and gaze on Thee.'

In the volume already mentioned Dr. Kirk has put forward strong and cogent reasons why the vision of God should be regarded as constituting the essence of the Christian ideal. He denies that the quest for it is selfish on the ground that the vision is corporate, and that out of this direction of heart and mind come greater saintliness and greater zeal for service. 'To look towards God, and from that "look" to acquire insight both into the follies of one's own heart and the needs of one's neighbours, with power to correct the one no less than to serve the other—this is something very remote from any quest for "religious experience" for its own sake. Yet this, and nothing else, is what the vision of God has meant in the fully developed thought of historic Christianity.'[1] The attitude described is that of worship; and, in the view of Dr. Kirk, 'worship' is a higher ideal than 'service'. Worship, he maintains, alone guarantees to service that quality of humility, without which it is no service at all. 'So far from being a selfish goal, worship is the only way to unselfishness which the Christian has at his command.'[2] Dr. Kirk recognizes that there are 'dilettantes of worship' and that there are those who, though they make little use of its time-honoured forms, serve their fellows with a humility which puts the ordinary Christian to shame. Yet the former are at best beginners in worship, and the latter 'are already in the attitude of worship towards their ideal'. With these exceptions the principle stands true. 'The danger of "service", as an ideal, is that it fosters the spirit of patronage: the glory of worship is to elicit the grace of humility.'[3]

Dr. Kirk is ready to describe the content of the vision of God in the widest terms. The mystical experience has been enjoyed 'wherever a man's mind has been uplifted, his temptations thwarted, his sorrows comforted, his resolutions strengthened, his aberrations controlled, by

[1] *Op. cit.*, 445. [2] *Op. cit.*, 447. [3] *Op. cit.*, 449.

the sight of innocence, purity, love, or beauty'.[1] These are the first traces of the vision of God. Dr. Kirk's claim is that 'what Christianity offers, with its fellowship and sacraments, its life of prayer and service, its preaching of the Incarnate Son of God, is the same vision in ever-increasing plenitude'.[2] He prefers this account of the Christian ideal to those mentioned at the beginning of the present chapter, since it suggests the necessity of contact or intercourse with God in the process of attainment, and it reminds us that we have already seen God in the face of Jesus Christ.[3]

Every student of the Christian ideal will desire to study Dr. Kirk's constructive argument for himself. Nevertheless, even the above summary is enough to show how essential the idea of the Vision of God is to the ideal. But is it a complete account of the goal? On this issue, I think, we have good reason to hesitate. The principal grounds on which the argument is based are capable of another interpretation, or at least of an interpretation which emphasizes more fully a different aspect of the ideal. Because one of two contrasted ideas, those, let us say, of worship and the service of humility, occupies 'a substantive position'[4] in relation to the other, it does not follow that we must choose between them. In point of fact, other possibilities are open to us. The ideal may be neither or both; and on the submission[5] that 'worship is the only way to unselfishness', it ought to include the two. Only if we are prepared to maintain that the adoration of God is a complete end in itself, are we entitled to give exclusive preference to the Vision of God as the Christian ideal. Dr. Kirk's discussion reflects a tendency so to

[1] *Op. cit.*, 464. [2] *Op. cit.*, 465.
[3] *Op. cit.*, 466 f. [4] *Op. cit.*, 447.
[5] *Ibid.*

think of worship;[1] but the worship which he actually describes is rich in moral and spiritual fruits, so much so that it can be said to create in us 'some likeness to the character of Jesus'.[2] But if this is true, as indeed it is, this likeness to Christ, or, if we prefer so to describe it, perfect love both to God and man, must be included in our statement of the ideal. The ideal ought not to be described as *either* the Vision of God *or* the service of humility, but as *communion with God reflected and expressed in perfect love*. With some reason it might be contended that, although worship stands in 'a substantive position' to perfect love, the latter, as the end realized in moral and spiritual life and character, has the greater claim to be regarded as the Christian goal. It is, however, a derogation of the idea of worship to suggest that it is only a means to an end; and for this reason it is better to include it, with the disposition in which it issues, within the orbit of the ideal. If we do this, we must think of worship as including meditation upon the love of God revealed in Christ, contemplation of the divine glory, and an adoration crowned in the life of perfect love.[3]

[1]See the statement on p. 447: 'We may leave on one side the scholastic arguments with which Aristotle, for example, outside the Christian Church, and S. Thomas within it, have maintained the thesis that contemplation is man's true end. A day may come when abstract reasoning is once more allowed its full weight, and then the Stagyrite and the Angel of the Schools will receive their due reward.' See also p. 451.

[2]*Op. cit.*, 467.

[3]Is it this preoccupation with the idea of the Vision of God, as constituting the Christian ideal, which leads Dr. Kirk to take such an unsympathetic view of Protestant teaching, to dismiss the German Pietists in three sentences, to make but two hurried references to the Wesleys, and this in respect of his discussion of antinomianism, and completely to ignore the Friends in general and George Fox, Isaac Penington, and Robert Barclay in particular? In this respect, as combining both the Catholic and the Protestant traditions, Dr. Flew's account of the *Idea of Perfection in Christian Theology* strikes a more 'Catholic' note.

A decisive reason, however, for extending our conception of the Christian ideal is the teaching of Scripture, as containing the revelation of God and as revealing the mind of the Church in its most creative period. The passages which support the inclusion of the idea of the Vision of God within the ideal are, as we have seen, of all-compelling force and value. Nevertheless, as providing direct support, they are few in number as compared with those which set forth the ideal of perfect love. If this is so, the claim of love to an essential place in the description of the goal, is beyond dispute, not merely because of the fact that 'so it is written', but because it is the teaching of Christ Himself and of those nearest to Him in mind and in spirit. Our next task, therefore, must be to examine the idea of sanctification conceived as perfect love.

(f) *Sanctification and Perfect Love*

The claim of the idea of love to be included in the statement of the Christian ideal is grounded in the words of Jesus in His reply to the question of the scribe concerning the first commandment. 'The first', said Jesus, 'is, Hear, O Israel; The Lord our God, the Lord is one: and thou shalt love the Lord thy God with all thy heart, and with all thy soul, and with all thy mind, and with all thy strength. The second is this, Thou shalt love thy neighbour as thyself' (Mk. xii. 29-31). 'There is none other commandment', He added, 'greater than these.' The same ideal is also implicit in the 'new commandment', in which the Fourth Evangelist interprets the mind of Christ: 'A new commandment I give unto you, that ye love one another; even as I have loved you, that ye also love one another. By this shall all men know that ye are my disciples, if ye have love one to another' (Jn. xiii. 34 f.).[1]

In pressing home upon the minds of his readers the claims of the ideal of love, St. Paul discloses how deeply he had entered into the teaching of Jesus. 'Above all these things', he writes to the Colossians, 'put on love, which is the bond of perfectness' (iii. 14). 'Owe no man anything', he counsels the Church at Rome, 'save to love one another: for he that loveth his neighbour hath fulfilled the law' (xiii. 8). The commandments relating to man are summed up in the words: 'Thou shalt love thy neighbour as thyself,' and love is 'the fulfilment of the law' (xiii. 9 f.).[2] How great a tribute he pays to the Thessalonians when he writes: 'Concerning love of the brethren ye have no need that one write unto you: for ye yourselves are taught of God to love one another' (1. iv. 9). When he speaks to them of the Christian warfare, he mentions first 'the breastplate of faith and love' (1. v. 8); and, significantly enough, immediately before one of his strongest exhortations to holiness, he says: 'The Lord make you to increase and abound in love one toward another, and toward all men, even as we do toward you' (1. iii. 12). Writing to the Galatians, he places love first in the list of the virtues which are 'the fruit of the Spirit' (v. 22), and attributes supreme value to the faith that works 'through love' (v. 6).

Besides reflecting the teaching of Jesus, this emphasis in his pastoral exhortations is the direct consequence of his belief that love is the key to the understanding of the redeeming work of God in Christ.[3] It is remarkable,

[1]Cf. also His teaching on the Golden Rule (Lk. vi. 31 = Mt. vii. 12) and on love to enemies (Lk. vi. 27 f. = Mt. v. 43), His use of Hos. vi. 6 (Mt. ix. 13, xii. 7), and the Parable of the Good Samaritan.

[2]To the same Church he says: 'In love of the brethren be tenderly affectioned one to another' (Rom. xii. 10).

[3]Cf. Rom. v. 8, 2 Cor. v. 14, Gal. ii. 20, Eph. v. 25.

however, that he makes only five direct references to love for God or Christ.[1] His reverence, as Dr. Moffatt suggests, imposed a restraint upon him in the use of love-language as addressed to God.[2] What moves the Apostle most deeply is the knowledge that God loves men. In addition to his references to the love shown in the Cross, this fact is seen in his description of believers as 'beloved of God' (1 Thess. i. 4, Rom. i. 7). Love, he believes, marks the activities of God, and underlies the unity which exists between the Father and the Son. Christ is 'the Son of His love' (Col. i. 13) and 'the Beloved' (Eph. i. 6). It is in the light of this thought and usage that all his counsels and exhortations to men to 'put on love' must be read. A spirit of overflowing and disinterested love is to him the inevitable relationship which must exist between men who are conscious of the amazing grace of God in salvation and inward renewal.

It might appear that St. Paul's teaching is the commendation of a primary Christian virtue rather than the unfolding of an ideal; but, in the light of his great 'Hymn of Praise to Love' in 1 Cor. xiii, this view is not tenable. It is the maturing of the Christian character in its loveliest and most perfect form, which he has in mind when he describes the love which is 'very patient, very kind', which 'knows no jealousy', 'makes no parade, gives itself

[1] Cf. J. Moffatt, *Love in the New Testament*, 154-63. Moffatt cites Rom. viii. 28, 1 Cor. ii. 9, viii. 3, xvi. 22, and Eph. vi. 24. The same is true, he shows, of other New Testament writings, apart from the Fourth Gospel and 1 John, *op. cit.*, 223-9. See also J. Weiss, *The History of Primitive Christianity*, 509.

[2] 'It is fair to argue that he employs the language of faith by deliberate choice, since it was free from the presumptuous idea of love-play on an equal footing with the Beloved,' *op. cit.*, 163. J. Burnaby speaks of the soundness of the instinct which finds obedience a safer term than love by which to denote the right relation of man to his Maker, but holds that obedience depends on love and not love on obedience, *Amor Dei*, 311.

no airs, is never rude, never selfish, never irritated, never resentful', the love which is 'gladdened by goodness, always slow to expose, always eager to believe the best, always hopeful, always patient'.[1] If Dr. Moffatt is right in his tentative suggestion that the words 'Faith and hope and love last on' are a quotation from some primitive Christian oracle or hymn,[2] St. Paul's climax: 'But the greatest of all is love', has increased force and leads naturally to his plea: 'Make love your aim, and then set your heart on spiritual gifts' (xiv. 1).

We are not on the same heights in other New Testament writings, if we except the Fourth Gospel and 1 John; yet St. James speaks of the command: 'Thou shalt love thy neighbour as thyself,' as 'the royal law' (ii. 8); and in the Epistle to the Hebrews, 1 and 2 Peter, the Pastoral Epistles, and the Apocalypse, although the ideal of love is not prominent, there are several passages of great beauty.[3]

In the Fourth Gospel and in 1 John this teaching finds its fullest expression. The Gospel frequently speaks of the love of the Father for the Son. Jn. iii. 35: 'The Father loveth the Son, and hath given all things into his hand,' is characteristic, and other passages of like tenor are v. 20, x. 17, xv. 9 and xvii. 23 f. In xvii. 24 the love is of the Father described as existing 'before the foundation of the world', and in x. 17 it is directly related to the death and exaltation of Christ: 'Therefore doth my Father

[1]Moffatt's translation.

[2]*The Moffatt New Testament Commentary; the First Epistle to the Corinthians*, 204.

[3]Love for God is mentioned in Jas. i. 12, ii. 5, 2 Tim. iii. 4 and iv. 8; love for Christ in 1 Pet. i. 8; and love within the Christian community in Heb. vi. 10, x. 24, xiii. 1, 1 Pet. i. 22, 2 Pet. i. 7, 2 Tim. ii. 22, and Apoc. ii. 4, 19. Moffatt points out that God's love is not mentioned in the Acts, James, the Pastoral Epistles (with the partial exception of Tit. iii. 4 f.), and 1 Peter; and that, while the writer of the Apocalypse mentions God's love for Christians, he does not call God their Father. *Op. cit.*, 213 f.

love me, because I lay down my life, that I may take it again.' The further thought of God's love for men is sublimely presented in iii. 16: 'God so loved the world, that he gave his only begotten Son, that whosoever believeth on him should not perish, but have eternal life'; and again in 1 Jn. iv. 10: 'Herein is love, not that we loved God, but that he loved us, and sent his Son to be the expiation for our sins.' Christ's love for men is also frequently mentioned, as, for example, in xiii. 1, xiv. 21, 23, xv. 9,[1] and in 1 John iii. 16: 'Hereby know we love, because he laid down his life for us,' His love is directly connected with His death. Besides these references to the love of God or of Christ, the great statement: 'God is Love' is twice made in 1 Jn. iv. 8 and 16.[2]

The love of men for God is rarely mentioned in the Gospel,[3] but in the Epistle it is a constant and distinctive theme. St. John speaks of the love of God as 'perfected' in men (1 Jn. ii. 5), and declares that, if any man loves the world, 'the love of the Father is not in him' (1 Jn. ii. 15).[4] In the Gospel, but not in the Epistle, there are several references to love for Christ, but in most of these cases some conditional statement is attached emphasizing the ethical character of the relationship implied. 'If ye love me', says Jesus to His disciples, 'ye will keep my commandments' (Jn. xiv. 15).[5] A further illustration of the need for a practical embodiment of this love is supplied in the conversation of Jesus with Peter by the Sea of Tiberias:

[1]Cf. also Jn. xi. 3, 5, 36, xiii. 23, xv. 12, xix. 26, xx. 2, xxi. 7, 20. For these references, and throughout the section, I am greatly indebted to Westcott's valuable note on 'St. John's Conception of Love', *The Epistles of St. John*, 130-3.

[2]See also the list of seventeen passages, given by Westcott, *op. cit.*, 133, in which the verb and the noun are used absolutely.

[3]Cf. Jn. v. 42.

[4]Cf. also 1 Jn. iv. 20 f., v. 1 f.

[5]Cf. also Jn. viii. 42, xiv. 21, 23 f., 28, xvi. 27, xxi. 15-7.

'So when they had broken their fast, Jesus saith unto Simon Peter, "Simon, son of John, lovest thou me more than these?" He saith unto him, "Yea, Lord; thou knowest that I love thee." He saith unto him, "Feed my lambs"' (Jn. xxi. 15).[1]

Finally, both the Gospel and the Epistle often speak of love within the Christian community. Of this love the references to the 'new commandment' are the best-known examples in the Gospel (xiii. 34 f., xv. 12), together with the saying: 'These things I command you, that ye may love one another' (xv. 17). In the Epistle the phrases, 'he that loveth his brother' (ii. 10; cf. iv. 21) and 'he that loveth not his brother' (iii. 10, 14, iv. 20), are almost formulae. Mutual love is the message heard 'from the beginning' (iii. 11); its visible expression is the sign that we have passed out of death into life (iii. 14) and the proof that we do the commandments of God (v. 2).[2] The lovely cadences of some of the sentences in 1 John linger unbroken in the mind by reason of the perfect union of their beauty and truth:

'Beloved, let us love one another: for love is of God; and every one that loveth is begotten of God, and knoweth God' (iv. 7).

'Beloved, if God so loved us, we also ought to love one another' (iv. 11).

'There is no fear in love: but perfect love casteth out fear, because fear hath punishment; and he that feareth is not made perfect in love. We love, because he first loved us' (iv. 18 f.).

The New Testament teaching, summarized above, can leave no room for doubt that love is an essential element in the Christian ideal. The question, whether the ideal is

[1]Cf. B. H. Streeter, *The Four Gospels*, 479-81. For the view that φιλεῖν and ἀγαπᾶν are practically synonyms, see J. H. Bernard, *I.C.C., St. John*, 702-4; E. Hoskyns, *The Fourth Gospel*, 667.

[2]Cf. also 1 Jn. iii. 23, 2 Jn. 1, 3 Jn. 1.

love for God or love for men, presents a false alternative; for there can be no true love for God which does not issue in love for men, and love for men which is not inspired and directed by love for God is sure to be found wanting or inadequate. God's love for men, which at first sight might not seem to belong to the ideal, is of first importance because, as Agape, pure self-giving, which wells out of the heart of God, and is made manifest in the Cross of Christ, it sets the standard of our love for God and for men.[1] Luther well describes this love as 'an overflowing love (*eine quellende Liebe*) welling forth from within out of the heart like a fresh streamlet or brook which ever flows on and cannot be stopped or dried up or fail, which says: "I love thee, not because thou art good (*fromm*) or bad, for I draw my love not from thy goodness (*Frömmigkeit*) as from an alien spring, but from mine own well-spring—namely, from the Word which is grafted into my heart".'[2] It goes forth lavishly and is open to every one who needs it, friend or foe, rich or poor. Because a man is a Christian 'and grasps the Word which in himself is quite pure, the same makes his heart also so pure and full of honest love, that he lets his love flow out unimpeded towards everyone, be the person who or what he may'.[3]

John Wesley set love at the centre of his doctrine of the Christian ideal. 'By Perfection', he wrote, 'I mean the humble, gentle, patient love of God and our neighbour, ruling our tempers, words, and actions.'[4] 'The heaven of heavens is love. There is nothing higher in religion: there is, in effect, nothing else; if you look for anything

[1]Cf. A. Nygren, *Agape and Eros*, Part I, *A Study of the Christian Idea of Love* (tr. by A. G. Hebert); Part II, *The History of the Christian Idea of Love* (tr. by P. S. Watson).

[2]Cited by Nygren, *op. cit.*, II, 512. [3]Cf. Nygren, *op. cit.*, II, 513.

[4]Wesley's *Plain Account of Christian Perfection*, cited by H. W. Perkins, *The Doctrine of Christian or Evangelical Perfection*, 219.

but more love, you are looking wide of the mark, you are getting out of the royal way. . . . Settle it then in your heart, that from the moment God has saved you from all sin, you are to aim at nothing more, but more of that love described in the thirteenth of the Corinthians. You can go no higher than this, till you are carried into Abraham's bosom.'[1] This teaching is seen at its best in the hymns of the Wesleys; as, for example, in Charles Wesley's lines:

'Lord, I believe a rest remains
To all Thy people known,
A rest where pure enjoyment reigns
And Thou art loved alone:

'A rest, where all our soul's desire
Is fixed on things above;
Where fear, and sin, and grief expire,
Cast out by perfect love.'

and in the more mystical hymn:

'My God! I know, I feel Thee mine,
And will not quit my claim,
Till all I have is lost in Thine,
And all renewed I am.

'Refining Fire, go through my heart,
Illuminate my soul;
Scatter Thy life through every part,
And sanctify the whole.

'My steadfast soul, from falling free,
Shall then no longer move;
But Christ be all the world to me,
And all my heart be love.'

It is possible, however, that John Wesley's translations

[1]Cited by W. B. Pope, *A Compendium of Christian Theology*, III, 95. R. N. Flew reminds us that this teaching appears in Wesley's first published sermon, the sermon preached at St. Mary's, Oxford, on January 1st, 1733, *The Idea of Perfection in Christian Theology*, 324.

from German hymns give an even nobler expression to this ideal, for example, in his rendering of P. Gerhardt's hymn, *O Jesu Christ, mein schönstes Licht*:

'Jesu, Thy boundless love to me
No thought can reach, no tongue declare;
O knit my thankful heart to Thee,
And reign without a rival there:
Thine wholly, Thine alone, I am,
Be Thou alone my constant flame.

'O grant that nothing in my soul
May dwell but Thy pure love alone;
O may Thy love possess me whole,
My joy, my treasure, and my crown:
Strange flames far from my heart remove;
My every act, word, thought, be love',

and in his translation of G. Tersteegen's *Verborgne Gottesliebe du*:

'Thou hidden love of God, whose height,
Whose depth unfathomed, no man knows,
I see from far Thy beauteous light,
Inly I sigh for Thy repose;
My heart is pained, nor can it be
At rest, till it finds rest in Thee',

and of J. Scheffler's *Ich will dich lieben, meine Stärke*:

'Thee will I love, my strength, my tower,
Thee will I love, my joy, my crown,
Thee will I love with all my power,
In all Thy works, and Thee alone;
Thee will I love, till the pure fire
Fill my whole soul with chaste desire.'

It is noticeable how in some of these hymns the mystical idea of the Vision of God is combined with that of

Perfect Love. This combination is particularly evident in Charles Wesley's hymn:

'Jesus, the First and Last,
On Thee my soul is cast:
Thou didst Thy work begin
By blotting out my sin;
Thou wilt the root remove,
And perfect me in love.

'Yet when the work is done,
The work is but begun:
Partaker of Thy grace,
I long to see Thy face;
The first I prove below,
The last I die to know.'

Further, the love described is the love of God Himself expressing itself in act, word, and thought.

While, however, love for God and for man may be emphasized by one teacher more than another, the place of Perfect Love in the Christian ideal is recognized by almost all who have sought to describe man's true end. The well-known words of Irenaeus concerning the Incarnation: 'Because of His immeasurable love He became what we are, that He might fit us to be what He is,'[1] and the equally great saying of Athanasius: 'He entered into humanity, that we might be made divine,'[2] describe an act which is at the same time an ideal, and even in the darkest hours of her history the Church has not lacked those who, inspired by the vision of Divine Love, have been constrained to tread the path of attainment. Even those who have preferred to give first place to the idea of the vision of God in their description of the ideal have no less enjoined the utter necessity of love. 'Augustine', Mr. Burnaby says, 'taught the Church that she is "really" one

[1] *Adv. Haer.*, v. praef. [2] *De Incarn. Verb.*, 54.

with Christ only in the measure in which she "realises" the love which is shed abroad in our hearts through the Holy Spirit which is given to us,'[1] and he claims that such a passage as the following is not to be dismissed as an example of his rhetorical fervour:

> 'God is Love. Why then should we go harking to the topmost heaven or the nethermost earth, seeking for Him who is with us, if we would be with Him? Let no man say, I know not what I am to love. Let him love his brother, and he will love that same love. He knows the love wherewith he loves his brother, better than the brother whom he loves. See, God may be held more known than a brother—more known because more present; more known because more inward; more known, because more sure. Embrace the love which is God: through love embrace God. He is that very love that links in the bond of holiness all the good Angels and all the servants of God, that joins us and them to one another in obedience to Himself.'[2]

Aquinas, also, who teaches that man's last end is contemplation, holds that love is the motive power of the contemplative life,[3] and although the love he describes falls short of the Agape of New Testament teaching,[4] it is none the less of essential importance in his exposition of the Christian ideal. In short, we may say that, however we define the ideal, it is impossible to exclude from it the idea of love, if we have regard to the distinctiveness of the Christian revelation. British theology has yet to come to terms with the powerful challenge of Anders Nygren in his *Agape and Eros*;[5] but, whatever conclusions may be reached, it will be unable to do other than agree with the

[1]*Amor Dei*, 179.

[2]*De Trin.*, viii. 11 f., cited in *Amor Dei*, 160 f. Cf. also p. 244.

[3]Cf. R. N. Flew, *op. cit.*, 234 ff.

[4]Nygren, *op. cit.*, II, 424-7, 433-9.

[5]Cf. P. S. Watson, *The Expository Times*, xlix, 537-40.

Swedish scholar's claim: 'We have . . . every right to say that the idea of Agape is not merely a fundamental idea of Christianity, but *the* fundamental idea *par excellence*. The idea of Agape is a new creation of Christianity. It sets its mark on the whole of Christianity. Without it nothing that is Christian would be Christian.'[1]

An outstanding merit of the ideal of Perfect Love is its non-dimensional character. In the nature of things Sinless Perfection must be attained at a definite point, either in this life or in the world beyond, however gradual may be the steps by which it is approached. The victory can be won partially over a period; it is completed only at a point. In like manner, the attainment of the *Visio Dei*, although it may be preceded by momentary experiences of illumination, is the last stage in a long and painful process which, in the teaching of the Mediaeval Church, follows the well-marked track of purification, illumination, and union with the divine. As the growing knowledge of God, the vision may be seen at all times, but in the fulness of its perfection it is an instantaneous gift of the divine love. Perfect Love is different from both these aspects of the Christian ideal. One stage of growth in love may be fuller than another, but, as love, each is perfect in its own order, just as the perfection of the bud shares in the glory of the perfect flower, and just as the opening theme in a symphony participates in the beauty of the final movement. Nor, in love, is a perfection ever reached beyond which a richer manifestation is not possible. God is love; and love has the infinitude of His Being. From this it follows that the ideal of Perfect Love is always attained and always attainable; it belongs both to this life and to that which is to come; it is here and yonder, at this moment and always.

[1] *Op. cit.*, I, 32.

(*g*) *Sanctification and the Community*

Not even yet have we seen the Christian ideal in its fulness: we still need to consider its corporate aspect. There is no statement of the ideal worthy of the name in which this aspect is not at least implicit. Even in the ideal of sinless perfection, in the pursuit of which the individual may easily be preoccupied with himself, his actions and his special temptations, a necessary social relationship is involved, not only because our sins affect others, but also because there is a heritage of good and evil into which we enter, and there are social sins in the responsibility for which we have our share. Again, the quest for the vision of God is a corporate undertaking. It is true that the end has often been sought by the solitary hermit; yet even he has found it impossible to deny compassion to the stranger, and so has discovered the need for charity in his search for God. More manifest is this social aspect of the quest in the long story of monasticism, in the recognition of the dignity of labour by the Benedictines and the love of learning among the Dominicans, and in the blessings of peace and ordered life preserved by the monks in a troubled and disordered world. Especially in worship is this corporate aspect of the ideal revealed, since worship is corporate by its nature, in that men seek God and adore Him together with a common aim and purpose. In worship the meaning of life is transfigured, service is cleansed of self-seeking, humility is received as a garment and love as a staff for the road. Men are seen as the children of God and the world as the place of His habitation; and, above all that is evil and sordid, shines the promise of the City of God. In the ideal of Perfect Love the social implications are so essential that, if regard is not paid to them, the ideal itself, not to speak of the possibility of its attainment, breaks in our hands. The love of God for man, that ceaseless and undeserved self-giving which finds its climax in the Cross of Christ, gives the inspiration and sets the standard of disinterested love for others which means hope for the hopeless, opportunity for the unprivileged, care for the weak, and every positive good for mankind.

If such is the nature of the Christian ideal, in whatever particular form it may be embodied, it cannot surprise us that its corporate aspects are especially prominent in the New Testament. Moreover, in its teaching regarding the Church, the New Testament describes an organism, the Body of Christ, in which the ideal can come to life, and grow, and yield its fruits for the healing of the world.

The New Testament passages we have examined are personal and direct; but they were addressed, not to isolated individuals, but to men living in fellowship with others in the first Christian communities. Most of these passages are in the plural. When Jesus said: 'Blessed are the pure in heart: for they shall see God,' He was not thinking of solitary seekers throughout the world, but of His disciples and followers already associated with Himself. This fact is clearly indicated in the Lukan Beatitudes, which are stated in the second person plural. The fact that Christ's ideal of love to God and one's neighbour is expressed in Old Testament commandments, and that He speaks of a 'new commandment', points in the same direction, for the ancient commandments were spoken to the people of God. It is in the New Israel which He establishes that men are to love God and their neighbour. The ideal belongs to the Kingdom. This communal aspect is even more apparent in the teaching of St. Paul, St. John, and the New Testament writers generally, since it is imparted in letters to the primitive Christian communities. Within these communities, living and worshipping side by side, men are to cleanse themselves from all defilement of flesh and spirit, 'perfecting holiness in the fear of God'.

Many of these passages gain a new interest when we read them from this point of view. What appears to be an exhortation to the individual is seen to be a call to the community and to the individual as a member within it. This view is confirmed by other New Testament passages still to be considered. The use of the term 'the saints' (οἱ ἅγιοι) is a case in point. Found frequently in the Pauline Epistles[1] and the Apocalypse,[2] and occasionally in the Acts, Hebrews, the Pastoral Epistles, and Jude,[3] this expression does not necessarily describe men of marked 'saintly' achievements; it denotes rather those who have been separated and called to share in the life of an elect and holy community, and who are therefore pledged to seek and to embody its holiness. The same meaning is also true of the phrase 'those that are sanctified' (οἱ ἁγιαζόμενοι).[4] It describes men who have been consecrated by God and dedicated to holy ends and purposes. The language is sacrificial. It illustrates the manner in which words and ideas associated with the Old Testament cultus were boldly appropriated by the New Testament writers and applied to the life of the Church conceived as the Israel of God. Several passages show how this language was pressed into the service of the Christian ideal, and always with a communal emphasis. Believers, for example, are exhorted to present their bodies 'a living sacrifice, holy, acceptable to God' (Rom. xii. 1); they are 'an elect race, a royal priesthood, a people for God's own possession' (1 Pet. ii. 9); and, as 'living stones', they are

[1] 38 times. [2] 14 times.

[3] Acts ix. 13, 32, 41, xxvi. 10; Heb. vi. 10, xiii. 24; 1 Tim. v. 10; Jude 3.

[4] Acts xx. 32, xxvi. 18; 1 Cor. i. 2; Heb. ii. 11, x. 14.

built up 'a spiritual house, to be a holy priesthood, to offer up spiritual sacrifices, acceptable to God through Jesus Christ' (1 Pet. ii. 5). They are members of 'the body of Christ', the Church, which Christ loved, and for which He 'gave himself up', in order that He 'might sanctify it', and present to Himself a glorious Church 'not having spot or wrinkle or any such thing', but that it should be 'holy and without blemish' (Eph. v. 25-7). This teaching has constantly to be borne in mind when we think of the Christian ideal. The personal element is not forgotten; on the contrary it is greatly enriched, because it is seen within the life of a corporate fellowship. Nowhere does the solitary pursuit of the ideal appear to be in sight. *Extra Ecclesiam nulla salus* is the law of sanctification as well as of reconciliation.

It ought to be unnecessary to add that nothing automatic or mechanical is involved in this teaching. The New Testament knows nothing of a sanctity, other than provisional or dedicatory, which is assured simply in virtue of membership with the Christian Society. It is true that there is an approach to this idea in Rom. xi. 16, where, in speaking of the Jewish people as the holy stock of Israel, into which the Gentiles as branches from a wild olive were grafted, St. Paul says: 'And if the first-fruit is holy, so is the lump: and if the root is holy, so are the branches.' Here, however, the Apostle is snatching at every argument which can sustain his faith that the rejection of Israel is providential and temporary, and that eventually it will be followed by their restoration. It is impossible to suppose that he is withdrawing that tremendous emphasis upon personal faith in Christ which is the foundation principle of his Gospel. Nor again is this teaching denied, or forgotten, when he speaks of himself as a minister of Christ, 'dealing in priestly fashion with the Gospel of God,'[1] that 'the offering up of the Gentiles might be made acceptable, being sanctified by the Holy Spirit' (Rom. xv. 16). St. Paul undoubtedly believes in the holiness of the Church, as the Body of Christ, and when he says to the Corinthians: 'But ye were washed, but ye were sanctified, but ye were justified' (1 Cor. vi. 11), he has in mind their entrance into, and participation in, this holiness; yet not for a moment does he renounce his passionate insistence upon the need for faith, perseverance, and obedience. Perhaps nowhere has he so happily combined this recognition of the personal and the corporate elements in the attainment of the ideal as in Eph. iv. 13: 'till we all attain unto the unity of the faith, and of the knowledge of the Son of God, unto a full-grown man, unto the measure of the stature of the fulness of Christ,' where the context clearly shows that it is the perfection of the Church which is meant.[2]

The Christian ideal, then, is for the individual members of an Elect Society. This fact does not imply any limitation of interest, since the Society is open to all men and the opportunity is that of each individual member. Far from confining the range of the ideal, this aspect provides for its endless enrichment. In seeking the goal the individual is not left to himself. He inherits a tradition of holiness, has access to common worship and united sacramental devotion, shares the fellowship of other members within the one Body, and is brought daily into union with its Living Lord. The Church is meant to be the home of sanctity, and its possibilities have not been fully

[1]Cf. Boylan, *Romans*, 303.

[2]So most commentators. Cf. J. Armitage Robinson, 99, 182; T. K. Abbott, 119f.; E. F. Scott, 211-5; G. G. Findlay, 249-58; C. H. Dodd, *The Abingdon Bible Commentary*, 1233; J. Scott Lidgett, *God in Christ Jesus*, 263; C. A. Anderson Scott, *Christianity according to St. Paul*, 156; *Foot-Notes to St. Paul*, 181.

explored until it is regarded as such and proved to be what it promises.

(*h*) *The Place of Sanctification in Modern Theology*

In view of our earlier investigation it is not necessary to discuss at length the position of sanctification in the orbit of the Christian experience. We cannot include it within the idea of reconciliation. It is true, as we have recognized, that the reconciling work of God is a sanctifying activity, in the sense that the believer is set apart for holy purposes; but, in the Christian experience, this divine hallowing needs to be worked out in a life of moral and spiritual progress moving steadily towards its goal. To include attainment within the idea of reconciliation is to rob the latter of its immediate and decisive character. Nevertheless, to exclude the thought of sanctification, even when we are thinking of reconciliation, is no less injurious. Reconciliation is meant to end in sanctity, and if it is not followed by sustained movement in this direction, it must lose its meaning as the restoration of the sinner to fellowship with God.

The same distinction must be made as regards justification. If sanctification must be distinguished from, and yet vitally connected with reconciliation, a like relationship is even more necessary if justification is to preserve its ethical and religious character. Doubtless it is an act of divine consecration, but fundamentally the two experiences are different; it is quite impossible to maintain that they are 'only different aspects of the same act'.[1] As a declaratory act of God, justification stands at the beginning of the Christian journey; as a work of grace, accomplished in us, sanctification relates to its entire course and to its goal.

[1]Cf. C. H. Dodd, *The Meaning of Paul for To-day*, 117f.

The character of sanctification, as well as the content of the ideal, compel us to give an important place to this teaching in the study of Christian doctrine. The work of Christ, for example, is but partially understood if it is not related to sanctification. All the more serious, therefore, is the neglect of this teaching, not only by individual theologians, but by large sections of the Church. At an earlier stage reference was made to the opinion that the doctrine of Perfection is 'a bypath in Christian theological systems'.[1] This description is not true, of course, of Christian devotion throughout the centuries, nor does it adequately describe the theology of the past if we include, as we must, the ideal of the vision of God. None the less, it is sufficiently true to be disquieting. For the most part it has been left to Catholic writers, Roman and Anglican,[2] to the German Pietists, the Friends, and the Methodists to preserve for the Church the ideal of sanctification. Any summary of this kind is tolerable only if important exceptions are also recognized. In Great Britain, for example, one cannot forget the brilliant pages of P. T. Forsyth's *Christian Perfection* (1899), and the more recent and comprehensive survey in A. E. Garvie's *The Christian Ideal for Human Society* (1930). Among German theologians also the ideal of perfection is strongly maintained in Schleiermacher's *The Christian Faith* and in the last chapter of Ritschl's *Justification and Reconciliation*.[3]

[1]See earlier, p. 190.

[2]Cf. Y. Brilioth, *The Anglican Revival: Studies in the Oxford Movement*, 46-52, 128, 260, 263.

[3]Schleiermacher describes redemption as the communication of the sinless perfection of Christ, mediated through the Christian community from conversion onwards. Ritschl explains perfection as dominion over the world, expressed by faith in providence, and manifested in patience, humility, prayer, and fidelity to one's vocation. Cf. Flew, *op. cit.*, 359-73, 378-93.

But when all is said the gaps are serious. It is a tragedy, the results of which we still feel, that Luther did not develop a doctrine of sanctification. In part, no doubt, this lack, for which there is no adequate compensation in isolated sentences which speak of Christian Perfection, is the price exacted by his vital emphasis upon the doctrine that justification is by faith alone (*sola fide*), and not by merit springing from the infusion of Grace or *Caritas* (*fides caritate formata*); in part, also, it is due to his instinctive reaction against wild forms of antinomianism; but perhaps most of all it is occasioned by his view of love as 'spontaneous and unmotivated'—to use the terminology of Nygren, with the result that he can speak of God's love for man with exultation, but only with increasing difficulty of man's love for God and his neighbour.[1] Whatever may be the true explanation, the whole Church of Christ has suffered from the want of a doctrine of sanctification in the Lutheran and Reformed Communions.[2] Other Communions, however, and in particular those already mentioned, dare not pride themselves on their fidelity to their historic witness; for, however explicit their credal confessions, in practice they have often lapsed into silence or have left the preaching of the ideal to Fundamentalists. In all cases the consequences of neglect are the same: want of height in spiritual attainment,[3] weakness in the

[1]Luther is compelled to speak of Christian love as something which has to come to us from heaven, and to liken the believer to 'a vessel or tube through which the stream of divine blessings must flow without intermission to other people'. Cf. Nygren, *op. cit.*, II. 517. Surely, this is not what Jesus meant by the commandment: 'Thou shalt love thy neighbour as thyself'!

[2]Cf. the well-known dictum of Harnack: 'Through having the resolute wish to go back to *religion* and to it alone, it (the Lutheran Church) neglected far too much the moral problem, the "Be ye holy, for I am holy",' *History of Dogma*, vii. 267.

[3]Cf. H. B. Workman, *The Evolution of the Monastic Ideal*, 334.

pursuit of social righteousness, failure in the formulation of doctrine. Only as the Church seeks sanctity is she blessed with saints, leaders, and theologians.

Happily, amidst much that weighs down and discourages the spirit of Christian men there are signs of hope in this respect. The rapid successive appearance of those studies of the Christian ideal, to which frequent reference has been made in the present chapter, reveals a renewed and growing interest in this theme, an interest which is all the more important because it is served by writers from different Christian communions, and because it rests upon earlier and long-continued investigations of religious experience in general and Christian mysticism in particular.[1] Is it too much to expect that the theology of the ideal will soon influence preaching and teaching, and thereby devotional practice and the pursuit of social righteousness? Be this as it may, such results are not likely to be healthy and continuous unless first the theological foundations are well and truly laid. And since sanctification is essentially the work of God, its connexion with the redemptive ministry of Christ is undoubtedly a question of first importance. Indeed, we apprehend neither sanctification itself nor the doctrine of the Atonement until we consider their mutual relationships.

It is hardly to be expected that New Testament teaching on this question will be as full as that which relates to forgiveness and reconciliation. St. Paul's Epistles belong mainly to the first generation of primitive Christianity, and it is natural that his doctrine of the Cross treats these great themes, together with that of justification. Had we more writings of the calibre of the Epistle to the Hebrews, the Fourth Gospel, and 1 John, it is safe

[1]Especially the works of William James, Baron von Hügel, Miss Underhill, and Dean Inge.

to say that there would be at our disposal fuller teaching about redemption and holiness. As it is, the New Testament teaching is of the greatest interest and importance. St. Paul associates crucifixion with Christ with the destruction of the body subjected to sin (Rom. vi. 6) and describes sanctification as the final purpose of reconciliation (Col. i. 21 f.). Most of all has he served the doctrine of the Christian ideal by dwelling, as he does, upon the love of God revealed in the Cross, and by his teaching that Christ gave Himself up for the sanctifying of the Church (cf. Rom. v. 8, Eph. v. 25-7). St. John also has laid the foundations of the ideal by his emphasis upon the love of God in the gift of His Son for the world (cf. Jn. iii. 16, x. 17; 1 Jn. iii. 16, iv. 10), by his assurance that, if we sin, we have an Advocate with the Father (1 Jn. ii. 1 f.), and by basing the sanctification of men upon the sanctifying of Jesus (Jn. xvii. 19). Finally, the writer of the Epistle to the Hebrews describes the God of peace, who can be invoked to make men perfect, as the God who brought from the dead the great Shepherd of the sheep 'with the blood of the eternal covenant' (xiii. 20). He speaks of Christ as 'the author of eternal salvation' (v. 9), who by His one offering has made perfect provision for the sanctified (x. 14), and can save to the uttermost because 'he ever liveth to make intercession' (vii. 25).

Here are the beginnings of the doctrine of sanctification, the material out of which it may be constructed, the guiding principles on which it depends. The most important principle of all is that the pursuit of the ideal is not man's unaided effort: attainment depends upon the work of God in Christ. But if this is true, we must gain a much richer appreciation of that work than is common in modern theology. We must indeed be able to see in the Cross the supreme revelation of love, but it must be seen as love which burdens itself with man's actual situation and counts no cost too great to secure man's perfection in love and that of the world in which he lives. More than this, however, is required if the process of sanctification is to move onwards towards fruition. It is not enough that the work of Christ should be seen only as a decisive deed upon which justification and reconciliation depend. Like fellowship with God, sanctification, as the conquest of sin, growth in perfect love, and the vision of God, requires a present and continuous ministry of Christ, which contains within itself the promise of victory over sin, the continued manifestation of the divine love, and the perfect disclosure of the face of God.

VI

ATONEMENT

We have now passed in review the leading aspects of the Christian experience, the remission of sins, justification, reconciliation, fellowship with God, and sanctification; and in each case we have found that they are directly related to the doctrine of the Atonement. It now remains for us to examine this relationship more closely and to consider what light it throws upon that doctrine.

It is necessary to state clearly at the outset that our purpose is not to discuss the grounds on which the doctrine of the Atonement rests, its place in the history of Christian thought, and its basis in New Testament teaching. These topics have been treated in the two works which preceded the present volume, and for the most part the results there reached will be assumed in the present discussion. The question for present consideration is whether these results are illuminated and confirmed from the standpoint of the Christian experience.

(*a*) *The Doctrine of the Atonement*

For the purpose of our discussion it is necessary to recall the outlines of the theory of the Atonement presented in *Jesus and His Sacrifice* and in *The Atonement in New Testament Teaching*, and to explain further some features which may be open to misunderstanding.

In *Jesus and His Sacrifice* the Passion-sayings in the Gospels were studied in the light of the teaching of Jesus as a whole, and against the background of Old Testament teaching concerning the Kingdom of God, the Messianic Hope, the Son of Man, the Son, the Suffering Servant, and the idea of Sacrifice. Jesus, it was maintained, believed that His sufferings would fulfil the Father's purpose for men, a purpose with which He was in complete harmony. In dying vicariously He would fulfil His Messianic destiny as He interpreted it. He would establish a new covenant-relationship between God and men through the power of His dedicated and surrendered life. In fulfilling this end He identified Himself with sinful men in the greatness of His love, entering into the consequences of human sin and bearing them upon His heart. As the Suffering Servant, He stood in a representative relation to His own, voicing their penitence, obedience, and submission to the will of God. This unique service for men He interpreted, not by the analogy of particular sacrifices, but in accordance with the sacrificial principle implicit in the worship of Israel, whereby the worshipper identifies himself with the offering made to God on his behalf. Accordingly, He instituted the Eucharist, in which a new direction was given to the earlier fellowship-meals He had celebrated in Galilee with His followers in anticipation of the great Messianic Feast. The Eucharist was meant to be a means whereby men should participate in the power of His self-offering, thus making it the vehicle of their penitent and believing approach to God. Fundamentally, this relationship was meant to be a faith-relationship to Himself, to be expressed daily in sacrificial living and service in the Kingdom of God within the fellowship of the Christian Society.

Such, in bare outline, is the reconstruction of the redemptive work of Christ for men presented in *Jesus and His Sacrifice*. In that volume it was fully recognized that a constructive element was present which needed to be supported by a fuller examination of New Testament teaching as a whole; but it was claimed that this view did justice to the sayings of Jesus Himself and to the indications, contained in the Gospels, of the manner in which He interpreted His redemptive mission for men.

In *The Atonement in New Testament Teaching* the fuller examination, projected in the earlier work, was undertaken. First, the ideas implicit in the earliest Christian preaching and belief were investigated, as they are disclosed to us in the Synoptic Gospels, the Acts, in various passages in the Pauline Epistles, the Epistle to the Hebrews, and in the Johannine writings, in 1 Peter and the Apocalypse, and finally in the later New Testament books, 2 Peter and the Pastoral Epistles. In this inquiry it was found that the beliefs of Jesus were preserved in the mind of primitive Christianity, especially His conviction that His death was the fulfilment of the divine purpose, that it was Messianic, vicarious, representative, and sacrificial, and was related directly to the fact of human sin. In the early Church it was recognized, although with diminishing clarity, that Jesus was the Suffering Servant of God, and with exultation His resurrection was looked upon as the culmination of His redemptive work. With growing conviction it was seen that His work was related to moral and spiritual ends, and that it was universal in its sweep and tendency. Other aspects, however, gained recognition more slowly. The intimacy of a personal faith-relationship with Christ Himself, as the victorious Living Lord, and the opportunities open to believers of sacramental communion with Him, the experience of mystical suffering in His service, the perception that the Cross was the final revelation of the love of God, these were ideas gradually embraced in the fulness of their meaning, as the true nature of Christ's Sacrifice was apprehended.

Secondly, the special teaching of St. Paul, the writer of the Epistle to the Hebrews, and St. John was examined. Resting upon, and indebted to, the primitive Christian faith, each of these writers develops distinctive aspects of the work of Christ. Powerfully influenced by his belief that God was active to redeem in Christ, St. Paul approaches the doctrine of the Cross from the standpoint of sin and the Law. In the death of Christ he sees the ground of man's justification and reconciliation with God, because in it God's righteousness was revealed and made effective. In the greatness of His love Christ had made Himself one with sinners and had suffered on their behalf. In describing this suffering St. Paul comes very near to the idea of substitution, but substantially his view is that Christ is man's representative, in the sense that His obedience and submission to the will of God made possible the free gift of God's salvation and restoring love. These gifts of grace, however, are not automatically bestowed; they depend upon a faith-relationship with Christ, sealed in baptism, quickened by the Spirit, sustained by the Eucharist, and expressed in a richly ethical and spiritual life. This reconciliation is universal in its scope, transcending the boundaries of race, class, and sex, and extending even to the universe itself.

The writer of the Epistle to the Hebrews apprehends the Cross in a manner no less distinctive. Approaching the doctrine from the standpoint of a sublime conception of God, and influenced by a Wisdom-Christology which strongly emphasizes the divinity and the humanity of Christ, he is deeply impressed by the power of sin as a barrier to fellowship with God. This barrier, he maintains, is removed by the finality of Christ's vicarious act in dying. Like St. Paul he interprets the act as that of a representative, but he describes it as that of a mediator and high priest. Christ effects man's deliverance by the offering of Himself in perfect obedience to the will of God. The conscience of man is cleansed, and a new and living way is opened to him into the world of eternal realities, into which he enters sustained by faith in the power of the unseen. The dominating ideas in the writer's theology are sacrificial, but he is not able to tell us how the self-offering of Christ is effective beyond saying that it expiates or covers sin, largely because he has no parallel to the Pauline teaching about faith-union with Christ, sacramental communion, and mystical fellowship in suffering with the Exalted Lord who still lives to make intercession for men.

The teaching of St. John has an individuality which is unmistakable. Dependent, like St. Paul and the *auctor ad Hebraeos*, on primitive tradition, he thinks of the Cross especially in the light of the Incarnation. The death of Christ is the supreme proof of the love of God, but it is also Christ's glorifying and exaltation. To some degree in the Gospel, but more fully in the First Epistle, its character is sacrificial. Christ is our Advocate with the Father and is Himself the Expiation for the sin of the world. All that He is and has accomplished for men, is to be appropriated by faith. In sacramental communion the believer feeds upon Him. He is the Vine; we are the branches. The inner witness is that God has given to us eternal life, and that this life is in His Son. 'He that hath the Son hath the life; and he that hath not the Son of God hath not the life.' In these words is sounded the characteristic Johannine note.

The unity and the distinctiveness of these three teachers is remarkable. What is wanting in any one of them is supplied by one of or both the others, and all rest in the faith of the primitive Church.

In the third place, an attempt was made to state the implications of New Testament teaching, to face its ultimate problems, and to expound a theory of the Atonement in harmony with its witness. Instead of restating this theory, it will be more useful to set down, in summary form, its leading ideas for purposes of reference when we examine further the various aspects of the Christian experience in relation to the doctrine. This summary is as follows: (1) The Atonement is the work of God in restoring sinful men to fellowship with Himself and in establishing His Kingdom; it is the reconciliation of men and of the world to God. (2) The Atonement is also the final proof of the love of God, both in itself, as a disclosure of His nature, and in the form it takes for man's renewal and recovery. (3) The Atonement is accomplished in the work of Christ, in that He reveals the love of God in His redeeming activity, and because in His life, death, resurrection, and exaltation He provides all things necessary for man's salvation. (4) This work of Christ is vicarious; it is wrought on behalf of men, doing for them what they are not able to do for themselves. (5) It is also representative. As the Son of Man, Christ acts in our name. He takes our side and becomes one with us, enduring the consequences of our sins, and expressing to the Father the obedience we ought to render, the penitence we ought to feel, and the submission to the judgment of God we ought to make, but which, in each case, we are unable to offer. (6) Christ's ministry is also sacrificial, not as a sin- or a guilt-offering, but because He poured out His life in willing surrender for men, in order that they may freely consent to all that He does for them, and thus make Him the means of their penitent and believing approach to God. (7) The Atonement is consummated when, through faith-union with Christ, men accept and embrace all that He has done on their behalf, when they make His self-offering their own through personal trust in Him, sacramental communion with Him, and sacrificial living in the fellowship of His sufferings. (8) While the Atonement is personal, in that it meets the spiritual needs of individual men, it is also communal, in that it is manifest in the life of the divine Society which is the Church, and in the renewed world which it makes possible.

Such, in broad outline, is the theory proposed, with the addition of explanatory phrases which, it is hoped, may elucidate further certain points in the argument. No further attempt will be made here to support this doctrinal construction, beyond the all-important inquiry whether it is adequate to satisfy the needs of the Christian experience as it is described in the New Testament. If it is found to correspond to that experience, and to meet its ethical and spiritual needs, there is added reason for accepting it as valid and true.

(*b*) *The Unity of the Christian Experience*

Before proceeding to the inquiry, it is necessary to emphasize the unity of the Christian experience in question. For purposes of investigation we have treated separately forgiveness, justification, reconciliation, fellowship with God, and sanctification; but it is not suggested that the Christian experience can be mapped out with the precision of a medical or geographical chart. The thoughts, feelings, and desires of men are strangely complex, and there is no single path which all tread with painful regularity. There is, of course, a relative order in the Christian experience. Reconciliation, for example, must precede fellowship with God, although not to the exclusion of an antecedent knowledge of Him gained from Christian tradition, the observation of nature, conscience, and the study of world history. Again, sanctification follows reconciliation, as justification precedes it, in spite of the fact that the latter may not be recognized until it is made the object of reflection. Further, it is impossible to say when the experience of fellowship with God merges into that of sanctification; indeed, sanctification may be described as the perfecting of fellowship. Finally, forgiveness, as the remission of sins, stands at the beginning of the journey; but it also belongs to its every stage, being more fully known in sanctification than at the moment of reconciliation.

Having recognized this unity and continuity of the Christian experience, we are compelled, as in the earlier chapters, to break it up for the purposes of investigation. We require to know how the remission of sins, justification, reconciliation, fellowship with God, and sanctification are each related to the divine ministry of atonement. Only so can we gain a more adequate knowledge of the mystery of the human heart and the amazing grace of God in the Cross of Christ.

(*c*) *Forgiveness and the Atonement*

We have already recognized that in modern theology forgiveness is the equivalent of reconciliation; and, as such, it will be considered later in Section (*f*). Here, however, forgiveness is in question as the remission of sins.

We have seen that the New Testament does not teach that Christ died in order that God might be able to forgive sins. The remission of sins is an act of God's free grace, whereby, in response to the cry of the contrite, He sets aside the barriers raised by our sins and makes possible our reconciliation to Himself. It might seem, therefore, that our sole need is that we should be assured of His gracious purpose, the significance of the Cross being that it gives us this knowledge. Calvary is the incredible revelation of a pardoning God. As the Israelites in the wilderness looked upon the brazen serpent, so we gaze upon the Cross of Christ, and, as we look, we are healed.

There can be no doubt that this teaching is of the very essence of the Gospel. It is not surprising, therefore, that many Christians, in recoil from unethical theories of the Atonement, and unwilling to probe further into its mysteries, are content with this Gospel. Nevertheless, it is not equal to man's need, unless we can go further and show in what manner the Cross makes known the pardoning God. Of the wonder of this message there can be no question; what is required is its enlargement in the interests of truth. This fact can be seen if we examine the experience of forgiveness more closely.

The remission of sins, it is recognized, depends upon repentance. Always an act of sheer grace, God's forgiveness is not largess bestowed indiscriminately. God cannot forgive the feebly penitent, or those who are not penitent at all, because so to act would be to act contrary to His nature as the God of righteousness and truth. Forgiveness of this kind would be the removal of great barriers which man has barely seen, or has not even descried. It is only when a man cries: 'God be merciful to me a sinner!' that God can, consistently with His love, remit sins.

We must be careful, however, not to misread this need for repentance. Repentance does not win forgiveness. So to think is to condition God's grace by man's worth, to affirm that we are forgiven because we are forgivable, in the sense of being worthy to be forgiven. Through repentance we are forgivable only in the sense that forgiveness is possible.

Thus far, there is general agreement; but is it adequately perceived how difficult repentance can be? In many cases, especially those of gross sins, the vision of divine love leads swiftly to repentance; but other sins, and these the most subtle—pride, uncharitableness, and self-complacency—are more intractable, because they are often hidden from us. Moreover, it is difficult to feel a sense of personal responsibility for social sins, to which we may not have contributed directly. Frequently, men find that they are not able to repent. The appeal: 'Repent ye, and believe in the good news,' either leaves them cold, or deepens a sense of frustration and defeat. How, then, is this need to be met?

In order to make repentance possible, we must be able to apprehend, not only that God loves, but how He loves, and what His love does. Probably, most of, if not all, those aspects of the Atonement enumerated in Section (*a*) are serviceable to this very end, and are therefore of great importance for the remission of sins. This claim does not mean that, before we can repent, we must first accept a theory of the Atonement. What it does mean is that we must be able to envisage a picture of God, and of the operations of His love, which ultimately is based upon that doctrine; for a Gospel without a theology is a reed shaken by the wind. For true repentance we need to know that, as the God of love, God has done all things necessary for our recovery in Christ who suffered for us even unto death. The more fully we understand what His suffering was, the contact with evil it entailed and the sharing in human desolation it involved, the more living our penitence becomes, not merely because our feelings are stirred and our pity stimulated, but because we perceive how evil sin is, and how much more deeply it is entrenched in our hearts than we had supposed. And especially is this effect likely to be produced in us, if we believe that this Sufferer is not simply a prophet, or a good man, faithful to his divine mission, but the Son of God, who came from the bosom of the Father and was incarnate for our salvation in flesh and blood.

There is reason to think that not even this revelation is all that the Cross does for us; but that, further, Christ Himself is the bearer of our penitence because of His self-offering for the sin of the world. The objection that vicarious penitence is a fiction rests upon an imperfect psychology and a small knowledge of life. If, among men, there are analogies[1] to such a ministry of corporate contrition, far more can this ministry be ascribed to Him who is the Son of Man and Lord of the Kingdom of God. But if so, in relation to Him, we are like mute poets who find their voice in the words of another. He who can be our conscience becomes our penitence. In Him, and through Him, we break the bands of our individuality, and share in His sorrow for the world. This view goes beyond the statements of Scripture and the confessions of the Church, and therefore the theologian can state it only as an opinion based upon his understanding of Christian experience and the meaning of the Cross. Only as it is confirmed by others, and throughout the years, can it attain the objectivity of theological truth.[2]

[1]Cf. H. R. Mackintosh, *The Christian Experience of Forgiveness*, 214.

[2]I have treated this question in *Jesus and His Sacrifice*, 309-12, and in *The Atonement in New Testament Teaching*, 292 f., but it is necessary to introduce it again in considering the remission of sins. Too often Moberly's critics assume that vicarious penitence is substituted penitence and fail to meet his claim that perfect penitence is not even conceivably possible except to the personally sinless. Cf. *Atonement and Personality*, 26-47.

There is still another consideration which bears upon the relationship between the Atonement and the remission of sins. The latter, we have seen, belongs to the further course of the Christian life, and not to its beginnings alone. It is anticipatory to reconciliation, but it accompanies our fellowship with God and the process of sanctification. The constant prayer of the Christian is: 'Forgive us our trespasses'. Since this is so, it follows that he needs a growing sensitiveness to evil, a truer understanding of himself, a better knowledge of life and of the world. This knowledge he gains in the Cross. Here he learns that sin can slay the Christ, that he himself is utterly dependent upon divine grace, that life's meaning is found only in sacrificial love. Hidden motives are laid bare, paralyzing sins which otherwise pass unnoticed are brought to light, values are recreated, judgments made more discriminating. Thus he gains a deeper sense of sin and an increased sense of his need for the divine forgiveness.

Finally, the Cross provides the supreme incentive for the forgiveness of others. Few things are so surprising as the difficulty which Christian men find in what is an elementary Christian duty. In this fact is explained the emphasis which Jesus in His teaching placed upon it. Not seven times, He taught, must we forgive, but seventy times seven. Happily, for His followers forgiveness is not laid down simply as a duty. Nor is His teaching ended even in the matchless prayer: 'Father, forgive them; for they know not what they do.' It is conveyed also by the silence of the Cross, by the appeal of the pierced hands. And beyond the motive, the method of the remission of sins is revealed to us. Consistently with love, we, no more than God, can ignore the barriers which wrongdoing builds; but we are not condemned passively to look upon them, and to wait for the repentance of those who have done us ill. We can bear the shame they ought to feel, not with the motive of shaming them, but as the burden of a love which makes their moral responsibilities its own. If there should be no response, our ministry, like that of Christ, is that of a 'lost love',[1] which goes on loving to the end; but if there is an answer to our love, we share in the joy of heaven over one sinner that repenteth, and understand, as never before, the majesty of the love of God.

(*d*) *Justification and the Atonement*

We turn next to the question of the connexion between justification and the work of God in Christ. Everyone who thinks carefully about New Testament teaching is compelled to face this question, especially if he is convinced that justification is of vital moment in the experience of forgiveness and reconciliation, that it is not to be grounded in works, and cannot be regarded as the equivalent of sanctification.

While it is not desirable to repeat our earlier discussion, it is necessary to recall to mind the peculiar nature of the problem which confronts us.

Justification, we have seen, is the act of God in accepting men as righteous on the ground of faith in Christ. As such, it is more than the remission of sins, although it implies and includes this gift of God. The righteousness in question is not fictitious, nor is it simply imputed to us; it is true righteousness, that of promise and potency rather than a righteousness of perfected achievement. It is the righteous mind of the man whose trust rests not

[1]Cf. A. Nygren, *Agape and Eros*, II. 514, who cites Luther: 'Nor is there any danger if it be in error; for it is of the nature of love to suffer betrayal, since it is exposed to all the uses and abuses of all men, the general servant of good and bad, faithful and unfaithful, true and false alike.'

in himself, but in Christ and His work. The righteousness is not the man's work, nor is it simply God's gift, but a righteousness which is dependent upon faith.

This teaching, we saw, raises in the acutest form the question of the relation between faith and righteousness. It is not a satisfactory answer to say that the faith is righteousness, unless we can show that its character, as such, is determined by the object in which it rests, that is, Christ as the bearer of salvation. Christ's work, therefore, is of essential importance to the ethical and religious character of justification. Only if His work has the quality of perfect righteousness can God accept as righteous the man who trusts in Him. This was the point reached in our discussion in Chapter IV, and we can now resume our argument, with the added advantage that we have set justification in its context, as a vital element in the Christian experience[1] closely related to the remission of sins, reconciliation, fellowship with God, and sanctification.

How, then, we ask, is justifiying faith related to the work of God in Christ?

This question, it should be observed from the outset, is both academic and practical. It is academic because our justification depends upon faith in Christ, and not belief in a theory of the Atonement. The response of faith may be much fuller than our theories, consistently interpreted, would warrant; for, in addition to our formal confessions, aspects of Christ's ministry preserved in New Testament

[1]But not necessarily a fact of which we are conscious, except in the light of its effects. This consideration makes it difficult to accept the claim of H. R. Mackintosh, *The Christian Experience of Forgiveness*, 3, that, while in theory the distinction between forgiveness and justification may be possible, 'it has not the slenderest bearing on experience'. Mackintosh, it should be remembered, accepts the usual Lutheran view that forgiveness = justification = reconciliation. This doctrinal equation robs justification of its meaning, and illustrates the danger of too exclusive a dependence upon experience as a basis for theology.

teaching, in Christian tradition, and in the hymns and worship of the Church, may be tacitly accepted, without being affirmed or articulated in our theories. Moreover, contact with Christ Himself brings us into touch with the actual saving realities of His work, however imperfectly we have apprehended, or stated, them. Further, the same consideration applies to the work of the Spirit in the creation of faith, since His ministry cannot be separated from that of the Father and the Son.[1] We have every reason to recognize the part of the Spirit in justification, inasmuch as His activity is dependent upon, and harmonious with, the Atonement,[2] both as a fact of history and as a present reality. All these considerations serve to remind us that no man is at the mercy of his theology, and that, in this as in other respects, man's weakness may be God's opportunity.

If, however, the question under discussion is academic, it is also and at the same time practical. From the considerations noted above we have no right to infer that theories of the Atonement are unimportant, since our faith-relationship with Christ may be vitally affected by the view we take of His work. Our faith, we have said, may be richer than our theories of His ministry warrant, but we are not thereby delivered from the perils of too limited an apprehension of our debt to Him. The work of the Spirit also, sovereign as it is, is conditioned by our

[1]It is one of the many outstanding merits of R. C. Moberly's theology that he so closely associates the work of the Holy Spirit with the Atonement. Cf. *Atonement and Personality*, 154-215.

[2]It was pointed out earlier (see p. 66) that Luther includes regeneration in his teaching concerning justification, and indeed he does so often; but he never abates his strong claim that justification depends on the work of God in Christ. Cf. Harnack, *History of Dogma*, vii. 209; R. S. Franks, *A History of the Doctrine of the Work of Christ*, i. 374; G. P. Fisher, *History of Christian Doctrine*, 274.

intellectual outlook as well as by our spiritual attitude. Moreover, it is much more likely that we shall appreciate the importance of justification itself, if we are able to give a satisfactory account of the manner in which it is related to the Atonement.

With these considerations in mind, we return, then, to the question: How is justifying faith related to the work of God in Christ?

The best way to treat this question will be to consider the main types among the theories of the Atonement represented in the history of the doctrine. The point for special notice is the influence likely to be exerted by the particular type in question, *when it is consistently held.*

I take, first, the purely revelatory type, the view namely that the Cross is the supreme revelation of the love of God. It does not need to be argued that this view is essential to justification; for how shall we dare to place complete trust in Christ unless He is the final revelation of the divine love? What, then, is the character of the faith of the man who receives this revelation? Its nature, undoubtedly, must be that of a grateful and penitent response to the love which is perceived. It may very well be that the response will be much richer than the revelatory theory, strictly interpreted, would warrant; being, in fact, a faith which God can accept as righteousness. But can it be so, if the revelatory theory is *consistently accepted*, as an adequate account of the meaning of the death of Christ? In this case, as it seems to me, the response will certainly reveal a righteous mind, and may well be a generative power for growth in righteousness. Nevertheless, the righteousness in question will be that of a man, with all the limitations which belong to human frailty. It will be a beautiful thing, the best of which he is capable, his personal attitude to God under the inspiration of a haunting vision of love, a mark of spiritual worth. But is it the righteousness proper to justification, a righteousness, not of his making, which gives him his standing in the moment of decision when, trusting no longer in himself and his deeds, he casts himself wholly upon God? Unless I am mistaken, there is a sense of incongruity in speaking of justification in this connexion; it is like introducing a foreign word in an alien context of thought. The righteousness in question is eschatological righteousness, that which is relevant at the End-time, when judgment is passed upon things done in the body. It is man's righteousness, and therefore capable of approval. It is something which the man does, and which consequently possesses merit. On this basis, God could pronounce men righteous, and therefore able to enter into fellowship with Himself, only by displaying a kindly tolerance inconsistent with His holiness and truth. Indeed, it is not surprising, but highly significant, that where a purely revelatory doctrine of the Atonement is maintained, justification is felt to have no meaning. It is the language of Canaan on the Acropolis at Athens.

I take, secondly, that type of theory which stresses the active element in Christ's ministry, which insists that the revelation of love is objective, in the sense that it is made in history under the conditions of flesh or blood; either by dwelling upon Christ's victory over sin, death, evil, and Satan, or by describing His ministry as one of sacrificial dedication to the recovery of men. There cannot be any doubt that these views are of much greater value for the understanding of justification. They stand much closer to New Testament teaching, in that they present the love of God as expressed in Christ, as well as revealed. It must further be said that, in the language of the Lutheran theology, they describe Christ's active obedience, that is,

His active fulfilment of righteousness, and His passive obedience,[1] His perfect endurance of suffering and death in conformity with His Father's will. In everything they affirm, they assert what is of essential importance to justifying faith. But do they provide an adequate basis for the interpretation of faith as the righteousness which gives man his standing, real yet unmerited, before God? It is precisely at this point that our doubts must arise. It is significant that those who hold these views, in so far as they speak of justification at all, think of it as the forgiveness of sins, or as God's mercy in restoring sinners to fellowship with Himself, instead of, in its Pauline sense,[2] the gracious act of God in accepting men as righteous in virtue of their faith in Christ. They think, that is to say, of what is implied or made possible by justification rather than of justification in itself. This fact suggests that the type of theory in question does not supply a rational basis for justification; and, when we examine the kind of faith which is presupposed, this fear is confirmed. An ethical account of the justifying activity of God cannot be given.

The reason for this denial is as before. When we believe because of what we perceive in Jesus and His Cross, in His victory over evil, His self-sacrifice, His perfect fidelity to His divine vocation, our response is subjective, except in so far as it is stimulated by what we see. Our faith is the expression, a necessary and desirable expression, of *our* mind and heart, of *our* gratitude, *our* trust in God's mercy, *our* desire for goodness and truth. Of this

[1] The use of the term 'passive' obedience was unfortunate, but it does not, of course, affect our argument.

[2] The one passage from which it might be argued that St. Paul identifies forgiveness and justification is Rom. iv. 7 f. But this basis is insufficient, for (1) he uses ἀφίημι nowhere else, (2) the passage is a quotation (Psa. xxxii. 1 f.), (3) his interest is plainly in the last line: 'Blessed is the man unto whom the Lord imputeth not iniquity.'

religious response we can indeed say that it is excellent so far as it goes. Nay more, it is an essential part of what the New Testament means by faith. But again, is it the faith on the ground of which we are justified? Can God declare us to be righteous because we are grateful, or trustful, or reverent, or well-intentioned? The greatest teachers of the past have not thought so. This fact is illustrated alike by the mediaeval theory, that man is justified by the infusion of divine grace, and the Lutheran view, that Christ's righteousness is imputed to him; for the interests of both theories were religious as well as controversial. In each case it was believed that the faith which justifies is not simply that of the individual. The modern view of faith, in so far as it represents faith as simply man's response to the divine appeal in Christ, is really a subtle, and therefore dangerous, form of justification by works, in which the claim to merit assumes the guise of faith instead of the grosser garb of meritorious deeds. If this be so, in its bearing upon justification, the modern conception is open to criticism no less than the theology of the past. The mediaeval theology destroyed justification by transforming it into sanctification; Protestant teaching mortgaged the religious future of the doctrine by undermining its ethical foundations; modern Christianity mortally wounds justification, so far as it does not ignore it, by its easy assumption that man can enter into fellowship with God, without a faith founded in Christ's righteousness and constituted thereby.

It may be objected that the issue has been stated too rigorously. Is the faith in question a purely human response? Is it not the work of the Holy Spirit, and therefore adequate for man's salvation? We have already recognized that, in the mercy of God, this may be so; but we must not too quickly assume that justification is adequately based if it rests on a faith prompted by Christ's victory over evil or His fidelity to His vocation, for we dare not claim that this type of theory adequately describes that atoning work in which, actually, the Spirit participates. Our inquiry is not concerned with the divine use of an imperfect faith, but with the kind of faith presupposed by a particular theory of the Atonement; and our conclusion must be that the theory under immediate consideration, when it is consistently held, supplies no basis for a faith which is to be counted as righteousness. As the victor over sin, and the Saviour who dedicates Himself to human recovery, Christ's righteousness is His own, His personal achievement, not a righteousness fulfilled in the name of mankind to which faith assents, and which it appropriates and makes its own. In consequence, faith is not given its divine opportunity to pass beyond the bounds of a personal response into the embracing of a righteousness, perfect and universal, but not meritorious, which gives man his standing with God.

In contrast with the types already examined, I take, thirdly, those which emphasize the representative nature of Christ's ministry, and are objective, in the sense that they presuppose a Godward, as well as a manward, direction in its range. The fact that some theories of this type are untenable, as, for example, theories of substitution and of vicarious punishment, is irrelevant, and does not therefore foreclose the discussion. In fact, the persistence of theories of substitution and of satisfaction in the history of Christian doctrine reveals the immense strength of a felt religious need; and the question is prompted, whether it is not possible so to present the representative ministry of Christ for men that this need is met, without the sacrifice of ethical and religious values. There is good reason to expect that such a theory is possible; for this type of doctrinal statement describes a work of Christ, apart from man, yet in his name, into which by faith he can enter, so that personal faith is rooted in the eternal and universal. In Section (*a*) I have summarized the outlines of a theory which has this character, and which I believe is harmonious with the teaching of Jesus and the belief of the primitive Church as it is reflected in the New Testament. Stated broadly, and omitting points which are necessarily speculative,[1] this view presents the work of Christ as that of the self-offering of the Son of Man, who, in the greatness of His love, burdens Himself with man's situation as a sinner, and suffers for him even unto death. It affirms, further, that, in the name of mankind and before the face of His Father, Christ expresses that mind concerning sin and righteousness, which in himself man has no power adequately to express, but into which he can enter through faith and trust in Him. Dependent utterly upon Christ, relying upon all that He has done for men, and committed to Him in complete loyalty, the believer shares in a corporate act of righteousness for which he can claim no merit. Of this view, as of those previously mentioned, we can say that any defects it may have are made good by fellowship with the Living Christ and the work of the Holy Spirit in the heart. But it can also be claimed, in contrast with other types of theory, that it supplies a fully ethical and religious basis for justifying faith. Grounded in Christ and in the realities of His saving work, faith can be accepted by God, in the perfection of His nature, as righteousness, because it reveals a mind resting in, and clothed with, Christ's righteousness. With such a faith, man comes before God, not simply as an individual, but as a member of the company of the redeemed, sharing in the

[1]As, for example, the description of Christ's self-offering as one of penitence, obedience, and submission to the will of God.

power of a racial act. Fully personal, faith is founded in the infinitude of righteousness, revealed and expressed by Christ in redemptive action. The believer comes to God, pleading no meritorious deeds, but with a faith affirmative of, and constituted by, God's righteousness in Christ, embodied in history, and eternally operative. In consequence, that act of divine love, whereby God receives him, and gives to him the right of entry into His fellowship, is not the compounding of a fiction, but ethical reality through and through.

In conclusion, it is to be observed that, in addition to its positive advantages, this type of theory includes within itself all that is of value in those previously examined. From the very fact that it describes a work of Christ directed Godwards, it presents the Atonement as the revelation of love, but with added force; it also sets forth a redemptive activity of God in Christ which effectually meets the spiritual needs of man in his penitent approach to God.

(*e*) *Reconciliation and the Atonement*

Continuing our inquiry, we consider next the experience of reconciliation. In what way does reconciliation depend on the work of God in Christ?

Our earlier investigation has something to contribute to the answer to this question. If we identify forgiveness and reconciliation, we must find room within the idea of reconciliation for the remission of sins and for justification. In order that he may be restored to fellowship with God, man needs a vehicle for his penitence and a standing with God for which he may claim no merit. Our submission was that both these needs are met in the representative ministry of Christ, provided that its benefits are appropriated by faith, and thus become an integral element in man's approach to God. If this argument is valid, provision for these needs is essential also to reconciliation. In his Christian experience the believer may, or may not, be conscious of stages in his return to fellowship with God; the remission of sins, justification, and entrance into fellowship may be coincident experiences, perceptible only when reflection is brought to bear upon them. Be this as it may, reconciliation is not a simple, but a highly complex experience which includes these elements. We must therefore conclude that whatever is necessary to each of them is essential to the whole; that, since the remission of sins and justification depend upon a representative and sacrificial ministry of Christ, the same is true also of reconciliation.

Apart, however, from this consideration, reconciliation in itself, as an act of divine love, has a direct relation to the work of God in Christ. It is agreed by all that reconciliation depends upon the amazing grace of God made known to us in Jesus Christ and supremely in His Cross. This conviction rests upon the teaching of Scripture, the hymns and confessions of the Church, the unanimous support of theologians and teachers, and the affirmations of multitudes of unknown believers. St. Paul expresses a fundamental Christian belief when he precedes one of his references to reconciliation (Rom. v. 10 f.) by the words: 'God commendeth his own love toward us, in that, while we were yet sinners, Christ died for us' (Rom. v. 8).

We have seen that many theologians are content simply to paraphrase this great passage, and to insist that the revelation was objective, in that it was made in history under the conditions of flesh and blood, that it extends to the entire life of Christ, and was consummated upon the Cross, where He dedicated Himself to the recovery of men. Saving faith is the response to this manifestation of love. When faith and love meet, reconciliation is effected, and man enters into fellowship with God.

The positive truth in this theology belongs to every doctrine of the Atonement worthy of the name. Sound, however, as this teaching is, it provides a sufficient basis for the doctrine of reconciliation only if we can answer the question: What makes the Cross the revelation of supreme love, and is our account of it adequate to human need?

That which makes the Cross such a revelation is certainly not the isolated fact that it discloses the divine heart; for, in this case, within the limitations of his finitude, man faces the task of essaying a repentance proportionate to his sin and the holiness worthy of a friend of God. So far from being a message of hope, the Cross, as a revealing of love *and nothing more*, is a ground for despair. It invites man to seek the impossible. The fact that this invitation could never be true of God, gives even a crude theory of substitution a dignity of its own. It is entirely true that, in responding to the divine love, man is aided by the grace of God. But the grace of God is not simply the release of spiritual power; it is the love of God operative in the Cross. In thinking, therefore, of the grace of God, we merely return to the original question: What is it that makes the Cross the supreme revelation of love?

Stated broadly, the answer can only be that the Cross must reveal God as meeting all the conditions vital to reconciliation. A loving heart is one which swiftly answers human need; and this principle must be true of God as well as of man. We are therefore bound to include in our answer everything which God has done, and is doing still, to restore men to fellowship with Himself. This divine activity is undoubtedly to be seen in the Incarnation, in all the earthly life of Jesus, in His acceptance of human limitations, His compassion towards sinners,

His conflict with temptation, His healing ministry, His constant attitude of unwearied love. Still more is it to be found in His death, as the consummation of His life, His final victory over evil, His eternal consecration to the recovery of men. All this is love divine, but it is not the fulness of divine love. In its entirety the love of God is manifest only as Christ goes all the way in meeting the cost of reconciliation, in His voluntary acceptance of the consequences of human transgression, in His bearing of the sin of men, and in His willingness to be the means of their penitent approach to God. 'Herein is love, not that we loved God, but that He loved us, and sent His Son to be the expiation for our sins.'

The New Testament is not uncertain in its interpretation of this supreme ministry of love. It sees Christ making Himself one with sinners, loving them so deeply as to plunge into the very shadows of the divine judgment which rests upon sin. It pictures Him before the Passion contemplating the drinking of the cup of sorrow (Mk. x. 38), straitened till His baptism of death be accomplished (Lk. xii. 50). It describes Him in Gethsemane drinking the cup, after prayer that it might be removed (Mk. xiv. 32-42), and crying upon the Cross, in the extremity of His desolation: 'My God, my God, why hast thou forsaken me?' (Mk. xv. 34). In the language of hyperbole, it declares that He was made to be sin on our behalf (2 Cor. v. 21), and that He became a curse for us (Gal. iii. 13). Its witness could hardly be more emphatic that He identified Himself with sinners and bore upon His heart the pain and desolation of sin. But even this is not all. The significance of what Christ endured is determined by what He is, by the fact that He is the Son of God, by His consciousness of His vocation as the Son of Man and Lord of the Kingdom. In the light of His Person, we must interpret His sufferings, not only as the cost of His personal fidelity to His mission, but as of supreme value to His brethren in all their relationships with God. He suffers, not only on their behalf, but in their name, and is thus their Mediator and Kinsman in things pertaining to God.

If, when we speak of the Cross as the revelation of divine love, we can interpret His service in this way, we give a worthy account of what the love does, and one that meets human need; for we can conceive no love greater than this, no more complete expression of the purpose of God in restoring men to fellowship with Himself, no better means for their recovery. The difficult points in the interpretation are the references to sin-bearing and to mediatorship; and it will be of advantage to treat these matters more fully. That, in the greatness of His love for men, Christ did in a true sense bear the weight of sin, few Christian thinkers would dispute. The point of difficulty is whether this suffering was submission to the divine judgment resting upon sin, and whether it is right to speak of it as penal suffering. Mediatorship involves the question whether there is a sacrificial element in Christ's work, so that, through His perfect obedience, we may find our way to God.

The problem of Christ's suffering is vitally affected by our view of the divine attitude to sin. My own belief is that a divine judgment falls upon sin, and that this judgment is more personal than the operation of a law of cause and effect in the moral universe. I believe also that it is possible for one who is not himself subject to that judgment to endure some of its consequences in the lives of others, to bear, in this sense, the sins of others, and that this he must do, if he truly loves those upon whom, primarily, the judgment rests. In this ministry of love he will not be careful to claim that the judgment is not personally upon himself; he will so far enter into the situation of another, or even of a community, that he will experience the judgment as falling upon himself. We are not debarred from pressing this analogy because Christ Himself was sinless, since actually it is sin in ourselves which prevents us from fulfilling this ministry beyond a certain point, and the degree to which we have any knowledge of it at all is the extent to which we have attained personal holiness of life. Only saints in the making can bear the sins of another; only Christ can bear the sins of the world. There does not seem to me to be any good reason why we should hesitate to think of Christ as submitting to the judgment which overtakes human sin. On the contrary, by reason of the greatness of His love, the perfect purity of His life, and the relationship in which He believed Himself to stand to men, there are the best of reasons why we should recognize this supreme service as the measure of our debt to Himself. Among Christians, at least, it ought not to be a subject for controversy, but a theme for adoring wonder, that Christ bore the sins of men.

In some respects, though not in all, it is a matter of secondary importance whether we describe Christ's suffering as penal. Much depends upon whether we think the suffering which attends sin is retributive as well as disciplinary. I have argued elsewhere[1] that it cannot be the one without being the other, inasmuch as disciplinary action which is not deserved is unjust. Apart from this question, the use of the term 'penal' with reference to the suffering of Christ, depends also upon whether it is right to use the adjective of a divine judgment the effects of which are shared. It has long been agreed that Christ

[1] *Jesus and His Sacrifice*, 286ff., *The Atonement in New Teaching*, 130f.

was not punished in man's stead. On this issue Calvin spoke the decisive word.[1] But it has not yet been shown that we are not entitled to use 'penal' to describe *participation* in the penal sufferings of others. James Denney did not hesitate to use the word of the sufferings of Christ, and he spared no effort to make his meaning precise. 'They were not penal', he wrote, 'in the sense of coming to Him through a bad conscience, or in the sense that God was angry with Him personally, as if He had really been a guilty man.'[2] These words are sufficiently clear, but equally clear is his positive explanation of the manner in which the term may be used. The Agony and the Passion, he declared, 'were penal in the sense that in that dark hour He had to realize to the full the divine reaction against sin in the race in which He was incorporated, and that without doing so He could not have been the Redeemer of that race from sin, or the Reconciler of sinful men to God'.[3] Prudential reasons, arising out of the fear of being misunderstood, ought not to lead us to abandon the word, until we have found a better;[4] and the reason why we cannot dismiss the matter, as merely a question of terminology, is that failure to use it is often accompanied with a faint appreciation of the wonder of Christ's self-identification with sinners.

The reality of Christ's sin-bearing is not only the proof of His love, but is also, as Denney has reminded us in the words quoted above, the experience which makes Him to be the Redeemer, the Reconciler of sinful men to God.

[1] 'How could He be angry with the beloved Son, with whom His soul was well pleased,' *Institutes*, II. xvi. 10. But Calvin speaks of Christ as abandoned and forsaken of God. Cf. A. Dakin, *Calvinism*, 58.

[2] *The Christian Doctrine of Reconciliation*, 272.

[3] *Op. cit.*, 273.

[4] Ritschl's suggestion that we should speak of the suffering of the innocent as 'affliction', is jejune. Cf. *Justification and Reconciliation*, 479.

It is because He is such, and is found to be such in the Christian experience, that we are justified in thinking of His ministry in sacrificial terms,[1] and in speaking of Him as the Mediator or the High Priest of our confession. We are restored to fellowship with God by Him, and not merely by reason of what He has revealed. He Himself, in virtue of His life and death, is our reconciliation, and through His ministry and service, we enter into communion with God, into peace, freedom, and the joy of sonship.

(*f*) *Fellowship with God and the Atonement*

The connexion of fellowship with God and the work of Christ is less obvious than it is in the case of the other aspects of the Christian experience we have hitherto considered. It is not surprising, therefore, that insufficient attention is often given to this theme, with a consequent loss in the interpretation of fellowship itself and of the doctrine of the Atonement. That a close relationship exists, we have already seen. We have found that, directly or indirectly, all the descriptions of fellowship in the New Testament, both individual and communal, are associated with the work of Christ for men.

In part, this relationship is due to the fact that fellowship with God depends on justification and reconciliation; and our earlier argument stands good that what is necessary to these experiences is required by the life in which they issue. There is, however, a special relationship to the Atonement arising out of the maturer expressions of the life of fellowship. These experiences involve an ever closer and more intimate communion of the believer with Christ and a deeper and richer knowledge of God. In consequence, when we are thinking of the possibilities of

[1]Apart altogether from the claim that Jesus Himself thought of His ministry in terms of the sacrificial category.

fellowship, it is not enough to think of the death of Christ as an event in the past: His work must also be envisaged as a present and continuous ministry. As possessing the note of immediacy, justification rests upon the decisiveness of Christ's deed; and the same is true also of reconciliation, as an act accomplished by God, and as the state of fellowship which He brings into being. In the life of fellowship, however, we need to think of Christ's work, not only as a deed, but also as a doing, a present ministry upon which we can continually rely, in the power of which we can share, and the spirit of which we can reproduce, in our own measure and aided by the Spirit of God, in daily life and practice.

Fellowship with Christ's sufferings, for example, is unduly limited, if it is only an imaginative sharing in the Gethsemane of history; and it is far less than the New Testament encourages us to expect, if it is no more than the pain of a costly fidelity. To possess the depth of meaning which belongs to this mystical experience, it must be participation in the power of that obedience of Christ which, even in His exaltation, still avails and speaks for men. In like manner, to be 'in Christ' is to have fellowship with One who still ministers to human need. To 'die' with Him is not only to die to sin, but also to share somewhat—just so much as we can bear—of His eternal self-offering. To 'rise' with Him is to enter into His present victory over evil and sin, and to anticipate the triumph which is still to come. To 'know' God is to apprehend Him in the Eternal Cross; and to 'see' Him is to behold Him in the face of the Lamb. In short, this interpretation of fellowship with God in Christ demands a corresponding interpretation of the Atonement as a permanent and continuous ministry of Christ for men, just such a ministry, in fact, as the New Testament implies when it speaks of Christ as our Advocate with the Father, and as One who makes intercession for us.

Of course, terms like 'Advocate' and 'intercession' are metaphorical; and they are misused if they are allowed to suggest thoughts unworthy of the Christian revelation of God. In the interests of this revelation we must guard against the idea that it is necessary to overcome a reluctance on the part of God to be gracious and compassionate towards men. The true meaning of this terminology is sacrificial, or, if the word is preferred, mediatorial. The words describe the high priestly service of One who places the power of His self-offering at the disposal of men, making Himself the medium and the means of their approach to God. In the experience of the Christian man this ministry is infinitely precious. On the one hand, it delivers him from the peril of supposing that communion with God is the fellowship of equals, and, on the other hand, it saves him from the despair of regarding communion as impossible for imperfect men. Positively expressed, Christ's present service is the supreme opportunity for fellowship with God. Apart from experiences, often momentary, of special illumination, the Christian's enjoyment of fellowship is a mediated fellowship. Only when the process of sanctification is complete do we see God face to face. There may be radiant souls for whom the divine light shines continually, but their experience gives us no warrant for believing that such is meant to be our normal lot. We discourage, and even torture, ourselves needlessly, if we think otherwise. Most men, and these by no means the least earnest or spiritually-minded, need a bridge for faith, an anchor for hope, a personal channel for the exercise of love to God. For this deeply human need Christ's present and abiding ministry is the indispensable medium.

It is easy to deceive ourselves by supposing that the reality of fellowship is diminished by the fact that it is mediate. The truth is that, as mediate, it becomes richer and deeper than it could ever be if the Christian experience were, not life 'in Christ', but the unaided flight of our spirit to God. The fear, that something of its purity and strength is lost by the medium by which it is effected, is groundless, because the medium is Christ Himself and His redeeming work. Even when the material forms of water and of bread and wine are used in the sacraments of the Church, both the cleansing and the feeding of the soul are His work, and they have all the spirituality which belongs to His dealings with men. The perils of materialism are painfully real, as the history of the Church reveals, but they are due to man's tendency to be unimaginatively literal, not to the fact that our fellowship with God is mediated; and from this danger our true safeguard is the spirituality of the doctrine of the Incarnation, as it is expressed by St. John in the words: 'And the Word became flesh, and dwelt among us, and we beheld his glory, glory as of the only begotten from the Father, full of grace and truth.'

It may be said that there is no need to think of His ministry, since fellowship with Christ Himself is enough for every spiritual need. If we are tempted so to think, we are in danger of making a misleading distinction. Can we so distinguish between Christ Himself and what He does? Are not He and His work inseparable? It is not credible that He, who in the days of His flesh went about doing good, should have no ministry for His brethren now. Every consideration of Christian devotion and belief must lead us to believe that He has a ministry still, and that His vocation is that of the eternal Saviour of men. If, then, we have fellowship with Christ, we have indeed enough for every spiritual need, but this very fact means that we are receiving the benefits of His continued work, whether we recognize it or not, but to a degree less than is possible if we have a true grasp of its nature. His ministry is still manward, in that it reveals the love of God and constrains the hearts of men, but it is also Godward, in that it avails for men in things pertaining to God. Such, at least, is the belief of those who sing with understanding the well-known lines:[1]

> 'And didst Thou love the race that loved not Thee?
> And didst Thou take to heaven a human brow?
> Dost plead with man's voice by the marvellous sea?
> Art Thou his kinsman now?'

Whether we can affirm a present mediatorial ministry of Christ for men, depends mainly upon two things: the conviction that, in His death, He acted representatively for mankind, and the assurance that He is the living and abiding Lord. If, upon the Cross, He consummated a perfect obedience as the Son of Man, if there He bowed beneath the burden of sin, and voiced the sorrow of men, there is no reason at all why so signal a service for men should be ended. On the contrary, as the Risen and Exalted Lord, His victorious life enables Him to continue this ministry for men, freed from the limitations of flesh and blood. No more than on earth is His service that of a substitute; it is sacrificial through and through, in that its meanings and its blessings can be appropriated by men. United to Him by personal faith, and permitted, like the disciples of old, to share in the new covenant sealed by His blood, we have every opportunity to make His Sacrifice the way to communion and fellowship with God.

[1] Jean Ingelow.

It must be recognized, however, that while fellowship with God is enriched and perfected by reliance upon the continued ministry of Christ, its enlargement depends upon His work in its totality, on earth and in heaven. In these pages, its heavenly aspects have been emphasized because, through misunderstanding, they are often neglected, to the impoverishment of our communion with God. Nevertheless, those aspects of Christ's Sacrifice which are more fully described in the New Testament, and especially in the Gospel Story, are of supreme value because, as wrought in history, they are brought powerfully before our notice and become formative factors in Christian life and experience. The imperishable story of the Cross, and of the stages in the life of Christ which led up to it, the darkness of Gethsemane, the desolation of Calvary, the triumphant 'It is finished', crowned by the glory of the resurrection, all convey such an incomparable manifestation of divine love that every picture we have formed otherwise of what fellowship can be is dissolved and recreated. Herein is made known the God with whom we have to do, the lengths to which His love can go, the burdens it can bear, the sacrifices it can make. 'Herein is Agape, not that we loved God, but that He loved us, and sent His Son to be the expiation for our sins.' The Christian heart is warmed by this revelation and expression of love, and in Christ seeks, not reconciliation only, but intimate fellowship with such a God. It dares to enter upon an amazing life, in which every day has its discovery, in which pain is transformed into joy, suffering into triumph, and sacrifice into glory. The *Via Crucis* becomes the highway to fellowship with God.

These discoveries of the possibilities of fellowship extend to our fellowship with men, for these also are revealed and made possible in the Cross. In the light of our fellowship with the Crucified, and of our knowledge of His abiding priesthood, we gain a truer understanding of sin and of its divisive power in social and international life, and a more adequate vision of the ways of love in uniting individuals and peoples. We gain also a greater patience and a deeper humility in all our dealings with human frailty. We are given no economic secret which can solve the problems of our disordered world, but we do discover the dignity of human freedom and possibilities of growth and development, without which the plans of statesmen are vain. Above all, our prayers for the Kingdom of God attain a greater power and meaning. We receive the faith that moves mountains, the hope that endures, and the love that never faileth.

(g) *Sanctification and the Atonement*

As the perfect flowering of fellowship with God, sanctification depends in the same manner upon the work of God in Christ; it is based upon that work as it is wrought in history, and it rests also upon the realities of Christ's present redemptive ministry fulfilled on high. In view of this relationship, it would be necessary to repeat the argument presented in the last section, if we were to discuss at length the relation of sanctification to the Atonement. It would be necessary to show how Christ's continued work is required by the process of purification, illumination, and growth in perfect love. Instead of repeating this argument, it will be better to supplement it by showing how the various aspects of the Christian ideal illustrate this relationship.

We have seen how vitally sanctification is connected with ethical progress in New Testament teaching. The New Testament knows nothing of a spiritual ideal which is not also fully ethical. There is no more obvious sign of failure to attain the goal than conduct which denies the eternal values of truth, beauty, and goodness. This admitted fact adds force to the plea that the work of Christ upon which sanctification depends must, as a revelation of love, be also a perfect embodiment of righteousness. Unless the reality of evil is met, and the inevitable connexion between wrongdoing and penalty is honoured, there can be no adequate foundation for a doctrine of attainment which stops at nothing short of perfect and positive righteousness. In the history of Christian doctrine this emphasis upon righteousness is no new demand, although it figures more prominently in the teaching of the past than in many modern theories. Usually, however, it is associated almost exclusively with the idea of reconciliation; but it is much more strongly based if it is also connected with sanctification. No one can do other than treat the problem of evil with the utmost seriousness, if his conception of man's recovery is not only restoration to fellowship with God, but also that of perfect fidelity to the highest ethical principles. Every consideration, therefore, which compels us to affirm that, in the redemption of mankind, it was necessary that the Son of God should identify Himself with sinners, and enter into the judgment which rests upon sin, receives an added force when the Atonement is approached from the standpoint of sanctification. Indeed, that demand would be invested with an austerity too painful to contemplate, if, as happily is not the case, we were forced to think of sanctification exclusively as a doctrine of ethical perfection.

The next aspect for consideration is sanctification as the work of the Spirit. The Christian ideal, we saw, is linked closely with New Testament teaching concerning life in the Holy Spirit. There is no warrant for thinking of sanctification as a catastrophic spiritual gift imparted only after frantic and importunate prayer; but it is the climax of regeneration and renewal, of the process of enlightening and strengthening, whereby the believer is empowered for every task, and, above all, of that outpouring of the love of God in the heart which, as St. Paul reminds us, is 'through the Holy Spirit which was given unto us' (Rom. v. 5). We have already maintained that this work is not to be thought of as operating apart from the work of Christ, but rather as intimately connected with it. Moreover, it is manifested both in the personal experience of the individual believer, and in the corporate life and worship of the Church, in baptism and in the Eucharist which is so vitally connected with Christ's death and redeeming ministry. All these considerations serve to remind us that sanctification, as the work of the Spirit, is dependent upon the Atonement, and that, if our apprehension of the scope of this doctrine is not sufficiently large to include this work, it needs to be extended. Especially is the conception of the work of God in Christ as a continuous ministry, based upon Calvary, reinforced and confirmed. Sanctification by the Spirit and the Atonement are not alternative, but coincidental, doctrines.

When we turn to the content of the Christian ideal, and think of it as the attainment of sinless perfection, whether in this life or in that which is to come, our sense of dependence upon the work of God in Christ is immeasurably increased. With what other feelings than those of utter despair can we contemplate this aspect of the ideal unless we have at our disposal an unceasing and eternal ministry of redemption? In this fact lies the secret of the strength and comfort of the assurance of the writer of the Epistle to the Hebrews that Christ 'abideth for ever', and 'hath his priesthood unchangeable', and that, therefore, 'he is able to save to the uttermost them that draw near unto God through him, seeing he ever liveth to make intercession for them' (vii. 24 f.). A priesthood such as this means the possibility of immediate access to God in penitence and faith, an increased sensitiveness to sin, a truer knowledge of ourselves, a confidence that all things needful are provided for an otherwise impossible goal. The blessings offered to us are more lasting than our need, stronger than our fears, superior to defeat, and unconquered by death. Moreover, in bestowing other aspects of the ideal, the vision of God and the gift of perfect love, the work of God in Christ gives with them power to overcome sin and the promise of final victory.

As the attainment of the vision of God, sanctification is dependent upon the Atonement, because in that redeeming activity God is most truly found. When we meditate upon the meaning of the Cross, even to the imperfect degree to which its secret has been imparted to us now, we know instinctively that we have seen God. What form the final revelation will take, when out of the world of shadows we shall attain to the glory of the beatific vision, we cannot tell. Yet here and now we have the assurance that we are nearest to it when we see God in the face of the Crucified. If this be so, our highest wisdom, as well as our privilege, in private devotion and in public worship alike, is to meditate, and to adore, as we contemplate the divine drama of redemption, which begins with Creation itself, and is continued in the mystery of the Incarnation, the story of the Garden, the Cross, and the Resurrection, and is crowned by the ministry of the Son on high. Here, as nowhere else, we see God; and, seeing Him, we have all things, the knowledge of life and death, of His purposes for the world, and of the means whereby they shall be brought to pass. It is by the way of the Cross, and in its light alone, that, through cleansing and sacrifice, we may hope to behold God in His eternal beauty.

Lastly, as perfect love, the Christian ideal is eternally bound to the Cross. However nobly man has dreamed of love, he has not seen it in its perfectness, except there, in the love of God in Christ. Poured out upon the thankless and the undeserving, willing, if need be, to appear as a defeated love, which yet does not know the meaning of defeat, this love of God is the supreme inspiration and power for the ideal of love between men and peoples. That love is meant to be the final law of life, is proved by the fact that lesser ideals, claimed as practicable, break down and prove wanting. No City of God can be built on other foundations. The Christian, therefore, can give his ultimate allegiance to no other end, since this is an end in itself. In pursuing this ideal, he cannot escape the Cross. Happily, however, he is not only given a vision of the divine heart, but is vouchsafed the proof of a love in action which finds him in his sins, bears his burdens, and brings him home to God. And yet, be it said with reverence, an expression of divine love in the past is not enough for man's need. It is not enough that love should have been embodied once, in perfectness of deed, upon the plane of history. What is needed is no addition to this work of love, as if it were otherwise than complete, but its still continued expression, operative for man's attainment of the ideal of love it enshrines.

Nowhere, perhaps, is this need so evident as when we think of sanctification as perfect love. The very greatness of God's love, presented to us as the Christian ideal, overwhelms us by its demand. How shall we display this selfless love to others, or even to God Himself? Is such a love possible?

The difficulty is not met by the answer that love to God

and man is not produced by ourselves, but must come to us from heaven.[1] If we are but the tube or channel through which the divine love flows, we cannot speak of love to God and our neighbour as *our* love, poor though it be, but only as God's love reversed and redirected. It is far better to think of wings than of a tube, of love as an upward flight rather than a downward stream, and of God as sustaining and purifying our love rather than as transmitting, through us, His own love. Doubtless, in its beginnings, our love will bear the marks of Eros. It will need to be cleansed from self-regarding motives, to become, not Eros, but Agape itself. But if it hovers in the heavenly places, upborne by the love of God Himself, it will shed its defects, becoming like that on which it rests.

The presumption, however, of this growth is that God's love is continuously active, active as in the Cross itself, today as yesterday swiftly responsive to human need. And while we may be sure that, from its very nature, God's love is such, eternally operative, eternally outpoured, our love will best become like His if it is confronted, not with an inference, or a doctrine, but with an experience of that love doing still all that Christ did on Calvary long ago. When we try further to describe this ceaseless service of divine love, we can but use the language of symbol, since it is the least inadequate form of speech. In this sense alone dare we describe it as the Eternal Sacrifice, meaning thereby love's self-offering within the riches of the Divine Being, that, namely, of the Eternal Son, an offering with which we can identify ourselves in the fellowship of faith, as uttering for us all that we would say, and all that we do

[1] This is Nygren's view, in dependence upon Luther. See earlier, p. 222. 'Christian love is not produced by us, but it has to come from heaven'; it is, 'so to speak, the extension of God's love'; the Christian 'is merely the tube, the channel, through which God's love flows', *Agape and Eros*, II. 515-7.

say as our union with Him is perfected. Such love begets love. As the love we behold and trust is Agape, perfect self-giving love, so our poor love is cleansed from dross, becoming that of the children of God. That this love overflows in love to man, even to the thankless and the unworthy, is simply its obedience to its nature, as perfected in our love to God Himself.

Our claim, then, stands, that the experience of sanctification is based upon the Atonement, and to this submission we must now add that the experience elucidates the ministry on which it depends. This is true whether we think of sanctification as ethical perfection, as the work of the Holy Spirit, as complete victory over sin, as the attainment of the vision of God, or as perfect love. Into the Christian ideal all these elements enter; but most of all its dependence upon the work of God in Christ is seen, and its illuminative power is greatest, when it is interpreted as perfect love to God and man.

(*h*) *Forgiveness and Reconciliation as the Heart of the Gospel*

In this concluding section it remains for us to reunite the various aspects of the Christian experience which have been treated separately, and to relate them as a whole to the doctrine of the work of Christ. The Christian experience, we have seen, is one of forgiveness and reconciliation, an experience which includes the remission of sins and justification, and which implies fellowship with God and sanctification. How is this experience, considered as a unity, dependent upon the Atonement? Such an inquiry can lead us to nothing less than the heart of the Gospel, the Good News of God for men. It must be our endeavour, therefore, at the close of our investigation to describe this Gospel in its fulness.

But before we treat this theme, it is necessary to consider a preliminary question, which deeply affects any attempt to state the Gospel, and is raised by our investigation as a whole. Is the Christian experience of forgiveness and reconciliation bound up with the acceptance of a particular theory of the Atonement? In particular, does it depend upon the recognition of the redeeming work of Christ as both manward and Godward?

This question is less easy to answer than might appear at first sight, and perhaps the best way of treating it is to consider two alternatives, each of which is true.

On the one hand, forgiveness and reconciliation, as a religious experience, cannot be determined by our ability or inability to accept theological propositions. 'Thou believest that God is one; thou doest well: the devils also believe, and shudder.' These words of St. James (ii. 19) decide this issue for ever. On the other hand, it is not true that our beliefs do not matter. Faith is always determined by its object, and while it is undeniably true that Christ can work upon the heart, irrespective of theology, it is no less true that our beliefs may retard and limit the full enjoyment of the Christian experience. What if our beliefs are so unenlightened or so conventionally heterodox that faith, as a conscious relationship, has no worthy object in which to rest! Our estimate of Christ and of His work fixes the character and content of our faith in Him; and, in turn, the quality and depth of our faith influence our attitude to sin, our conformity to the divine will, our aspirations after holiness, and our attainment of abiding fellowship with God. We appear, then, to reach an impasse. A definite creed is not essential, and yet is of essential importance! What is the solution of this dilemma?

However much we may be tempted to do so, we cannot

gain intellectual relief by denying either of the alternatives we have outlined. Salvation does not depend on orthodoxy, and it is not independent of belief. Part of the solution lies in the different senses in which the word 'essential' is used in the dilemma stated above. Belief is not essential if it is merely a matter of cold intellectual assent; but it is of essential importance as providing a rational basis for the kind of faith exercised, and sometimes in order to make faith possible, especially in the case of the man whose religion is strongly controlled by reason.

A further explanation has been suggested earlier in our investigation, which applies to all theories of the Atonement, including that supported in this work; the view, namely, that the deficiencies of an imperfect creed can be overcome by the grace of God, that our response to the work of God in Christ may be richer than our affirmation, that, in a word, we may believe more than we confess. To this statement we must also add the fact that, whenever we believe in Christ, and trust ourselves to Him, He works upon our life with all the power which belongs to His actual redemptive activity, however little we may have apprehended its true character. As soon as we believe in Christ, that activity, whether it is recognized by us or not, is operative in our Christian experience, in spite of the fact that its power may be restricted by our intellectual prejudices and preoccupations. This is a consideration of infinite comfort to the theologian who is prepared to confess that, conceivably, he may be mistaken, or who admits that in important respects his theology has been inadequate to the facts of Christianity.

Perhaps the truest way of putting the matter is to say that the vital thing in Christian practice is to make the kind of response, or to have the faith-relationship, which is rational if Christ has done all things necessary to salvation.

Once we have made this response, the issues are in the hands of God. This attitude does not mean, and must not be allowed to mean, that all theories of the Atonement, our own included, are matters of minor importance. Whatever theory he holds, the theologian must claim, and must feel himself entitled to claim, that the view he accepts accounts best for the blessings springing from faith in Christ, because it supplies the most satisfactory explanation of the work of God in Christ. Unless he believes this, he has no right to accept a theory at all, much less to commend it to the acceptance of others. He will admit that every theological construction, including his own, is the work of men who know in part and understand in part, and that, when that which is perfect is come, then that which is in part shall be done away; but he has no right to admit that another theory is as good as his own. In accordance with this point of view, it is here claimed that, while the acceptance of a mediatorial theory of the Atonement is not a necessary condition of the Christian experience, the quality and the range of the faith-relationship, which is the basis of forgiveness and reconciliation, presuppose such a theory, or its rational equivalent; and that, other things being equal, this faith is most likely to be exercised, when a Godward, as well as a manward, explanation of Christ's redeeming work is accepted fully and unreservedly.

Now that we have considered the relation between faith and belief, we can return to the question proposed at the beginning of the section. The test of a theology is the extent to which, after full investigation, it permits us to describe the Gospel. We ask, therefore, What is the Gospel, and in what manner does it depend on the work of God in Christ?[1]

[1]Perhaps the final test of the theologian would be his ability to write a tract.

(1) In the first place, the Gospel is the good news that the barriers to fellowship with God are set aside when we loathe our sins and long to be delivered from them. It is the declaration that, in response to our faith in Christ, God is ready to receive us, to clothe us with the garment of His righteousness, and to give to us the possibility of communion with Himself. It is further the assurance that He actually restores us to this fellowship, giving us peace with Himself, freedom from fear, sin, and death, and, above all, the joyous life of true and abiding sonship. The Gospel is also the announcement of a life of progressive fellowship, in which through faith and worship we know Him increasingly, and have fellowship with His Son in suffering, in joy, and in service. It is, finally, the promise that, here or hereafter, we can attain to complete victory over sin, that we shall surely receive the beatific vision of God and know the meaning of perfect love. All this is the Gospel, but it is not all the Good News.

(2) The Gospel is, further, the assurance that all these gifts of the Christian experience come to us, not only as individuals, but pre-eminently as members of the divine Society which is the Church, the Body of Christ. That sins are remitted, that men are put right with God and restored to the life of fellowship, we learn through the Scriptures; but, apart from the needs of the primitive Church, we should have had no Scriptures, and in these writings are made known both the revelation of God and the discoveries of the Society itself. These primary experiences, therefore, are personal and communal. Still more evident is this debt to the Church in the richer experiences of communion with God and perfection in love. Through repeated acts of worship, in Baptism and the Eucharist, and in manifold relationships with our fellow-

members within the Body, we discover the possibilities open to us and the means to their attainment. In the Church we inherit the treasures of Christian tradition, the wisdom of its doctors and teachers, the inspiration of its poets, the sanctity of its saints. We are put, as it were, to school. We learn how to forgive one another, how to accept the unworthy as worthy, to restore men to fellowship with ourselves, to grow with them in attaining the knowledge of God, to aspire to the Christian ideal, and to find its realization in daily life. These experiences are gained in a Society which is the home of the Spirit, the temporal manifestation of the Kingdom and the earnest of its fulfilment in heaven and on earth. This, too, is the Gospel. Yet there is still more.

(3) The Gospel is also the good news that what the individual man experiences in himself, and discovers in the Church, is meant to extend to all mankind in its social relationships, in the life of communities and nations, in the whole universe of living men and created things. It is the message that barriers between nations can be removed, that unworthy peoples can be deemed worthy and restored to fellowship within the family of nations, that mutual co-operation is possible and world unity is not an empty dream. Anything less than this is an imperfect Gospel; it is also bankrupt statesmanship, since the alternative is a world in perpetual fear and expectation of woes to come. As St. Paul saw it, the Gospel is the message of the reconciliation of all things in heaven and on earth. This also is the Good News.

Grand and moving, however, in their personal and communal implications, as all these conceptions are, they are still not the whole Gospel. They describe the expression which it takes in life and the extent of its manifestation, but not the divine activity by which alone the Christian experience is brought into being; and without this vital element the Good News is but half told.

(4) The Gospel, further, is especially the message that, in Christ, God has done, and is doing still, all things necessary to meet man's need, to remove his desolation and to establish his blessedness. With God lies the initiative; in Him alone is man's hope. The Gospel is the announcement of His saving work in Christ, in His life, His cross, His resurrection, and His continued ministry on high. This claim is valid of the Christian experience in its most personal aspects and in its widest manifestations.

At every stage of our inquiry we have been compelled to think of this redeeming work of God in Christ, because upon it, at every point, the experiences we have described depend. While this work is not limited to the Cross, it finds its centre and focus there; and, in a summary statement, it is in terms of the Cross that its results can best be described. In disclosing the reality of the love of God, the Cross awakens and deepens penitence, and, as expressing divine sorrow for the sin of the world, it supplies a vehicle for a human contrition which is communal as well as personal. As embodying the perfect obedience of Christ, it provides an object for faith so ethical and spiritual that, with complete self-consistency, God can receive the unworthy as righteous, in virtue of the righteousness to which they freely consent. As giving effect to a love which makes itself one with sinners, it restores them to fellowship with God, to freedom, and true sonship. As the symbol in time of an abiding ministry for men, it sustains continued growth in the knowledge of God and ensures the attainment of perfect love to God and man.

Of this message, to a far greater degree than of all that has been previously described, we can say that it is the good news of the Gospel, since it is the foundation upon which all things else depend, and without which they cannot come into existence. Nevertheless, vital as it is, even this message cannot be said to be the fulness of the Gospel until it is made plain how the blessings assured by the Cross become operative in the Christian experience, both personal and collective.

(5) In addition, therefore, to all that has been described, the Gospel is the good news that the blessings offered to us, in the work of God in Christ, spring from the faith-relationship between believing men and Christ Himself. Both elements, the work and the faith, are essential. Christ does not save us apart from faith: faith does not restore us apart from Christ. He became one with us: we must become one with Him. Without the affirmation of this dual process of self-identification, and the results which follow from it, there is no complete statement of the Gospel. We must be careful also to give a sufficient depth of meaning to the idea of faith in Christ, since the content of this phrase, which describes the deepest element in Christian experience, may range from respect for a human personality to adoration for a Divine Redeemer. It is in the latter sense alone that faith in Christ, whilst beyond value in all its forms, is of the essence of the Gospel, for Christ and His work are one. Faith, moreover, is not a purely human response, because its character is determined by its object, Christ Himself as active to redeem. In this sense it is the gift of God.

The part of faith is to receive Christ as the bearer of all the blessings which He brings, and to appropriate these blessings as its own. Does He reveal the love of God? Faith is the reverent acceptance of that love, the adoring recognition that it exists, and the reception of its power. Does He suffer for us? Faith is our response to His suffering in repentance and hope. Is He obedient unto death, sorrowful, and submissive, in the name of mankind, with whom He has made Himself one? Faith finds His obedience the highway and the means of a penitent approach to God. Is His outpoured life the medium by which men may enter into communion with God? Faith lays its hand upon His self-offering, entering into its significance, and making it the sacrifice by which man draws near to God. In His exalted life, does He still continue to minister for men? Faith relies upon this ministry and receives its gifts, finding deeper and richer fellowship with Him and daily progress in the knowledge of God; and this it continues to do until, in the mercy of God, we see Him face to face and know the life of perfect love.

Like the light which came to Saul of Tarsus on the Damascus road, faith may come to us as a flash, while we read the Gospel Story, while it is described to us by others, or as we meditate upon its meaning. Again, faith may steal upon us so gradually that we cannot tell how or when it came. In either case it is present only in its beginnings, with much imperfection and an intermingling of earthly dross. If it truly rests upon the work of Christ in all its fulness, it is a life process, determined from beginning to end by the ministry of Him on whom it depends. Thus it is that, on the one hand, faith is the most personal and intimate of all forms of the Christian experience, and, on the other hand, it is communal, since it is enriched daily by the teaching and worship of the Church, its sacramental rites and its fellowship, and by the manifold experiences of sacrificial living in the world of men. A relationship which begins in time, it persists through death, and continues in eternity.

Such, then, is the Gospel; no small or insignificant thing, but the most momentous tidings that men can receive, both as individuals and as members of communities. The Gospel concerns man as an individual, since it tells of his deliverance from the hampering folds of sin, the full development of his personality, his well-being in time and in eternity. It also concerns him vitally as a member of human society, since it makes possible his true fellowship with God and men, determines the character of his institutions, and establishes the true relationships of nations and peoples. In each of these, its principal aspects, it is in the fullest sense a Gospel of forgiveness and reconciliation. Always it is experienced as something new, as something inexpressibly rich, which issues, as by some inner and divine necessity, in the utmost variety and growth. In its final significance, it is the promise, not of a return to some fabled perfection lost in the beginnings of the race, but of the fulfilment of the mind and purpose of God for man before the world was or earth received its form. This assurance is not easily gained ; it is the vision for those who have eyes to see ; and for them, only because, like Stephen of old, they behold the heavens opened and the Son of Man standing on the right hand of God.

INDEX OF NEW TESTAMENT REFERENCES

Matthew:
iii. 2 - - - - 8
11 - - - 9
iv. 17 - - - 16
v. 8 - - 146, 186, 199
9 - - 111, 113, 147
11 - - - 161
43 - - - 204
44 f. - 111, 113, 147
48 - - - 185
vi. 9 - - - - 113
11 f. - - - 138
12 - - 12, 15
14 f. - - 12, 17
33 - - - 59
vii. 11 - - 111, 113
12 - - 176, 204
20 - - - 174
ix. 13 - - - 204
x. 13 - - - 102
20 - - - 180
37 - - - 161
40 - - 138, 161
xi. 19 - - - 40
20 - - - 9
21 - - - 16
xii. 7 - - - - 204
32 - - 12, 15, 180
37 - - - 41
41 - - - 16
xvi. 19 - - - 13
xvii. 26 - - 109, 111
xviii. 5 - - - - 161
15-22 - - - 12
15 - - - 12
18 - - - 13
20 - - - 162
21 f. - - 12, 175
22 - - - 15

Matthew:
xviii. 23-35 - - -12, 18
24 - - - 18
27 - - - 12
28 - - - 19
32 - - 12, 15, 19
35 - - 12 f., 17, 19
xix. 21 - - - 186
xxii. 40 - - - 186
xxiii. 30 - - 131, 133
xxv. 35 - - - 161
46 - - - 186
xxvi. 28 - - 11, 14
xxviii. 20 - - - 162

Mark:
i. 4- - - - 3, 8
15 - - - 16
ii. 1-12 - - - 11
5 - - - -11, 15
7 - - - - 3
9 - - - - 11
10 f. - - -11, 13
iii. 28 - - 11, 13, 15
29 - - 11, 180
iv. 12 - - - 3, 8
vi. 12 - - - 9
35-44 - - - 164
vii. 15 - - - 176
21 f. - - - 175
viii. 1-9 - - - 164
34 - - - 176
35-7 - - - 176
38 - - 138, 161
x. 15 - - - 175
17 - - - 186
30 - - - 186
38 - - 176, 250
xi. 25 - - 11 f, 15, 17

Mark:
xi. 26 - - - 12
xii. 29-31 - - 186, 203
xiii. 11 - - - 180
xiv. 24 - - 11, 14, 152
32-42 - - - 250
xv. 34 - - - 250

Luke:
i, ii. - - - - 165
i. 77 - - - 3
79 - - - 101
ii. 14 - - - 101
iii. 3 - - - - 3, 8
iv. 18 - - 11, 180
21 - - - 59
v. 10 - - 131, 133
21 - - - 3
32 - - - 16
vi. 27 f. - - 175, 204
31 - - 176, 204
35 - 111, 175, 187
36 - - - 185
vii. 29 - - - 40
35 - - - 40
42 - - - 6
43 - - - 6
47 - - -12, 15
48 - - -13, 15
49 - - - 13
x. 5 f. - - - 102
13 - - - 16
29 - - - 40
xi. 4 - - 12 f., 15, 17
13 - - - 111
20 - - - 59
32 - - - 16
xii. 6 f. - - - 147
10 - - 12, 15, 180
12 - - - 180
24 - - - 147
27 - - - 147
50 - - - 250
xiii. 3 - - - - 16
5 - - - - 16

Luke:
xv. 7 - - - - 16
10 - - - 16
11-32 - - 20-3, 113, 147
20 - - - 22
22-4 - - - 21 f.
xvi. 9 - - - - 186
15 - - - 40
19-31 - - - 19
30 - - - 19
31 - - - 16
xvii. 3 f. - - 12 f., 15, 17
7-10 - - - 175
xviii. 14 - - -20, 40
xxiii. 34 - - 12 f., 15
xxiv. 47 - - - 3 f., 8
49 - - - 181

John:
i. 12 - 111, 113, 116
14 - - 150, 199
18 - - 150, 199
iii. 5-8 - - - 182
16 - - 207, 224
18 - - - 60
34 - - - 182
35 - - - 206
36 - - - 60
v. 20 - - - 206
24 - - - 59
28 f. - - - 58
37 - - - 150
38 - - - 144
42 - - - 207
vi. 40 - - -58, 60
44 - - - 58
46 - - - 150
47 - - - 60
54 - - - 58
56 - - - 143
63 - - - 182
vii. 39 - - - 182
viii. 31 f. - - 109, 144
36 - - - 109
42 - - 113, 207

John:
x. 1-16 - - - 153
17 - - 206, 224
xi. 3 - - - 207
5 - - - - 207
36 - - - 207
52 - 111, 113, 116
xii. 45 - - 151, 199
xiii-xvi. - - - - 153
xiii. 1 - - - - 207
23 - - - 207
34 - 179, 204, 208
xiv. 7 - - - 150, 199
9 - - - 150, 199
10 - - - 144 f.
12 - - - 207
15 - - 179, 207
20 - - - 145
21 - - 179, 207
23 - - - 207
26 - - - 183
27 - - - 103
28 - - - 207
xv. 1-8 - - - 153
2 - - - - 188
4 - - - 143, 145
5 - - - - 143
6 - - - - 143
7 - - - - 143 f.
9 f. - - 145, 206 f.
12 - - 179, 207 f.
13 - - - 175
14 - - - 179
17 - - - 208
26 - - - 153
xvi. 8 - - - - 183
13 - - - 183
27 - - - 207
33 - - - 103
xvii. - - - - 153
19 - - 188, 224
21 - - - 145
23 - - - 145 f.
24 - - - 206
26 - - - 145 f.
xix. 26 - - - 207

John:
xx. 2 - - - - 207
19 - - - 103
22 f. - - - 183
23 - - - 13
xxi. 5 - - - - 111
7 - - - - 207
15-7 - - - 207 f.
20 - - - 207
22 - - - 58

Acts:
i. 8 - - - - 181
ii. 1-13 - - - 184
38 - - 2-4, 8, 181
42 - - - 132
iii. 19 - - - 9
iv. 31 - - - 184
v. 1-11 - - - 184
31 - - - 2-4, 8
vi. 1 - - - - 184
3 - - - - 181
5 - - - - 184
vii. 55 - - - 184
60 - - - 15
viii. 22 - - - 3 f., 8
x. 36 - - - 102
43 - - - 2-4
44 - - - 181
47 - - - 181
xi. 12 - - - 181
17 - - - 181
18 - - - 9
24 - - - 184
xiii. 24 - - - 9
38 - - - 2, 4
39 - - 41, 44
52 - - - 184
xvii. 30 - - - 9
xix. 2 - - - - 181
4 - - - - 9
xx. 21 - - - 9
22 f. - - - 181
28 - - - 155
xxvi. 18 - - 2, 4, 8
20 - - - 9

Romans:
i. 7 - - - - 205
17 - - -48, 51
18-32 - - - 89
32 - - - 48
ii. 4 - - - - 9
13 - - -43, 57
16 - - - 58
26 - - - 48
iii. 4 - - 47, 63
5 - - - 51, 63
20 - - - 42
21 - - - 51
22 - - - 51
24 5, 42 f., 45, 47, 135
25 f. - 43, 45-7, 51
26 - - 44 f., 48
28 - - - 43 f.
30 - - - 44 f.
iv. 2 - - - - 42
3-12 - - - 53 f.
5 - - - - 43 f.
7 - - 3, 34, 54, 243
9 - - - - 51
11 - - - 51
13 - - - 51
19-21 - - - 56
22 - - - 53 f.
23-5 - - - 54
25 - - -45, 50
v. 1 f. - - 104, 106 f.
1 - - - 44 f., 107
2 - - - - 107
5 - - - 185, 262
6-9 - - - 89
8 - - 204, 224, 248
9 - - -44-7, 90, 95
10 f. 85, 87-91, 92, 95, 248
10 - 85 f., 89, 96
16 - - 45, 48 f.
18 - - 45, 48 f.
19 - - 43, 48, 57
vi. 1-7 - - - 193 f.
1-14 - - - 137
2 - - - 190 f., 193

Romans:
vi. 3-11 - - - 163
4 - - - - 140
6 - - 140, 190 f., 224
7 - - - - 47
8 - - - - 140
11 - - 136, 190 f.
12 - - - 192
13 - - - 97
14 - - 176, 190 f.
18 - - - 109
19 - - - 187
20 - - - 109
21 - - - 110
22 - - 109, 190 f.
vii. 12 - - - 177
14 - - - 177
viii. 1 - - - - 136 f.
2 - - - - 109
4 - - - 48, 177
6 - - - - 103
7 - - - - 92
9-11 - - - 137
9 - - - 136, 181
11 - - - 181
14 - - - 115
15 - - - 114
16 f. - - - 115
16 - - - 181
17 - - - 140
19 - - - 115
21 - - 110, 115
23 - - - 5, 114
26 - - - 182
28 - - - 205
30 - - - 42
33 - - 42 f., 57
ix. 4 - - - - 114
8 - - - - 115
26 - - - 115
30 - - - 51
x. 3 - - - - 51
4 - - - - 51
6 - - - - 51
xi. 15 - - - 90
16 - - - 218

Romans:
xi. 17 - - - 131
28 - - - 88
xii. - - - - 177
1 - - - 97, 217
6-8 - - - 185
10 - - - 204
13 - - 132, 134
xiii. 8 - - - - 204
9 f. - - - 204
13 - - - 178
xiv. 10 - - - 58
12 - - - 58
17 - - 103, 136
xv. 2 - - - - 177
3 - - - - 177
7 - - - - 177
13 - - - 102 f.
14 - - - 177
16 - - - 219
26 - - 132, 134
27 - - - 132
33 - - - 103
xvi. 20 - - - 103

1 *Corinthians:*
i. 9 - - - - 133
30 - - 5, 136 f.
31 - - - 136
ii. 1 - - - - 150
9 - - - - 205
iii. 16 - - - 182
iv. 4 - - - 43, 47, 57
5 - - - 44, 58
vi. 11 - - 182, 219
19 - - - 182
vii. 11 - - - 84 f.
35 - - - 178
viii. 1-3 - - - 148
3 - - - - 205
ix. 23 - - 131, 134
27 - - - 192
x. 16 - - 47, 133
18 - - - 131
20 - - - 131
24 - - - 177
32 f. - - - 177
xi. 1 - - - - 177
25 - - - 152
27 - - - 47
xii. 3 - - - 136, 182
27 - - - 152
xiii. - - 177, 205, 210
12 - - 148, 198
xiv. - - - - 185
1 - - - - 206
26 - - - 165
33 - - - 103
40 - - - 178
xv. 3-5 - - - 163
22 - - - 135
xvi. 22 - - - 205

2 *Corinthians:*
i. 7 - - - - 131
22 - - - 182
ii. 2 f. - - - 149
7 - - - - 6
10 - - - 6
17 - - - 109
iii. 18 - - 147, 199
iv. 4 - - - - 149
6 - - - 147, 199
v. 5 - - - - 182
10 - - 58, 62
14 - - 86, 204
17 - - - 136
18-20 - 85-7, 88, 95
18 - - - 90
19 - - 90, 95, 135
20 - - - 85
21 - - 51, 86, 250
vii. 1 - - - - 187
3 - - - - 140
9 f. - - - 9
viii. 4 - - - 132, 134
9 - - - - 177
23 - - 131, 134
ix. 9 - - - - 51

2 Corinthians:
ix. 13 - - 132, 134
xii. 13 - - - 6 f.
21 - - - 9
xiii. 11 - - - 103
13 - - - 132 f.

Galatians:
ii. 7 - - - - 148
9 - - - - 132
11-18 - - - 184
16 - - - 42-5
20 120, 139-41, 148, 204
21 - - - 51
iii. 2 - - - 181
5 - - - - 52
6 - - - - 52
7-9 - - - 52
8 - - 42, 44 f., 53
11 - 43 f., 48, 53
13 - - - 250
21 - - - 51
24 - - 44 f., 176
26 - - - 115 f.
28 - - - 154
iv. 5 - - 114, 116, 176
7 - - - - 115
9 - - - - 148
28 - - - 115
v. 1 - - - - 109
5 - - - -51, 57
6 - - - - 204
13 - - 109, 177
22 f. - - - 177
22 - 103, 181, 204
25 - - - 181
26 - - - 181
vi. 1 - - - - 177
6 - - - 132, 134
16 - - - 102

Ephesians:
i. 5 - - - 114, 116
6 - - - - 205
7 - 2, 4 f., 34, 47

Ephesians:
i. 13 - - - 182
14 - - - 5
22 f. - - - 137
23 - - - 152
ii. 4 ff. - - - 140
6 - - - 140
11-22 - - - 93
12 - - - 96
13 - - 91, 47, 104
14-7 - - 100, 104-6
14 f. - - - 91
15 - - 92, 104
16 - - 85 f., 91-3
17 f. - - 92, 105
17 - - 91, 104
18 - - 93, 182
19 f. - - - 154
19 - - - 99
21 f. - - - 154
21 - - - 99
iii. 4 - - - - 150
9 - - - - 150
16 - - - 182
18 f. - - - 150
iv. 3 - - - - 182
4 - - - - 182
12 f. - - - 187
12 - - - 152
13 - - - 219
18 - - - 96
30 - - -5, 181
32 - - 6 f., 18
v. 1 - - - - 115
2 - - - - 177
11 - - - 132
14 - - - 165
19 - - - 165
22-vi. 9 - - 178
25-7 - 155, 218, 224
25 - - 177, 204
30 - - - 152
vi. 15 - - - 102
19 - - - 150
23 - - - 102
24 - - - 205

Philippians:
i. 5 - - - 132
7 - - - - 131-3
11 - - - 51
ii. 1 - - - - 132 f.
4 - - - - 177
5-11 - - 165, 177
14 f. - - - 115
19 - - - 136
20 - - - 148
24 - - - 136
iii. 8 - - - - 147
9 - - - -51, 71
10 - - 133, 147
12 f. - - - 192
iv. 1 - - - - 136 f.
7 - - - - 103
8 - - - - 178
9 - - - - 103
13 - - 136, 152
14 - - - 132
15 - - 132, 134

Colossians:
i. 13 - - - 205
14 - - 2, 4 f., 34
15 - - - 149
18 - - - 152
19-22 - - - 93-9
19 - - - 150
20 f. - - -85, 91
20 - - 47, 104 f.
21 f. - - 195, 224
22 - - - 187
24 - - - 152
26 f. - - - 150
28 - - - 187
ii. 2 - - - - 149 f.
9 - - - - 150
12 - - - 140
13 - - 6 f., 140
iii. 1 - - - - 140
3 - - - - 148 f.
11 - - - 154
12 - - - 177
13 - 6 f., 18, 177

Colossians:
iii. 14 - - 177, 204
15 - - - 103
16 - - - 164
18-iv. 1 - - 178
iv. 3 - - - - 150
12 - - - 187

1 *Thessalonians:*
i. 1 - - 104, 136 f., 149
4 - - - - 205
6 - - - - 177
iii. 8 - - - - 136
12 - - - 204
13 - - 187, 194
iv. 1 - - - - 136
3 - - - 187
9 - - - - 204
12 - - - 178
v. 8 - - - - 204
19 - - - 181
23 - 103, 187, 194

2 *Thessalonians:*
i. 1 - - - - 149
iii. - - - - 103

1 *Timothy:*
ii. 1-vi. 19 - - 178
1-11 - - - 179
iii. 16 - 40, 165, 183
v. 22 - - - 132

2 *Timothy:*
i. 14 - - - 183
ii. 11-3 - - - 165
11 - - - 140
12 - - - 140
22 - - - 206
25 - - - 9
iii. 4 - - - - 206
iv. 8 - - - - 206

Titus:
ii. 1-iii. 2 - - - 178
ii. 1-10 - - - 179

Titus:
iii. 4-7 - - - 165
4 f. - - - 206
5 - - - - 183
7 - - - - 41

Philemon:
6 - - - - 132
16 - - - 137
17 - - 131, 134

Hebrews:
i. 2 - - - - 116
5 - - - - 116
8 - - - - 116
ii. 4 - - - - 183
10 - - 116, 188
14 - - - 132
iii. 6 - - - - 116
7 - - - - 183
iv. 3 - - - - 149
14 - - - 116
v. 5 - - - - 116
8 - - - - 116
9 - - - 188, 224
vi. 1 - - - 9, 189
4-6 - - - 196
4 - - - 181, 183
5 - - - - 149
6 - - - 9, 116
10 - - - 206
18-20 - - - 149
vii. 2 - - - - 102
3 - - - - 116
24 f. - - - 263
25 - - 189, 224
28 - - 116, 188
ix. 8 - - - - 183
22 - - - 3
x. 14 - - 189, 224
15 - - - 183
18 - - - 3
24 - - - 206
29 - - - 116
33 - - - 131

Hebrews:
xii. 2 - - - - 188
5 f. - - - 116
7 - - - - 116
8 - - - - 116
14 - - - 197
23 - - - 189
xiii. 1-6 - - - 179
1 - - - - 206
16 - - 132, 134
20 - 103, 189, 224

James:
i. 4 - - - - 188
12 - - - 206
25 - - - 109
ii. 1-9 - - - 179
5 - - - - 206
8 - - - 109, 206
12 - - - 109
14-26 - - - 179
21 - - - 41
24 - - - 41
25 - - - 41
iii. 1-12 - - - 179
iv. 1-6 - - - 179
5 - - - - 183
v. 15 - - - 3 f.

1 Peter:
i. 2 - - - - 183
8 - - - - 206
9 - - - - 217
12 - - - 183
14 - - - 116
22 - - - 206
ii. 5 - - - - 218
ii. 11-iii. 12 - - 178
13-iii. 9 - - 179
16 - - - 109
iv. 13 - - 131, 133 f.
14 - - - 183
v. 1-5 - - - 178
1 - - - 131, 133
14 - - - 102

2 *Peter:*
i. 4 - - - 131, 133
7 - - - - 206
21 - - - 183
iii. 9 - - - - 9

1 *John:*
i. 1-4 - - - 151
3 - - - - 132 f.
6 - - - 133, 146
7 - - - - 132
8 f. - - - 196
9 - - - - 3 f., 8
ii. 1 f. - - 196, 224
3 - - - - 179
4 - - - - 179
5 f. - - 145 f., 207
6 - - - - 144
7 - - - - 179
10 - - - 208
12 - - - 3 f.
14 - - - 144
15 - - - 207
24 - - - 144, 146
27 - - - 144
28 - - - 144
iii. 1 - - - 111, 113
2 - 111, 113, 151, 188, 199
3 - - - - 188
6 - 144, 188, 190, 195
7 f. - - - 179
9 - 144, 188, 190, 195
10 - 111, 113, 208
11 - - - 208
14 - - - 208
15 - - - 144
16 - - 207, 224
17 - - - 144
22 - - - 179
23 - - - 208
24 - 144, 146, 182
iv. 2 - - - - 182
6 - - - - 182
7 - - - - 208
8 - - - - 207

1 *John:*
iv. 10 - - 207, 224
11 - - - 208
12 - 144, 150, 188
13 - - 144, 182
15 - - - 144
16 - - 144-6, 207
18 - - 188, 208
20 - - 150, 207 f.
21 - - 179, 208
v. 2 f. - - - 179
2 - - 111, 113, 207 f.
6 - - - - 182
8 - - - - 182
16 - - - 196
18 - 188, 190, 195
20 - - - 145

2 *John:*
1 - - - - 208
2 - - - - 144
9 - - - - 144
11 - - - 132

3 *John:*
1 - - - - 208
15 - - - 102

Jude:
3 - - - - 217
19 f. - - - 183

Apocalypse:
i. 9 - - - - 131
ii. 4 - - - - 206
5 - - - - 9
16 - - - 9
19 - - - 206
21 - - - 9
22 - - - 9
iii. 3 - - - - 9
19 - - - 9
20 - - - 153
iv. 11 - - - 165
v. 9 f. - - - 165

Apocalypse:
v. 12 f. - - - 165
ix. 20 f. - - - 9
xi. 17 f. - - - 165
xv. 3 f. - - - 165
xvi. 9 - - - - 9
11 - - - 9
xviii. 4 - - - - 132

Apocalypse:
xix. 6-8 - - - 165
xxi. 2 - - - - 155
7 - - - - 116
9 - - - - 155
xxii. 4 - - - - 199
11 - - 41, 60
17 - - - 155

INDEX OF PROPER NAMES

Abbott, T. K., 91, 92, 94, 96, 97, 98, 105, 219.
Akiba, 158.
Angus, S., 159.
Aquinas, 65, 198, 202, 213.
Aristotle, 202.
Athanasius, 212.
Augustine, 65, 198, 212.

Baeck, L., 26.
Barclay, R., 202.
Barth, K., 73.
Beet, J. A., 43, 98, 106, 107.
Benedict, 198.
Bernard, J. H., 41, 111, 113, 208.
Bernard, St., 198.
Bigg, C., 183.
Billerbeck, P., 17.
Bousset, W., 159.
Boylan, P., 39, 44, 47, 50, 106, 219.
Brilioth, Y., 221.
Büchsel, F., 5, 46, 85, 90, 91.
Bultmann, R., 146.
Burnaby, J., 205, 212.
Burton, E. de W., 36, 37.

Calvin, 29, 70, 253.
Clemen, C., 159.
Conybeare, F. C., 97.
Creed, J. M., 120.

Dakin, A., 253.
Dalman, G., 146.
Dante, 199.
Davey, F. N., 146.
Davidson, A. B., 156.
Deissmann, G. A., 46, 114, 135, 136, 137, 138.
Denney, J., 49, 50, 86, 88, 89, 106, 121, 122, 123, 126, 253.
Dibelius, M., 92, 94, 105, 132, 148, 174.
Dimond, S. G., 103, 165.
Dodd, C. H., 35, 36, 38, 70, 71, 97, 98, 219, 220.
Dominic, 198.

Ellicott, C. J., 94, 105.
Ewald, 94.

Faber, F. W., 199.
Farmer, H. H., 126, 127.
Findlay, G. G., 104, 106, 219.
Fisher, G. P., 240.
Flew, R. N., 1, 8, 137, 153, 181, 186, 192, 197, 202, 210, 213, 221.
Foerster, W., 88, 92, 104, 106.
Forsyth, P. T., 221.
Fox, G., 202.
Francis of Assisi, 198.
Franks, R. S., xvi, 1, 65, 67, 240.

Garvie, A. E., 120, 121, 221.
Gerhardt, P., 211.
Gloege, G., 153.
Goodspeed, E. J., 91.
Gore, C., 194.

Harnack, A., 66, 67, 120, 222, 240.
Hauck, F., 132.
Haupt, P., 94.
Headlam, A. C., *see* Sanday.
Hebert, A. G., 209.
Hegel, 120.
Hendry, G. S., 93.

Herrmann, W., 120, 121, 166, 168.
Hofmann, J. von, 98.
Hort, F. J. A., 96, 106.
Hoskyns, E., 146, 208.
Howard, W. F., 91, 113, 131, 138, 160.
Howe, J., xxi.
Hügel, F. von, 223.
Hunter, A. M., 165.

Ignatius, 160.
Ignatius, of Loyola, 198.
Inge, W. R., 223.
Ingelow, J., 258.
Irenaeus, 198, 212.

James, W., 223.

Kaftan, J., 120.
Kennedy, H. A. A., 159.
Kennett, R. H., 25, 156.
Kirk, K. E., 146, 147, 148, 158, 198, 199, 200, 201, 202.
Klöpper, 94.
Knox, W. L., 159.
Kosnetter, J., 8.

Lachmann, C., 106.
Lake, K., 41, 102, 132.
Lidgett, J. S., 112, 116, 154, 219.
Lightfoot, J. B., 49, 91, 94, 96, 97, 98, 132, 207.
Loewe, H., 158.
Lofthouse, W. F., 112.
Loofs, F., 82.
Luce, H. K., 6.
Luther, 46, 66, 82, 209, 222, 238, 240, 265.

Macdonald, A. B., 164.
Mackintosh, H. R., 67, 236, 239.
McGiffert, A. C., 41.
Manson, T. W., 12, 17, 26, 113, 186.
Martineau, J., 197.
Matthews, W. R., xviii.
Meecham, H. G., 50.
Melanchthon, 67.
Meyer, H. A. W., 43, 88, 97, 98, 105, 106.
Michael, J. H., 147, 178.
Milton, 199.
Moberly, R. C., 28, 30, 236, 240.
Moberly, W. H., 1.
Moffatt, J., 94, 104, 105, 106, 147, 174, 205, 206.
Montefiore, C. G., 146, 158, 175.
Moore, G. F., 26, 27.
Moulton, J. H., 85, 105, 106, 134.
Moulton & Milligan, 6, 55.
Müller, J. T., xix, 82.

Nygren, A., 73, 209, 213, 222, 238, 265.

Oesterley, W. O. E., 26.
Oman, J., 76, 123, 124, 125.

Penington, I., 202.
Perkins, H. W., 190, 197, 209.
Philippi, F. A., 37, 49.
Platt, F., 190.
Plummer, A., 6, 43, 85, 147, 182.
Pope, W. B., 75, 210.
Procksch, O., 187.

Rashdall, H., 174.
Rawlinson, A. E. J., 148.
Redlich, E. B., 1, 17, 18, 174.
Reitzenstein, R., 159.
Ritschl, A., 29, 46, 75, 77, 118, 119, 120, 121, 154, 170, 221, 253.
Ritschl, O., 67.
Robertson, A., 43, 182.
Robinson, J. A., 91, 92, 95, 105, 134, 219.
Robinson, T. H., 26.
Ropes, J. H., 188.

Sanday, W. (and Headlam, A. C.), 36, 37, 38, 47, 48, 49, 50, 65, 69, 88, 106, 107, 136, 194.
Scheffler, J., 211.
Schleiermacher, F., 221.
Scholefield, 94.
Schrenk, G., 36, 38, 41, 45, 48, 49, 50.
Schweitzer, A., 138, 139, 149, 159, 160, 161, 164.
Scott, C. A. A., 46, 88, 95, 106, 114, 132, 137, 174, 177, 194, 219.
Scott, E. F., 91, 92, 94, 95, 96, 98, 105, 132, 148, 153, 174, 219
Sharp, D. S., 134.
Skinner, J., 156.
Smith, C. R., xx.
Smith, D., 46.
Smyth, N., 174.
Soden, H. von, 94.
Stewart, R. W., 121, 166.
Strachan, R. H., 147.
Strack-Billerbeck, 175.
Streeter, B. H., 10, 12, 208
Taylor, V., 43, 47, 50, 128, 131, 174, 176, 180, 226, 227, 228, 236, 252.
Temple, W., xviii, 1.
Tersteegen, G., 211.
Tischendorf, C., 106.

Underhill, E., 223.

Vincent, M. R., 131, 132.

Wand, J. W. C., 178, 183.
Watson, P. S., 209, 213.
Webb, C. C. J., xviii.
Weiss, J., 50, 135, 136, 141, 175, 205.
Wesley, C., 210.
Wesley, J., 75, 192, 196, 202, 209, 210.
Westcott, B. F., 105, 106, 111, 207.
Williams, N. P., xix.
Wilson, T., 159.
Winer, G. B., 49.
Workman, H. B., 198, 222.

PRINTED IN GREAT BRITAIN BY ROBERT MACLEHOSE AND CO. LTD.
THE UNIVERSITY PRESS, GLASGOW